B&T 16,50

D1546056

MONSTERS *of* AFFECTION

Dickens, Eliot & Bronte on Fatherhood

DIANNE F. SADOFF

The Johns Hopkins University Press / Baltimore & London

Copyright © 1982 by The Johns Hopkins University Press
All rights reserved
Printed in the United States of America

The Johns Hopkins University Press, Baltimore, Maryland 21218
The Johns Hopkins Press Ltd., London

Library of Congress Cataloging in Publication Data

Sadoff, Dianne F.
    Monsters of affection.

    Includes index.
    1. English fiction — 19th century — History and
criticism. 2. Fathers in literature. 3. Psychoanalysis and literature. 4. Dickens, Charles,
1812-1870 — Knowledge — Psychology. 5. Eliot, George,
1819-1880 — Knowledge — Psychology. 6. Brontë,
Charlotte, 1816-1855 — Knowledge — Psychology.
I. Title
PR878.F37S2   823'.8'09352   82-15378
ISBN 0-8018-2793-0   AACR2

Contents

Acknowledgments

This study of fatherhood owes its existence and inspiration to many of my own "fathers," to each of whom I owe a different kind of debt. First and foremost, to J. Hillis Miller, whose National Endowment for the Humanities Summer Seminar at Yale University in 1977 focused my thinking about paternal thematics and literary structures; since that summer, Miller's support and generosity have provided sustenance when I most needed it in the long process of writing this book. To my graduate school teachers, Barry Westburg, William Rueckert, Carlisle Moore, and William Cadbury, I owe my interest in Victorian literature, in Charles Dickens, and in literary theory. To my husband, Ira Sadoff, I owe the most important debt: a belief in the necessity of my commitment to writing and a conviction that my work was valuable. I would also like to thank then academic dean of Antioch College Frank Wong for providing me a two-year leave of absence from teaching to write much of this book and Julie Cannon of Colby College for typing it.

Parts of this book have been published in different form in *PMLA*, *Genre*, and *Papers on Language and Literature.*

MONSTERS OF AFFECTION

INTRODUCTION

Narrative, Psychoanalysis, and the Nineteenth Century

T HIS BOOK found its structure when I stumbled on
an essay by Jean Laplanche and J.-B. Pontalis on fantasy and the origins
of sexuality. Although primarily concerned with Freud's theory of seduction and its relation to fantasy, the essay contains a short discussion of
primary fantasy and the Oedipus complex which I immediately realized
stood as theoretical underpinning for the work I was struggling to do.
My material suddenly took shape; its boundaries and limitations became
clear as well as its resonance—its triangular articulation of literary texts,
writerly lives, and theoretical speculation. Laplanche and Pontalis's
several paragraphs served my need for structure because they articulated
the themes my writing pondered: an obsession with triangulation—with
rivalry and desire in the family; with the problematic of origins and
retroactivity; with the ways in which a text (in psychoanalysis, a fantasy)
mediates experience through the agency of language and narrative structure (in psychoanalysis, storytelling and symbolism).

My meditations here take as theoretical center Freud's primal fantasies,
all of which recount the origin of the subject and define retroactivity as
an interpretive strategy that allows us to move forward in our lives by
reinventing our pasts in the light of new information. These primal
fantasies include three scenes: the primal scene, seduction, and castration.
Each represents or symbolizes an enigma that confronts the child who
fantasizes—or the author who looks back and writes, however obliquely,
about his or her past experience. Problematic events for which the subject,
child or writer, needs explanation get narrated as stories that seek the
origin of that event; the issues of a life are shaped by these moments of
emergence, these beginnings of a personal history.[1] Moreover, writing
stories not only retroactively reinvents the past but also attempts to

1

engender the subject who writes. The narrative project employs language and fictive structure to shape a life both in story and in fact.

Each of Freud's primal fantasies structures a different life story, its beginnings, middles, and ends. In the primal scene, the child sees or hears the parents making love and assumes violence enacted against the mother. This real or fantasied scene unites the child's perceptions, fears, and explorations of the world around him with emerging thoughts of the mystery of his own origin—"Where do babies come from?" It articulates the "biological fact of conception and birth with the symbolic fact of filiation," unites the parents' act of intercourse with the child's intellectually unformulated but nonetheless intense feelings about his place in the father-mother-child triangle. In the real or fantasied scene of seduction, the child has been or imagines she has been seduced by her father or a figure of authority from the class of fathers. This scene or fantasy articulates the child's suddenly experienced sexuality, the origin of her desire, with her feelings of love for and/or hatred of her father. In the castration enigma, the child imagines he will be castrated by his father for his undefined desire to be close to and cared for by his mother or imagines she has been wounded by her love for her mother and embarks upon love for her father. This scene is always fantasied; neither boy nor girl is castrated, though the boy may fear he will be and the girl may fear she has been. The fantasy of castration articulates the child's first perception of the real difference between the sexes with the symbolic loss of love from father or mother and the repression of desire by the child.[2] Each of Freud's primal fantasies as I have discussed it conjoins or mediates the real and the symbolic, the theme of origin with the triangular structure of the Oedipus complex.

After so schematic and theoretical a psychoanalytic beginning, let me explain that I do not equate the "child" of my discussion with the writers I will write about in this book. Rather, I understand Freud's "primal fantasies" as a metaphor in literary criticism which facilitates interpretation of certain recurring problems in a novelist's work. I do not intend to imply that writing is regressive, because I believe it is not; nor do I mean to imply in appropriating psychoanalysis as a tool for literary interpretation that the writer is "neurotic." Psychoanalysis has infiltrated our contemporary idiom and scene precisely because it interprets such various experience. We all have childhoods as well as adult problems; in the psychologist's office or to our friends, we tell stories about the first as a method of interpreting the second. Freud's theoretical justifications for primal fantasy, moreover, discuss kernels of childhood material he gathered from his patients' storytelling. The novelists about whom I will tell stories in this book, and to whom I will attend as they tell stories, all seek in narrating to find that kernel, that explanatory origin, which will structure themselves as subjects and shape their lives. They tell stories to conjoin the real and the symbolic, to interpret their pasts and themselves, just as Freud's hypothetical child fantasizes about his own origin (the primal scene), the origin of her desire (the scene of seduction), or the origin of the differences between the sexes (the castration enigma). As metaphor, each primal fantasy defines an area of speculation and recollection upon which my authors center their attention and toward which as end they pursue their narrative goals.

Charles Dickens's narrative project, for example, takes as its central metaphor the primal scene. His novels track down the father's sexual and violent rape or wrong as narrative origin, deny the hero could have been conceived by that sinful figure, structurally and surreptitiously kill the father, and proceed to engender the hero as subject with language; the figure of the daughter serves to efface these sonly activities. George Eliot takes as metaphor the scene of seduction. Her heroine desires a "sort of father" yet defines him as a figure of law and authority; narrative structure seeks to undercut his authoritative word and so to usurp it textually as the discourse of a male narrator, the authority of a male author. Charlotte Bronte takes as metaphor the enigma of castration. She represents desire at the level of language, her metaphors are the male gaze and the female voice; castration symbolizes the father's punishment of the daughter who loves him and her self-denying desire for his love. Language is also a tool for mastery, however, and after turning castration against the father, the daughter eventually defines herself as no longer desiring a father or his representative; she becomes a single woman not identified by her status as daughter. In each of these nineteenth-century narrative projects, a writer retroactively reinterprets his or her past and by telling stories attempts to dramatize his or her origin and desire. Because different material is at stake for these writers, different metaphors of origin and different primal fantasies center their narratives and my interpretive attention. If I have chosen to discuss these three writers to the exclusion of other nineteenth-century novelists, it is not because others do not share Dickens's, Eliot's, and Bronte's concerns. Jane Austen, Anthony Trollope, and Elizabeth Gaskell, to name only three, wrote narratives deeply concerned with origins and paternal thematics. In shaping this project, however, I chose to work with three writers I believed to represent these concerns, each of whom illustrates one of my own commitments to metaphors of origin and desire.

My title indicates the connections between fatherhood and structures of desire which center my text. The fathers who appear as characters in my authors' texts, as in my own, are necessarily figurative; around these fathers, configurations of desire organize themselves. The storytelling sons and daughters whose novels I examine may write against or attempt to punish the father who prohibits, may fix in memory whether nostalgically or parricidally the father who abandons or deprives. In my own father-ridden text, I am concerned not as much with explication as with authorship and the urge to fictionalize, with the ways in which Dickens, Eliot, and Bronte narrate their conflicts and fears about fathers through the textual fathers we encounter in their tales. Fictional fathers serve as indicators of a writer's motivation for undertaking a narrative project, serve as interstitial figures mediating between a writer's text and his or her experience. Yet the father about whom my writers write is not necessarily John Dickens, Robert Evans, or Reverend Patrick Bronte but an imaginary figure invented by the writer when he or she was a child and confronted afresh as adult and author. We can list abstractions for which these fictional fathers stand: for Dickens, the father appears as an image of improvidence and profligacy, both monetary and sexual; for Eliot, sternness and authority; for Bronte, punishment and mentorship. None of these writers paints, as Eliot so astutely defines it, a "portrait" of a father but instead renders his or her own conflicts with desire and prohibition, authority and inadequacy, cultural law and the structures of a community. The father as a narrative figure focuses these concerns.

As my last set of terms indicates, I am also concerned in this book with the symbolic father, the concept of paternity in the dominant ideology of Victorian England in the arenas of politics, sexuality, and religion. Yet this book takes as its theoretical focus not social history but psychoanalysis, so I do not discuss political, religious, and historical events contemporary with the Victorian narratives I examine. When contemplating this project and making the first choices about its focus and scope, I realized not only that one book could not do everything but that I as critic could not. My interest in Freud and psychoanalysis is now a decade old; my interest in social history is newer. Nonetheless, this book examines Victorian texts, and my theoretical adherence to psychoanalysis rather than social history should not obscure the fact that my interpretive strategies and commitments appear particularly relevant to narratives written in nineteenth-century England. The reasons are twofold. First, the structure of and ideology about the family in Victorian England permeates these texts and could generate narrative in identical ways in no other period or place; second, the appearance of psychoanalysis as a science at the end of the nineteenth century seems to have been an outcome of the conflicts and cultures of nineteenth-century Europe rather than a harbinger of twentieth-century interest in sexuality. Freud, as so many anti-Freudians like to remind me, was a "Victorian" with all the pejorative connotations that term signifies to the modern and non-scholarly imagination.

I would like to say a bit about my understanding of family history and the necessity to see my particular concerns as representative of nineteenth-century values. The new social history in general and Peter Laslett in particular have shown the evolutionist conception of family structure to be unsubstantiated by the data and records of domestic habitation, especially in England.[3] Laslett bases his criteria for a structural definition of the family on coresidence or shared location, on shared activity or function, and on relationship by marriage or kinship. Despite the growth of nonmarital and nonkinship groups in the twentieth century, marriage and monogamy now, as in the nineteenth century, retain their strength as ideology though society currently tolerates a wide range of deviance from that ideology. Laslett contends that what we loosely call the "nuclear family"—the coresident conjugal group or "simple family household" —has always been the primary or dominant familial institution and that evolutionist theories of structural change from extended family to stem-family to the modern companionate family are based not on fact but on ideology. "Modernization" of the family and industrialization as an indicator of that change, Laslett concludes, have no appreciable effect upon the structure of the family group. Laslett concedes, however, the necessity to differentiate between family structure and family experience. In the nineteenth century, the presence of lodgers, servants, relatives, and long-term guests made family interaction different from family intimacy as we know it in the twentieth century. Although they do not alter the predominance of the simple family household as the basic familial structure, these differences alter the quality and experience of family life and indicate historical change in ideology about the family and its functions. Family structure, then, remains intact over historical time whereas family ideology, which is based in part upon or which generates social and economic realities, changes dramatically.

Laslett's work portrays the stem-family concept (married parents residing with one married offspring, often male, and his offspring) as rooted in nineteenth-century values. The belief that the stable stem-family replaced the stable patriarchal family, after which industrialization and modernization created the unstable nuclear family, confounds structure and ideology. Moreover, this belief results from a nostalgic desire that the family be the secure patriarchal institution nineteenth-century idealists imagined it had been in preindustrial Europe, rather than an expanding and contracting group based on the developmental cycle of households. The socially conservative desire for a more stable patriarchal family likewise appears intimately associated with the dominant nineteenth-century ideologies of domesticity and female chastity, the cults of motherhood and childhood innocence—all of which embody a particularly Victorian abstraction bearing no relation to the structure and perhaps little to the daily experience of family life.

And what about fathers? The stem-family concept is patriarchal and therefore patrilineal. The house and property of the father succeed intact to his (usually oldest) son. Although Laslett pays scant attention to this aspect of stem-family ideology, it goes hand in hand with the "cults" I named above. The sometimes exaggerated authority of the father, the patriarch, the paterfamilias, is a staple of Victorian literature and historiography.[4] What gives this myth its power, I think, is Victorian ambivalence about such paternal authority: the desire for its stability, decisiveness, and cultural validity side by side with the hatred of its narrowness, stubbornness, and social domination—oppression—of those without such authority. Moreover, just as the desire for social stability informs the study of family history as the stem-family concept, so does the desire for paternal authority shape our contemporary thinking about the family. A prominent Marxist historian of the family, Christopher Lasch, concludes his two most recent books with an unstated but nonetheless recognizable call for the return of paternal authority.[5] Although Lasch stops short of believing fathers can reassert the power in the family they once maintained without challenge, he implies this desire throughout his diagnosis of the family as no longer a "haven in a heartless world": the invasion of family functions by the liberal "helping" professions; the rise of peer-group socialization; the invitation into family processes, by wives, of male obstetricians and doctors as allies against husbands; the increased absence of the father from family life. Although Lasch knows the ideology of paternal authority belongs to the nineteenth rather than the twentieth century, he nevertheless pays tribute to its power by reviving it in socially conservative and nostalgic Marxist history of the family.

I would like to return to my second justification for the methodology of this study of fictional fathers. Psychoanalysis, like the stem-family concept, is a nineteenth-century phenomenon. In terms of historical shifts in ideology, Freud's work is prepared for by the eighteenth-century challenges to political authority in France and those throughout Europe in the mid-nineteenth century. According to Fred Weinstein and Gerald Platt, this Enlightenment and Revolutionary challenge made possible Freud's investigation of authority in the family. Eighteenth- and nineteenth-century examination of political authority, Weinstein and Platt believe, made the figure of the father in the family vulnerable to criticism and challenge. In addition, the changes industrialism and urbanization wrought in the social sphere changed the functions of family members but did not alter the structure of the nuclear family. The father became "systematically differentiated from the household," and so affectual ties in the family changed as family experience altered. This change allowed sons to compete with fathers, rather than to identify with, imitate, and follow them in class status, vocation, and marital advisement. We can view something of this shift in the Victorian novel: Pip's fear of entrapment as apprentice in Joe's forge; battles between upper-middle-class fathers and sons in Trollope's or Thackeray's narratives. These changes in the political and economic spheres, then, with their concomitant effects upon family functions, experience, and ideology, facilitated Freud's attention to the relationships between fathers and sons and the structures of the Oedipus complex.[6] Freud's self-analysis, for example, focused primarily on his rivalry with his father for his mother's affection and on his numerous battles with brothers, mentors, and father-supplements. The implications for the study of psychoanalysis are enormous: Freud's psychoanalytic theory normally takes as subject the male child, and his cultural and anthropological speculations model social contracts on the dialectic of identification and rivalry between fathers and sons—the sacrificial totem meal, for example, in *Totem and Taboo*.

Although the father and his authority became available for psychoanalytic investigation, the accompanying role of the mother and her nurturance did not.[7] Freud's contemporaries and followers, Karen Horney, Helene Deutsch, and Jeanne Lampl-de Groot, criticized him for ignoring the preoedipal phase of a child's development. In his late essays on femininity, Freud therefore reconsiders the Oedipus complex with the daughter as subject and in doing so details the desires, punishments, and oppressions of the daughter in patriarchy. In Freud's masculine and patriarchal view of a paternalistic culture, however, the daughter has no function; unlike the son, she cannot question the father's authority, nor can she as an adult free herself from her self-definition as "daughter." Apart from his personal misogyny, Freud's attitudes accord with the roles of women in nineteenth-century life; rather than excoriate Freud for his failure to attend to female psychology, we must view his psychoanalytic theory as a first, if problematic, step in the consideration of ideology about the female. Freud "repressed" the feminine partially because his culture did so. Moreover, according to Weinstein and Platt, the preoedipal nurturing functions of the mother to the exclusion of the father may be related to changing ideology about the middle-class family and so have emerged as the father's function in the family altered. And despite the suffrage movement, the liberation of women in the nineteenth century was still problematic: the "Woman Question."[8]

Freudian theoretical texts, a nineteenth-century phenomenon themselves, render psychoanalytic criticism particularly well-suited to the interpretation of nineteenth-century narrative. Because I am concerned in this book with gender and family, Freud's writings on female psychology and the Oedipus complex serve my argument well. I employ as theory Freud's texts which announce "female sexuality" or "femininity" as their topics, as well as those which do not but nevertheless attend to the female as subject—if only because Freud's hysterical or fantasizing patients were in certain instances female. I am also concerned to view Freud primarily as a writer rather than a clinician or neurologist. Freud's case histories reveal him a consummate storyteller; his letters to Wilhelm Fliess, a lively metaphor-maker; his dream texts, an imaginative interpreter; all his collected papers, a writer willing to admit his elisions and self-deceptions, the need for revision, and the necessity for the writer to be vulnerable and self-reflexive. As writing, his work represents a remarkable achievement.

If Freud's writing is not immune to feminist criticism, however, neither is it to structuralist revision or deconstruction.[9] Like all writerly texts, Freud's text's metaphors and embedded narratives often contradict his stated scientific assumptions. From a structuralist perspective, Freud relies too completely on the concept of "personality" in his speculation about the etiology of neurosis. As Augustus Napier and Carl Whitaker point out in their narrative and theoretical case history of a family therapy, the family as an intersubjective structure or system tends to designate certain of its members to act out the group's dysfunctions.[10] Although I do not explicitly refer to systems theories of family therapy in this book, this perspective supplements my own thinking with Freud. More important, the French "return to Freud" serves my interpretive strategies in this book. Jacques Lacan and other structuralist psychoanalysts rewrite psychoanalytic theory from the perspective of the Oedipus complex, the signification of the phallus, and the originating role of the father in the onset of neurosis and so help me speculate on oedipal identification and rivalry in my novelists' texts. Lacan's introduction of Ferdinand de Saussure's linguistic theories into psychoanalysis makes his work central to my interpretive project. Despite his willful obscurantism as a writer (no Freudian vulnerability appears in Lacan's texts!), Lacan's theory that the unconscious, like language, works by the structured laws of condensation and displacement (in linguistic terminology, metaphor and metonymy) rationalizes the connections between fantasy and fictional prose.[11] His differentiation of real, imaginary, and symbolic realms also makes available to the literary critic levels of interpretation which supplement singular use of Freud's texts. The world of images, ghosts, doubles, and mirrorings (the imaginary) and that of cultural system and linguistic structure (the symbolic) enrich interpretation that articulates the novelist's need to write his or her version of personal experience and cultural system with the mediating role of language.

Yet Lacan's texts, like Freud's, demand criticism as well as interpretation. Lacan, like Freud, focused attention on the father and repressed the feminine. Indeed, his written work demonstrates his willingness—his desire—to sneer at the female and at feminist theory. Like Freud, Lacan speculates only about the male subject. His obsession with the phallus and with his total authority in the French return to Freud portrays an amusing and undisguised castration anxiety. Whereas Freud, as I have tried to demonstrate, repressed the feminine partly because of his historical and cultural context, Lacan's twentieth-century contempt for the female appears antediluvian. Partially because of his masculine bias, however, I find Lacan's writings useful in discussing father-son conflicts in Dickens's texts because I view Dickens the writer as a son who fathers himself. In considering Charlotte Bronte's narratives, on the contrary, I find useful as corrective to Lacan's masculine bias the writings of American, English, and French psychoanalytic feminists.[12] Although Luce Irigaray and Julia Kristeva, to name two such writers, may glorify the feminine and so comply with the dominant ideology of the female as totally sexual, different from the male (and so capable of oppression), and an object of fetishization, they nevertheless change the texture of feminist discourse by including in its purlieu psychoanalysis, linguistics, and Marxism. These writers remind us that gender has not been sufficiently theorized in most humanistic and social-scientific scholarship.

I would like to conclude this introduction by preparing my reader for the structure of this book. I have chosen not to consider my writers in the chronological sequence in which they wrote but rather to shape the book by my theoretical and psychoanalytic concerns. Each chapter conjectures about a writer's career in its entirety but without a necessarily chronological consideration of the narratives; in a similar way, the book as a whole meditates a particularly nineteenth-century mythology without assigning a necessarily chronological sequence to such consideration. I place the chapter on Charles Dickens first because his metaphor for origin and desire, the primal scene, concerns the origin of the subject himself. George Eliot's metaphor, the scene of seduction, involves a later problem of emergence or origin in the psychoanalytic structuring of a subject's experience. Charlotte Bronte's enigma of castration and sexual difference represents yet a later moment of origin and desire. Moreover, my theoretical material becomes more speculative as the reader moves on in this book; I intend the early chapters to prepare for the combination of psychoanalytic and feminist discourse in the chapter on Charlotte Bronte, although I hope the reader need not read this book sequentially to assent to its theoretical perspective.

Charles Dickens:
Authors of Being

IN THE FIRST CHAPTER of *Martin Chuzzlewit*, the narrator's "history" proves the "Chuzzlewits to have had an origin." Yet Dickens's parodic "pedigree" both affirms and repudiates genealogy as a structure of origins. The novel's apparently naive narrator places the family's "ancient origin" in initiatory situations provided by myth, religion, and English history: the family "descended in a direct line from Adam and Eve"; a member came over from France with William the Conqueror; one burned with Guy Fawkes. Dickens chuckles at his narrator's tautological, mythologically inconceivable, and historically impossible declarations of origin. We chuckle too when the narrator "demonstrates" the aristocratic heritage of the Chuzzlewits: Toby Chuzzlewit proves his class and legitimacy by whispering on his deathbed the name of his grandfather, "Lord No Zoo"; Diggory Chuzzlewit gives gifts of plate, jewels, books, watches, and finally clothing to his "uncle" (the pawnbroker) and is forced by his friends to "dine with Duke Humphrey" (to go hungry).[1]

A recurring figure in Dickens's narratives also emerges here with the mention of Adam and Eve: "It is remarkable that as there was, in the oldest family of which we have any record, a murderer and a vagabond, so we never fail to meet, in the records of old families, with innumerable repetitions of the same phase of character" (1). The sequential family tree appears a structure of repetition as well as of descent. And jokes about the original father and mother inevitably remind Dickens of Cain, with whose sins against the family, with whose exile, Dickens's imagination discovered great sympathy. Despite the outright laughter this chapter's double significations provoke, Cain's presence as son and criminal affirms Dickens's guilt and anxiety as well as his intense curiosity about origins.

Dickens's glancing reference to the serious connections among genealogy, repetition, and criminality appear in one of his greatest initiatory tours de force. Joking about origins provides the novelist (and critic) with a narrative point of departure. The study of genealogy, however, demands interpretation, and Dickens's naive narrator misinterprets his already questionable "documentary evidence": he relies on Toby's deathbed whisper because it was copied and witnessed with six signatures and on Diggory's evidential correspondence to friends and relatives. Yet we are forced to interpret Toby's whisper as the misunderstood words, "Lord knows who"; we understand Diggory's correspondence as begging letters, a form of discourse with which Dickens himself was all too familiar. This narrator, this genealogical detective, however, not only reads misunderstood language and metaphor literally but he also emends his evidence. In a family "anecdote," a Chuzzlewit woman now four generations dead once asserted that her "fourth son" carried a "dark lantern of undoubted antiquity" on the "fifth of November when he was a Guy Fawkes"; our narrator decides the woman really said, "this lantern was carried by my forefather" on the "fifth of November" and "*he* was Guy Fawkes." Dickens's joke about narratorial emendation, however, creates transformations and displacements that betray his serious concern about genealogy: the play on four (generations and sons) and five (of November) transforms "son" into "father" and transforms the Chuzzlewit ancestor from member of a group into its leader, its originator. Genealogical joking seeks in structural shifts and language displacements a father who initiates. Toby Chuzzlewit on his deathbed seeks to name the "secret of his father's birth" (4); Dickens's narrative structures seek, as I shall hope to persuade my reader, the father's secret of the son's birth.

Narrative Search for the Father

The discovery [that Ralph Nickleby is Smike's father] is made, Ralph is dead, the loves have come all right, . . . and I have now only to break up Dotheboys and the book together. — The Letters of Charles Dickens, *ed. Madeline House and Graham Storey*

The structure of genealogy creates a metaphysics of origin and identity: known paternity signifies an offspring's legitimacy and a progenitor's authority. Many of Dickens's characters, however, appear without origin, either literally or metaphorically. Oliver Twist is alphabetically named by a beadle in the absence of a father and the death of a mother; Pip derives his notion of father and mother from the "turn of the inscription" on the family tombstone; Esther Summerson feels guilty because of her parentage yet somehow innocent. Dickens's orphans, however, appear destined to find their fathers and so to determine their origins and confirm their identities. Origin initiates identity and accounts for character as a logical unfolding in time. Dickens clearly subscribes to this genealogical belief: Oliver is indeed his father's son, although he does not know it until the end of his narrative; his origin and paternity promise and deliver a certain character that remains inviolate in the face of criminality and poverty, and so he finally inherits his true patrimony.[2] Narrative sequence represents this belief in the metaphysics of origin and identity: events originate, unfold over time, and acquire significance through sequence. Narrative teleology means events in narrative become understood as the reader moves from origin to end, associating and accumulating the repeated evidence of pattern, of signification, inherent in narrative event. Like the discovery that Oliver's origins confirm his represented character, the end of a novel reveals the coherence of origin and sequence from the vantage point of end.[3]

In his novels of real or metaphorical orphanage, Dickens indeed represents narrative sequence as an eventual revelation of origin over time which appears congruent with ends. Readers of Dickens's novels learn quickly to recognize his recurring clues to the secrets of origin. Esther Summerson, not wanting to know her origin and having no family relations according to law, experiences uncanny moments in which the sight of her unknown mother reminds her of herself. *Barnaby Rudge* presents the appearance and reappearance of the "mysterious stranger," whose figure we trace and retrace, reading him as a clue that, connected with clues to other narrative contexts not yet revealed, will resolve the novel's mysteries. These Dickensian clues accumulate in a linear version of narrative discovery, imitate or represent the metaphysics of narrative temporality in which significance is created by virtue of pure sequence. If we read these clues rightly, interpret sequence with the tools of repetition, we understand the solution of mystery, the narrative's teleology and signifying structures. Like the solution of mystery, narrative sequence acquires its teleology by virtue of ends that credit and confirm origin.

In Dickens's novels, the drive toward discovery of origin and so the confirmation of identity focus on the figure of the father. At the end of narrative, the mystery of parentage yields up the name of the father, he who originates character and so identity, he who initiates the events of narrative and so sequence. At the end of *Nicholas Nickleby,* we discover that Ralph Nickleby is Smike's killing father. At the end of *Barnaby Rudge,* we discover that John Chester is Hugh of the Maypole's father and that Chester's machinations account for the complications of plot in the novel: he paid Mrs. Rudge and Barnaby to leave London; he sent Gashford and Hugh to burn the Warren; he separated Emma and his son; he told the story, before the novel began, that Haredale killed his own brother. At the end of this novel, we also discover that the "mysterious stranger" is Barnaby's father, that Barnaby's identity as madman originates in his father's murders, and that those murders initiate the events culminating in the narrative itself and create the situation that Chester then manipulates. Just as the father begets children who figure in stories, he initiates narrative event and so sequence. Learning the father's name at the end of narrative confirms identity and demonstrates that narrative sequence reveals its significance over time.

The metaphysics of origin and narrative sequence most clearly appear in *A Tale of Two Cities*. Scenes of "shadowy" recognition, like those between Esther and Lady Dedlock, alert the reader to an unknown relationship between Charles Darnay and Dr. Manette. These scenes derive their mysterious power from the sequential revelation that Darnay, whom we first assume to be an Englishman, is a French aristocrat, the Marquis's nephew, a descendant of a degenerate and corrupt class. As these clues accumulate, they promise to reveal his true name and so his father's name, his place in a genealogy, his origin. The "substance of the shadow" between Darnay and Dr. Manette comes to fruition in Manette's prison narrative, which accuses and curses all descendants of the aristocratic Evremondes as murderers and identifies Darnay as one of those descendants. This embedded narrative makes the genealogical assumption that fatherhood as origin indeed confers identity: Darnay is an Evremonde and so partakes of their essence, their "substance." In Manette's narrative, the father also begets the events of narrative: Dr. Manette attends and treats a woman raped and a brother wounded by the Evremonde twin brother whom Manette terms "younger." When Manette attempts to report this act to the authorities, he is imprisoned in the Bastille, and the narrative is later used by the Defarges to condemn the descendants of Evremonde. In its relationship to the larger narrative, this act of sexual violence causes the sister of the murdered boy and girl — Mme Defarge — to take personal and political revenge against the Evremondes and against their entire class, because the double rape and murder also represents the symbolic rape of the peasant class by the aristocracy.

The "source" of *A Tale of Two Cities*, then, appears to be a rape and murder by twin Evremonde brothers. The "elder" brother is Charles Darnay's father, the "younger" the current Marquis. Although Darnay's father does not literally beget the events of the larger narrative, he appears symbolically responsible for the rape and murder: Carton himself forces the reader to identify the twin brothers. "Why need I speak of my father's time, when it is equally yours?" he asks his uncle. "Can I separate my father's twin-brother, joint inheritor, and next successor, from himself?"[4] Dr. Manette's narrative answers emphatically, no, and so Darnay's father begets the events equally with his twin brother. Another father, Gaspard, or "Jacques," kills the rapist and murderer for killing his son; and a father-in-law's narrative condemns Charles Darnay by the laws of genealogy—the nephew-son must "die for the sins of his forefathers" (344).[5]

A Tale of Two Cities discovers at its end that at its origin the father begets the events of narrative. Yet this "begetting" also calls into question the metaphysics of identity. Only because his literal father's twin or double has raped and murdered can Darnay be saved by substitution of *his* double; yet because his literal father symbolically raped and murdered, the revolutionaries must condemn him to death. Darnay both is and is not responsible for the sins of his forefathers. The novel both affirms and dissimulates the genealogical myth of origins that confer identity. In addition, the "begetting" of narrative event finds its origin in rape and murder, not in the begetting of a character who will figure in narrative and whose identity will appear in the unfolding of narrative to be continuous and coherent with his origin. Unlike *Oliver Twist*, in which revelation of paternal origin confers and confirms identity, virtually all Dickens's narratives, like *A Tale*, discover a father's rape, murder, or adultery at the source of narrative event.

Narrative doubling and repression of the father as origin disguise or deny the consequences of the sins of the father. The double father in *A Tale*, for example, upsets the metaphysics of origin and identity upon which the novel first appears to count. *Little Dorrit* and *Bleak House* demonstrate great ingenuity in denying a son or daughter full knowledge of his or her paternity or in denying the reader full knowledge of a character's knowledge. These narratives mystify origin and interrogate the notion that the father originates character and narrative event. The rhetoric of narrative deferral and repression of paternity as origin appears in *Bleak House*'s refusal to name the father in texts about his sins. In her childhood, Esther reports, her godmother told her to "pray daily that the sins of *others* be not visited upon your head, according to what is written" (my italics). When Esther discovers her mother, she remembers these words in terror. Yet "what is written" in Numbers 14:18 confirms that the sins of "the *fathers*" shall be visited upon the children. Only after interpreting herself as the figure who walks on a symbolic Ghost's Walk and so brings calamity on the Dedlock house does Esther admit what is written, "the sins of the *fathers*," yet she admits it only to deny that her transcendent "Heavenly Father" holds her responsible for her birth, her identity as conferred by her literal paternal origin.[6] Dickens's narrative must discover this rhetorical substitution of the "other" for the father despite its denial.

The Old Curiosity Shop radically represses and excludes the father as origin of identity and narrative sequence. The circumstances of the novel's composition as well as its status as an early novel, of course, account for a good deal of this repression. Although "Abel" Garland appears as one of Dickens's benevolent and early "good daddies," the narrative expunges his counterpart's role as Cain and as evil father. Quilp in his "Wilderness," Quilp as the Marchioness's father, Dickens only implies. In fact, when Quilp demonically offers Dick, as "Abel" Provis Magwitch will later offer another boy, to become his "second father," Dick discovers the joys of orphanhood, of being "left alone."[7] We now know Dickens intentionally mystified Quilp's fatherhood by cutting Sally Brass's confession that she is the Marchioness's mother and by implication Quilp her father. Yet Dick Swiveller names the Marchioness "Sophronia Sphynx" and so signifies her dilemma, the mystery of her parentage, as well as implying a resemblance to Sally Brass, whom Dick earlier calls the "sphynx." Dick also correctly imagines that Quilp himself can solve the entire Sphynxian mystery.[8] In this novel, the gaze is a metaphor for sexual aggression, for rape, and Quilp's evil sexual energy, his ogling Sally Brass (among others) metaphorically identifies him as the figurative father Dickens renders in *A Tale* and in *Barnaby Rudge*.

Dickens excludes Quilp's fatherhood of the Marchioness to disguise fatherhood in the allegorical structure of the novel. If the novel names Quilp "father," his pursuit of Little Nell becomes a figurative version of paternal seduction or rape, and the narrative allegory of flight to the country to reform, to transcend the vices of the (grand)father would be contaminated by the "second" or double father as a figure of criminally sexual origination. Nell's story, a "kind of allegory" (13), takes as narrative sequence the "journey," a wandering from place to place without goal. Yet the clear and proper goal of Nell's allegory is death; Nell chooses to die (the grave is "garden," she perceives), chooses to die in spring. Her narrative, then, must never concern itself with origin, only with transcendent end, and so Dickens carefully kills off Nell's literal and metaphorical ancestors both male and female aside from the gambling-obsessed grandfather, who provides the occasion for both allegory and death. To separate origin from end in the narrative and to drive Nell's narrative sequence only toward death, Dickens doubles the figurative father, separates Nell from Quilp, and dedicates her to the (grand)father who drives the novel toward its end.

Dickens's double plotting in *The Old Curiosity Shop* mystifies the figure of the father as originator and associates his metaphorical double with death. In this novel Dickens wants to prove that identity conferred by character and end bears no relationship to that conferred by origin. Nell's innocence and the Marchioness's sympathy deny the genealogical myth that the father's evil, his sexual begetting, transmits itself to his progeny. This denial turns *Oliver Twist* on its head, just as Magwitch later turns Pip on his head in the graveyard of his father. Like the doubling of the figure of origin in *A Tale of Two Cities*, this apparently double plotting protects Dickens against the discovery toward which his narrative structure drives: the sins of the father who begets, who originates.

Bleak House carries this doubling of narrative sequence to its logical conclusion: the dual narrative. The search for the begetting father as originator of character and event takes place only in the omniscient narrative, clearly separated from Esther's narrative, in which Nemo would be named as "Captain Hawdon" and as "father." Esther asserts that she seeks no knowledge of her parentage, but Esther's narrative, despite her stated intentions in writing it, relentlessly discovers to her her mother.[9] Esther finds her mother only by virtue of events that occur in the omniscient narrative: Lady Dedlock's recognition of Captain Hawdon's handwriting; Tulkinghorn's consequent—and later Bucket's—detective work. In her own narrative, Esther represses her daughterhood by defusing Guppy's attempt to follow up on her own resemblance to the portrait of Lady Dedlock. At the end of the novel, however, the two narratives recounting different events tend toward the same end, the pursuit of Lady Dedlock by Bucket and Esther, which culminates in the discovery of Esther's dead mother by the graveyard in Tom-all-Alone's.

What of the father? The omniscient narrative makes clear Nemo's role as engenderer both of Esther's identity and of narrative event. When the omniscient narrator demands to know the connections between the place in Lincolnshire and the whereabouts of Jo in Tom-all-Alone's (197), the novel offers as answer this implication: the burial ground in Tom-all-Alone's is the locus of that connection, the place from which disease spreads and to which discovery tends. And when Esther and Bucket track Lady Dedlock, who tracks Captain Hawdon, Esther by metonymic displacement tracks Nemo, her father. He lies dead in the burial ground in Tom-all-Alone's, whose bars Esther's dead mother embraces. The father represents the link between classes, the connection between narratives; his presence in that burial ground accounts for all other events consequential upon and to discovery: sexual wrong and origination. By virtue of narrative structure and metaphor, *Bleak House* seeks the father as origin but denies that search in Esther's narrative.

Both narratives, however, attenuate the clear distinction Dickens attempts to draw by virtue of the dual narrative between the knowledge of origination and its refusal. Taylor Stoehr believes that because the issues of class and sexuality remain separated by the double narrative, Esther never knows the identity of her father.[10] Although Esther neglects—as usual—to tell us what she knows and declines to make judgments about character and identity, we do not know whether she knows her father's identity. George Rouncewell, apparently knowing the connection between Esther and his old friend Captain Hawdon, sends Esther a letter "both straightforward and delicate" (747)—and therefore virtually unreadable without the knowledge of fatherhood to which it alludes—apologizing for his cooperation in Tulkinghorn's hounding of Nemo. Does Esther therefore know her father as the figure the novel tracks down? We do not know, because George's letter, sent in the omniscient narrative, never arrives in Esther's narrative. On the other hand, John Jarndyce, in offering Esther the ambiguous role of "mistress of Bleak House" through marriage to his substitute, Allan Woodcourt, signifies Woodcourt's legitimacy as husband when he says Woodcourt "stood beside your father when he lay dead—stood beside your mother" (753). Jarndyce clearly knows the law-writer who died at Krook's house was Esther's father. Esther, of course, refuses comment. Does Jarndyce know, however, that Nemo is buried in Tom-all-Alone's filthy and disease-ridden burial ground? Does Esther? The narrative refuses to answer.

Bleak House, then, represents, through its disguised and displaced metonymies of narrative, the father as origin and his discovery as end point. Yet Esther's narrative, which excludes mention of her father as the origin of herself, also excludes mention of his end and finally refuses to close itself either dramatically or grammatically. At the conclusion of her narrative, does Esther literally recover her beauty or metaphorically reconfirm it through the admiring gaze in the mirror of her husband at herself? The reader will never know, for Esther ends her writing with the words "even supposing—." Narrative end is deferred and identity suspended; narrative origin remains absent, implied by but untold in its own story. The double narrative of *Bleak House* tracks the father's sin, his identity as Nemo or "no one," but Esther, the novel's heroine, refuses to partake in the search. The narrative represents Dickens's double attitude toward the project upon which all his novels embark: the attempt to come to terms with the father as his own metaphorically sinful and diseased origin and the desire not to know what it all means.

Dickens undercuts the metaphysics of origin and identity, the structures of genealogy, not only through narrative and figural doubling but also by exploiting the double temporal perspective inherent in that metaphysics and those structures. When in *A Tale of Two Cities* present narrative time (the Marquis's time) appears equally past narrative time (Darnay's father's time), Dr. Manette's story collapses end on origin and so disrupts the temporal structures and sequential principles of narrative.[11] When in *The Old Curiosity Shop* figurative fatherhood becomes associated first with origin, then—and more forcefully—with end, only schematic allegory can save the metaphysics of narrative temporality from disruption. Dickens's narrative clues to fatherhood or parentage create narrative sequence and lead to discovery of origin and identity, but they also subvert narrative sequence and so call into question in another way origin and fatherhood as sufficient to confer identity. While moving forward in narrative reading time, clues to the mysteries of parentage move relentlessly backward in narrative causal time. The writing of narrative combines the drive toward discovery at the end, in the future, with the tracking back toward origin, in the past. A mystery is solved when knowledge of the past gathers in the narrative present and predicts an unknown future. This double narrative temporality appears, when represented in the single temporality available to writing, as dialogical; a story drives toward end, while preparing for that by establishing the retrospective evidence of origin throughout the narrative. "Plot" and "story" inhere in one narrative.[12]

In *Little Dorrit,* this double temporality disguises the father as a figure of origin and radically disrupts or attenuates narrative sequence. The novel's tortured entanglements and mystifications of plot make temporal sequence appear virtually pointless. Arthur Clennam, searching for a vocation after his father dies, finds himself blocked by feelings of guilt and fear. Because his mother treats Amy Dorrit well—and no one else—Clennam associates her with his feelings of paralysis: have any actions of his mother's and his dead father's caused William Dorrit's imprisonment for debt? Clennam's absolutely unmotivated connection of Amy with his dead father indeed proves true, as Dorrit metaphorical orphanage, transgression, and reward mirror Clennam orphanage, repression, transgression, and punishment. Arthur's mother was not Mrs. Clennam but instead an orphaned woman who had met Clennam's orphaned father at Frederick Dorrit's dancing studio and later committed adultery with him. When Uncle Gilbert's codicil, stolen by Mrs. Clennam, comes to light, Amy Dorrit inherits his wealth: the will enriches Frederick Dorrit's daughter or niece if there is no daughter in an effort to cure the wrong done to and by a nearly niece. The almost ridiculous entanglements of the codicil's dissemination of wealth parallel the entanglements of the novel's plot, and both exploit the double temporality of narrative and of genealogical structures to mystify a father as origin.

Clennam's search for a vocation dissimulates his narrative search for his father's guilt. If readers feel mystified by the novel's plot, so also its hero remains mystified about his father's sexual crimes. Dickens keeps Clennam conspicuously absent from the denouement, the scene in which Clennam's parentage is related by Rigaud alias Blandois alias Langier. Despite Clennam's tracking his father's adultery via its connection with Amy Dorrit, only Rigaud, Clennam's dark double, learns the facts of that parentage, learns of Clennam's father's adultery; Clennam never knows the facts of his engendering, and he marries Little Dorrit, who equivocally promises to protect him from knowledge of it, at least within the limits of this narrative. The retroactive search backward in narrative time for the facts of origin appears frustrated by the narrative's forward temporality, by the narrative denial of paternity at its end, and by the symbolic marriage of Arthur and Amy, which attempts to cure the sexual sin at the novel's absent origin. Plot confounds story.[13]

Little Dorrit, The Old Curiosity Shop, and "Esther's narrative" all banish the originating sexual act of fatherhood from their texts. Origins prove absent, despite their initiatory role in creating the narratives we read. Esther's narrative, for example, banishes her own origin from its events and denies her father any part in the begetting of herself. Her text thus asserts her status as a subject without origin, while at the same time demonstrating the narrative's project as retroactively seeking origin. In *Little Dorrit,* as in Esther's narrative, that retroactive project calls itself into question and exposes the search for the father as origin as a search for nothing, for "no one." As the principle of narrative retroactivity and sequence in *Little Dorrit* is named by its own discarded title, "Nobody's Fault," so Arthur Clennam, his origin banished from the text which seeks it, begins to resemble "nobody." In *Bleak House,* the begetting father has become "Nemo," no one. The retroactive tracking of the father as origin tracks emptiness. The novel's apparent repression of the "sins of the fathers" by terming them the "sins of others" appears, finally, felicitous rather than fortuitous. These narratives seek at their origins absence, the dead or unknown father; the text dissimulates its origin, its retroactive project.

As Dickens's narratives banish origin from their texts and structures, they disclose the facts of origin in stories at their ends. The facts of paternity in *Little Dorrit,* as in *A Tale of Two Cities* and *The Old Curiosity Shop,* are disclosed not in the narrative's action, but in embedded narrative: Rigaud tells Clennam's story at the end of *Little Dorrit;* Dr. Manette's narrative, Darnay's; the single gentleman, Nell's. These stories within plots recount those absent origins of narrative and disclose the mysteries of fatherhood. They symbolize the narrative project as retroactive yet double. Dr. Manette's prison narrative is read aloud at a trial during the Reign of Terror, was written during December 1767, and refers to as well as intends to repeat verbatim the events of 22 December 1757. As the narrative seeks to trace identity to its origin, so the structures of narrative retroactively embed earlier narrative. The exposure of narrative temporality as double, or dialogical, culminates in this reversal of narrative time, this recounting of absent origin at a text's end. Cynthia Chase terms this typically Victorian narrative structure "metaleptic."[14]

This metaleptic revelation of the facts of origin in embedded story identifies origin and known paternity (and so legitimacy and authority) as fictional. Just as origin is banished to absence before the beginning of narrative proper, and end is deferred or suspended, the narrative project refers not to the knowledge it desires to discover but to a story of that knowledge. *Little Dorrit* discovers in its present father, William Dorrit, as well as its absent father, Mr. Clennam, that fatherhood lacks substance, that engendering is corrupt and debased, that origination partakes of sexual inauthenticity and illegitimacy. Rigaud's recounting of this tale, however, remains discontinuous with the narrative in which it appears; because Clennam never knows about his father's adultery, the story refuses to refer to the subject in the novel for whom it would create a metaphysics of origin and identity. By analogy, the novel itself appears a storied search for fictional origins. Dickens's embedded stories of origin, then, expose the fictions of origin and sequence upon which narrative depends.

The single gentleman's embedded story of Nell's origin in *The Old Curiosity Shop* identifies this problematic relationship between origin or genealogy and narrative sequence. The single gentleman tells this tale: a younger and an elder brother loved the same woman, and the younger sacrificed himself so his much-loved elder brother could marry her; she died, leaving an infant daughter, who grew up, married unwisely, and whose husband beggared both herself and her father (the elder brother); she and her husband died, leaving two children, now orphans, to the father's (elder brother's) care. The reader gradually comes to recognize these facts, although they appear unrelated to the novel we read; the reader names these unnamed characters by comparison, by the metaphorical act of reading things similar and different. Although we are never told who these characters are, we know the two orphans are Nell and Fred Trent and the elder brother is Grandfather Trent. The single gentleman might have disclosed the names of his characters, but the listener, Abel Garland, like the reader, comes to recognize these people, and, expressing human sympathy, tells the storyteller he knows the rest. The narrative remains unfinished. Yet it not only resembles the novel of which it is a part, it also tells the story of what happens before the novel we read begins. It leaves off where *The Old Curiosity Shop* begins. It tells the source of Nell's story, its beginning, her engendering. Like the novel we hold in our hands, this story focuses on what it excludes yet metaphorically defines the structures of father, brother, and daughter. Narrative discloses and disguises the facts of genealogy.

The single gentleman's narrative also identifies the problematic of fictional referentiality, of inside and outside, of narrative structure and experiential structure. As the repeating father-daughter structures in the single gentleman's narrative resemble those same structures in *The Shop's* narrative, so the structures of father and daughter in the novel relate to structures that resemble it outside the narrative. These structures or their analogues might refer to Dickens's own experience, to the same structures in his other novels.[15] Yet as they metaphorically relate outward, they also call attention to themselves as fictions, as stories embedded in larger structures. Once more, Dickens demands to know origins, to portray the structures of genealogy, while at the same time demonstrating that knowledge and its portrayal as fictional.

Finally, however, we wonder why the fictive narrative of a father engendering children and therefore a narrative's events and sequence appear so important to Dickens. We might begin with Steven Marcus's and Albert D. Hutter's insights about the primal scene in *Oliver Twist* and *A Tale of Two Cities* respectively. Hutter notes the emphasis in *A Tale* on public and private versions of spying, on staring and transformation into the Gorgon's Head and its analogues, on gazing spectators at Darnay's trial. These gazes function as synecdoche for the novel's represented primal scenes, which combine the child's gaze with the parents' sexual activities. Hutter identifies as represented primal scenes Dr. Manette's experience with the Evremonde brothers' rape of the peasant girl and, as parody, Young Jerry Cruncher's spying on his father's mysterious night-time activities in the graveyard and his witness of his father beating his mother on their bed for her "flopping tricks" (448-54). These scenes occur at night, combine the language of sexuality and violence, and render seen (and "scene") what is not meant to be seen.[16]

Marcus identifies in *Oliver Twist* two scenes of half-sleep in which Oliver sees or thinks he sees Fagin, with whom Oliver enjoys a surreptitious identification in this narrative, as several critics have pointed out. In the first, at Fagin's hideout, Oliver watches Fagin open a jewel box full of trinkets, brandish a knife, and read a secret document; in the second, at the Maylies' country house, Oliver watches Fagin at a window while nodding over a book. Marcus identifies the symbolism in the first scene as related to the primal scene: a female shape, a figurative father's aggression, and the document about patrimony or sonly identity. The second scene Marcus relates to the narrative's complex transformations of Dickens's autobiographical fragment about his experience at the blacking warehouse and his father's imprisonment for debt: the figurative father watches the child here, as Dickens's father watched him tie up blacking bottles in the warehouse window. This inversion of the primal scene—the father gazes at the child—identifies a father's betrayal and a son's imagined replacing of him. Marcus believes these primal scenes reveal Dickens's feeling of identification with the father he imagined had betrayed him.[17]

These primal scenes in *Oliver Twist* and *A Tale* combine figures of fathers with the urge to expose (or see) and with the necessity to conceal (or transform). Like Dickens's embedded stories of genealogy and origin, the primal scene links fatherhood with engendering. Both primal scene and embedded story demonstrate a problematic reason for writing narrative: to expose or discover while questioning the figure of the father as origin. I am not saying, however, that Dickens's embedded stories are identical with the primal scene but that they display similar metaphorical functions in the novels. Jean Laplanche and J.-B. Pontalis's ideas about the primal scene as symbolic structure may help clarify this resemblance. The primal scene, like the other primal fantasies of seduction and castration, is a fantasy of origin. It represents the origin of the individual, the father begetting and the mother—as the gazing child assumes—being beaten. The child who watches, remembers watching, or fantasizes watching this scene might think retroactively that he himself was conceived in this way. The function of the primal scene in the field of fantasy, as I said in my introduction, accounts for the origin of the subject himself. The primal scene represents the conjunction of the biological fact of conception and birth with the symbolic fact of filiation;[18] the father as originator retroactively explains the mystery of a son's making. In writing narratives that create disguised primal scenes and embed stories about the father as genealogical and narrative origin, Dickens the writer accounts for his own origin and imagines his engendering. Dickens attempts by writing narrative to answer the question, "how did I get here?" just as do his betrayed orphans, those figures for himself as "small Cain." Some of Dickens's orphans, like Oliver, inherit their unstained birthrights themselves unstained; some, like Esther, refuse to define those birthrights yet acquire metaphorical fathers; some, like Pip, come into their own as orphans and so write their own fictions. All, however, seek in narrative as their creator seeks through narrative to "take their place," as Esther puts it, in this world which disguises, displaces, and decenters origin, mystifies what it means to be a subject to oneself and in narrative.

The Dead Father

I conducted myself—much more like a Parricide than a person of independent property," said Mr. Toots, with severe self-accusation.
—*Charles Dickens,* Dombey and Son

Jacques Lacan contemplates the structural importance of the father in the dissolution of the masculine Oedipus complex by reminding us of Freud's insistence on the affinity of the father with death in *Totem and Taboo:* Freud's "reflection led him to link the appearance of the signifier of the Father, as author of the Law, with death, even to the murder of the Father—thus showing that if this murder is the fruitful moment of debt through which the subject binds himself for life to the Law, the symbolic Father is, in so far as he signifies this Law, the dead Father."[19] The son's working through of his oedipal burden, then, demands the double work of identification with the father and rivalry with him for the love of the mother. Subsequently the son needs to replace or supersede the father so he can enter into his own social and sexual life. The figure for such replacement, for the son's becoming a person capable of assuming his own authority, of taking his own place, is the dead father. The father's figurative murder by the son enables individual growth, health, and normality; it enables the son to enter as well into the social structures of lawful order by affirming the symbolic structures of the family as excluding incest. This is the "fruitful moment of debt" of son to father.

Lacan speaks, of course, not merely of the literal father in his structuring of the Oedipus complex but of the son's imaginary relationship to the father as an idealized figure and of his symbolic relationship to cultural and religious assumptions about the structures and significations of paternity. We cannot, then, when we think about language and authorship, merely trace symbolic structures back to "real" fathers as origins but must see the real, imaginary, and symbolic aspects of oedipal work as structurally interrelated. When we consider Charles Dickens as son and author, what we know of the relationship between Dickens and his father must figure into our exploration of his narratives. Dickens's ambivalent relationship to John Dickens as causing the proliferation of doubled father surrogates in his novels, especially the early ones, has become a critical commonplace. Yet this description of good daddies and bad, this investigation of Dickens's version of the "family romance," must be defined in terms of the structures of oedipal work. Two critics have recently done so. Albert D. Hutter, discussing Dickens's reconstruction of his childhood experiences at the blacking warehouse in the autobiographical fragment, identifies Dickens's suffering at the warehouse and his adult obsession with its memory as anxiety about finding himself while yet a boy in the place a father should occupy. The young Charles, the only member of the family living and working outside the debtor's prison, experienced not only a severe deprivation of intimacy and caring but also realized a fantasy of the oedipal period of a son's life: the replacement of his own father.[20] Pearl Chesler Solomon, discussing Dickens's social criticism and its relation to his ambivalent feelings toward John Dickens, defines the blacking warehouse incident as a "declassing" and an imagined betrayal by the father. Solomon relates the structure of oedipal desire for the child-mother in *David Copperfield* to David's guilt about replacing his father and his resulting need to supplant and supersede surrogate fathers—Murdstone, Micawber, Mr. Dick, and the "masculine" Aunt Betsey. In superseding these figures of fatherhood, Solomon argues, David enables himself to become successful and portray himself to himself as responsible for his own creation. David's figurative fathers punish and threaten the ambitious, desiring boy whose real father could not; Aunt Betsey encourages the ambitious, desiring boy to supersede herself as father—"just a woman"—and so allows him not to face the full implications of his worldly success. Like David, Solomon argues, Dickens superseded *his* father, felt guilty about it, and resented his impecunious father because he recognized yet repressed his own resemblance to John Dickens.[21]

Considered together, Hutter's and Solomon's theories about father and son include the aspects Freud identifies as important in the dissolution of the masculine Oedipus complex: identification or resemblance, replacement, and supersedence. Yet both critics elide a figure central to the "fruitful moment of debt": the dead father. A son's superseding a father involves his calling into question paternal authority and precedence; a son's supplanting a father implies displacement by force, fraud, or innovation; a son's replacing a father defines that place as empty, that father as absent. All three versions of father-son relationship, then, represent conflict—a son disillusioned with paternal authority, a son killing the idealized image of a father. In terms of narrative sequence and structure, Dickens's search for the father as originator of identity and initiator of narrative event discovers an absent origin, a dead or murdered father, a metaleptic temporality. This structural discovery of the murdered father coincides with Dickens's textual thematics of parricide: a son confronts his desire for paternal murder, and his narrative recalls the figure of the murdered father from the grave.

The son, then, murders the father at the "fruitful moment of debt." This murder, however, appears figurative, fantasied, wished. Guy Rosalato discusses the ways in which this fantasy of murder transforms the relationship between father and son by virtue of "sacrifice." Rosalato, like René Girard, believes all sacrificial structures kill the father through substitute victimage. In the case of Abraham and Isaac, for example, Abraham makes a covenant with the Father, God, which he confirms with the sacrificial murder of his own son, Isaac. Yet through the mechanism of substitution—the ram for Isaac—God takes death upon himself. Abraham as father takes death upon himself by recognizing in his near-murder of his son his own mortality and his eventual supersedence by his son. Rosalato calls God before the covenant the "Idealized Father," all-powerful, jealous, the sole and original lawgiver. The "son," Abraham, can only wish this Father murdered; yet in order to make a covenant with the Father, Abraham must murder his son, his own fatherhood.[22] The substitution of the ram as sacrificial victim mediates the murder. As John T. Irwin puts it, "Through the use of a substitute, the murder of the father can be accomplished in an indirect, in a symbolic manner, so that the figure of the Dead Father takes the place of the figure of the Murdered Father. Through the symbolic substitution inherent in the mediating sacrifice, the Oedipal situation is surmounted, and [the son] passes into the patrilineal situation."[23]

Rosalato's sacrificing father elaborates Lacan's symbolic father. Both theories of the father-son oedipal relationship require a mediating third term that transforms the oedipal battle into an alliance, which allows the son to move into and accept the symbolic structures of law and sexuality. For Lacan, the third term appears as the signifier of the phallus and castration; for Rosalato, the mark of circumcision, the near-castration. Both, however, invoke the order of symbolism, the laws of language, to explain the son's transformation of the murdered father into the dead father, the son's fantasied wish to kill his father into a symbolic understanding of fatherhood.[24] In Dickens's narratives that deal with parricide, just such a transformation must take place. When at the origin of his fictions Dickens discovers the father dead, he in fact discovers the murdered father, the murdering father, the corrupt father, the debunked and no longer idealized father. The thematics of parricide in Dickens's narratives attempt to transform this father into the symbolic father. Narrative structure itself mediates the oedipal conflict; the text performs the act of parricide which turns the murdered father into the dead father. In this way, Dickens's parricidal narratives rework and attempt to symbolize the "fruitful moment of debt."

For Charles Dickens the "symbolic debt" was also economic. The exaggerated struggle he and his father undertook when both were adults centered on money, a literal representation that the father and son continued to work through the structures, the figurative "debt," of the oedipal situation. The debting began early. In 1824, Dickens's father was imprisoned for debt, and Charles went to work. In 1826, his father's successful stint as a journalist came to an end, and Charles's second period of education ended with it. In 1834, John Dickens was again arrested for debt, and his son Charles now paid his bills, taking over the pecuniary role of father to his father in earnest, not fantasy. After a crisis in which his father applied to Chapman and Hall for money in 1837, and the appearance of more debts in 1839, Dickens moved his father and mother to a cottage at Alphington. In 1841, the banishing of the debt-ridden father to the country failed, and as his father took out debts on his son's now-famous name, Dickens made his private trials public (as he later would do when he and Kate separated) and advertised in the papers that he would no longer pay his father's debts. He urged his father to go abroad and offered to pay a yearly sum to keep him there. When his father refused to go abroad or to stay at Alphington, Dickens hired him in 1843 at the *Daily News* and once again replaced his father as provider — as "boss" — to his own father, now dependent upon him as is a son.[25]

Dickens's attempts to banish his father represent a figurative parricide of sorts, an acknowledgment that doing away with the father in whatever form is closely linked to debt, both literal and symbolic. The near-homonyms, "death" and "debt," "parricide" and "parasite," as my epigraph to this section intends to imply, identify the father-son oedipal struggle as "economic." I mean my term to suggest both the structural and figurative senses of "economic" here. Figuratively, between father and son in the oedipal situation, Lacan's concept of "symbolic debt" defines the son's placement as subject within the social and cultural structures of law and authority. Structurally, Freud's third definition of the psychic processes, his "economic" point of view, defines psychic energy as quantifiable, as capable of increase, decrease, and equivalence. Central to Freud's notion of libidinal economy is the concept of circulation, of values "capable of being exchanged for one another," "susceptible of displacement and equivalence within a system."[26] When I use the term "economic," then, to describe the father-son oedipal relationship, I intend to articulate the concepts of symbolic debt, the son's figurative murder of the father, and the systematic oedipal structure in which terms for equivalence, displacement, and exchange—or circulation of value between son and father—define intersubjective and structural transformation.

Dickens continually imagines the father-son relationship as an economic one. His recurring prodigal sons and fathers (Pip, Rob the Grinder, Steerforth, Eugene Wrayburn, Micawber), his figurative Cains (Clennam, Quilp, Rob the Grinder again, Florence Dombey, himself) allude to biblical figures in stories that articulate economic sins of ingratitude against the family and particularly against the "Father," with death, usually of a substitute (the calf, Abel) for the son or Father. In his first, almost spontaneously written novel, *Pickwick Papers,* Dickens structures his interpolated tales to articulate such economic issues of debt and death, to associate and transmute the figurative, structural, and narrative elements of his own blacking warehouse father-son experience: prison, debt, betrayal, revenge. In "The Convict's Return," a son remembers his abandoning father's "cruel" and "unnatural" ill-usage of his mother, turns criminal, and is arrested; during his resulting term of transportation, his mother dies, and the son's letters fail to reach the mediating clergyman who tells the tale. When he returns home, the convict-son finds a loving father and son inhabiting his old home; he accidentally meets his own father and metaphorically murders him—strangles but does not immediately kill him. In "The Old Man's Tale about a Queer Client," a son imprisoned for debt vows to revenge his incarceration and the death of his wife and child; after his release, he refuses to save the life of his father-in-law's only son and with his accidental patrimony, hounds his father-in-law to death for debt.[27] In both of these tales, Dickens portrays an imprisoned son, a betraying father, a debting father, and a revengeful son—quite a different interpretation from the nostalgic autobiographical fragment's "small Cain" who never hurts anybody and who protests too much that his father did not betray him. The interpolated tales rather baldly represent the debt-death, parasite-parricide equivalences and do so primarily because of their status in the text of *Pickwick Papers.* The critical terminology we use to describe these tales as "insertions," as "corruptions" of the text in which they appear, identifies them as self-reflexive fictions: they tell stories within the posthumous papers of the Pickwickians and pointedly define themselves as fictional. Their exemplary nature as narratives identifies their narrative structures of revenge as the mediator of the father-son economic.

The "symbolic debt" of son to father in *Pickwick Papers* finds its comic parody in Sam and Tony Weller's jovial relationship. Late in the novel, when his benevolent master is in prison for debt and misinterpretation of a woman's language, Sam Weller persuades his father to lend him money and subsequently to imprison himself, the "prodigy" son, for debt (634-46). This symbolic debt involves no revenge, no betrayal. At Dingley Dell, Mr. Wardle hosts the profusely eating-and-drinking Pickwickians, and a gentleman recites his poem, "The Ivy Green," about host and parasite, yet the equivalences Dickens imagines in the interpolated tales between "parasite" and "parricide" fail to apply here. In fact, in the 1841 preface to *The Old Curiosity Shop*, Dickens imagines his novel a feast, himself as author the host, his reader the happy consumer — the "parasite"?[28] The father-son economic demands a structure of betrayal and revenge, a narrative structure with victimage at stake, for the equivalence to assert itself, for an "economic" to operate its transformations. The interpolated tales, skeletal narratives in which "plot" and "story" coincide, identify Dickens's discovery that narrative itself represents the act of parricide, that the murdered father becomes the dead symbolic father in the structures of the text.

Barnaby Rudge, as Steven Marcus has already suggested, represents Dickens's anatomy of the father-son economic, of sons and circumstances murdering fathers, and of the text symbolizing the dead father.[29] Among the novel's characters, the struggle of the father-son economic is structured by the language of desire and prohibition: fathers repress their sons' desires (their "no" is Lacan's pun in "nom-du-père").[30] John Willet denies Joe's maturing into manhood and loudly demands his son's "silence," claiming his own superiority in "argeyment"; John Chester interferes in Edward's courtship of Emma Haredale and sneeringly asks his son not to be "prosey." Both sons disappear from the novel at the end of part one, leave home on the same fictional day in order not to attempt murder against the father who prohibits.

This novel, then, appears to refuse, figuratively, to murder fathers. Yet the text symbolizes parricide in its displacements of the father-son economic. In the absence of fathers, sons' desires transform the language of the father-son economic: Barnaby Rudge's idealized desire for his mother appears in his madly metaphorical speech; Hugh of the Maypole's "rape" of Dolly Varden in the woods is accomplished metaphorically through aggressive rhetoric. The lack of the "paternal metaphor" creates such metaphorical expressions of desire. In the absence of fathers, the narrative also provides these metaphorical sons with displaced oedipal relationships and structures. Desire takes as its object a father's daughter rather than a mother; metaphorical parricide, a master or aristocrat. Sim Tappertit's rallying cry in his 'Prentice Knights meeting names three kinds of violence against the master-fathers: beat them, burn their houses (as Hugh and Sim later burn the significantly named "Warren"), and carry off their daughters (as Hugh and Sim kidnap, ogle, and threaten Emma Haredale and Dolly Varden after burning the Warren). This metaphorical rebellion against or murder of the figurative father, however, appears frustrated by the novel's structure and by Dickens's metaphor of the Gordon riots as parricidal. When the riots get bloody, Dickens calls in the heretofore ineffective law to repress and punish the rioters and ends up demonstrating that symbolic parricide merely results in the figurative son's turning his violence against himself.

The narrative structure, however, murders fathers despite the problematic political metaphors of the riots, despite the "good" sons' decision to refuse parricide. Joe Willet and Edward Chester return home to "save" fathers from the riots and to discover themselves magically in possession of daughters, Dolly and Emma. Edward's father is murdered by Haredale, himself a figurative father to Emma. Joe's father has been figuratively murdered by narrative sequence and circumstance, has lost his ability to speak, is shorn of his "gift of argeyment" as a result of Hugh's gang's plundering and burning of the Maypole. At the end of the novel, an inverted primal scene represents the father watching the son express his desire to a daughter: John Willet dumbly gazes at Joe kissing Dolly and speaking "in the most impassioned manner"; Joe asks his now speechless father to "say a word . . . if it's only 'how d'ye do,'" but John Willet fails to understand the necessary articulation of language which mediates desire in this primal scene stood on its head and so continues to sit motionless, watching.[31] John Willet loses the linguistic power he defines at the novel's opening as the domain of the father, and his son at the narrative's end appropriates it.

The narrative's paradoxical parricide in the father-son economic finds at its center the "magic name" of the father. In the heart of Newgate, the son and father for whom the novel is named meet in a scene of shadow and silence. When Rudge tells Barnaby, "I am your father," Barnaby springs toward Rudge, whom he identifies as the robber, but then embraces him. The son speaks "not a word" in answer to his father, as Grip the raven dances around father and son and encloses them in a "magic circle" (478). This scene of magic and embrace identifies the paradox of the father-son economic. Within the structures of parricide, at its heart, its center, is desire for the paternal embrace, for imitation of and identification with father by son. In *A Tale of Two Cities*, this desire appears as comic parody, as Young Jerry Cruncher thinks of entering his father's mysterious nighttime business and sits in front of Tellson's Bank in perfect imitation of the father. Yet the plethora of orphans and fatherless sons in Dickens's narratives demonstrates that despite this desire, the paternal metaphor proves inadequate. The son fails to resemble his father; the father fails to love his son. The son must continue metaphorically to murder the "real" father in an effort to transform him into the symbolic and dead father.

The father-son economic in Dickens's narratives, then, attempts to pay off the "symbolic debt" by figuratively performing the murder of the father. Yet the dead father in Dickens's novels refuses to accept his role as symbolic father. Throughout Dickens's narratives, the murdered father returns; throughout Dickens's career as a writer, the father-son economic returns as material for narrative. The father has not been murdered, but repressed; his return both within the structures of individual narrative and throughout a career of writing narrative identifies the text as a repetition of the son's attempt to symbolize the father and so position himself as subject in a social, cultural, and linguistic system. In *Barnaby Rudge, David Copperfield,* and *Great Expectations,* the apparently dead father haunts the murdering son. This temporal doubling of the father matches his "spatial" doubling or surrogate figures—the good daddies and bad seen throughout Dickens's novels. Only at the end of his career, in Pip's excoriating self-criticism, does Dickens discover the narrative metaphors and structures that finally keep the dead father in his symbolic place.

Barnaby Rudge once more identifies the structures and metaphors of this thematic. The "mysterious stranger" reappears throughout the narrative, a ghostly figure of temporal doubling, and is finally identified as the "dead" father. This mystery about fathers and murder declares itself at the novel's point of departure. A stranger asks at the Maypole if Emma Haredale's father is alive; John Willet responds, "He is not alive, and he is not dead— . . . Not dead in a common sort of way" (10). Although the landlord means by his comment, "Haredale was killed in a singular manner," his language can also signify, "Haredale appears dead, yet is really alive." This double signification mediates the novel's father-son economic and allows for the structure of repetition or temporal doubling, for the return of the repressed figure of the father. Just as structural doubling of narrative sequence calls into question the father as a figure of origin in Dickens's narratives, the multiplicity of the signification in the texts' parricidal language creates the moment in which the dead father returns. When Freud discusses the ways in which the familiar becomes "uncanny," he links double signification, the figure of the double, the return of the repressed, and the death of a father.[32] Although Freud himself "represses" the dead father in his essay, dropping his early discussion of the "Sand-Man" with its reappearing figure who signifies the father's death and consigning its interpretation to a long footnote, that interpretation nonetheless roots the ghostly father in what I have called the father-son economic. In *Barnaby Rudge,* the first appearance of this "stranger" at the Maypole who inquires about dead fathers introduces the reader to a sense of the uncanny and signals the entire symbolic of the double, repression, and the murdered father. This stranger, although neither Willet nor the reader yet knows it, is himself the returning apparently "dead" father, the "murdered" and murdering father. Although we at first think him Emma Haredale's "dead but not in a common way" father, his reappearances, especially at Barnaby's home, gradually identify him as Barnaby's "dead but not in a common way" father. After killing his master, Rudge had killed the gardener and exchanged clothes with the dead man to signify his own death, as Rogue Riderhood would much later attempt to "kill" himself in *Our Mutual Friend.*

The murdered father returns because of a structural relationship to his son, and that relationship creates a system of metaphors to which Dickens will return in *Great Expectations'* farcical representations of *Hamlet:* the father as ghost. As surely as the "dead of night" sets in, Rudge wanders the streets as "spectre," "ghost," and "shadow." After leaving the Maypole, he is beaten by his son at a crossroads; like the paradigmatic Oedipus, Barnaby thinks his antagonist a thief and fails to know him as his father. Rudge thereafter appears at his wife and son's home as a "ghost," surrounded by secrets and himself the figure of a "riddle"; there he watches his son imitate himself and appear "so like the original he counterfeited" that he himself, the dark figure "peering out behind" Barnaby, appears to be Barnaby's "own shadow" (43-46, 133). The metaphor of the father as ghost, as these passages indicate, springs from the oedipal work of the text. Father and son have a symbolic debt to settle, although in this narrative Dickens disguises that debt as Barnaby's madness and displaces its work onto other sons. The narrative nevertheless attempts to pay off the symbolic debt of son to father and to transform by textual parricide the murdered father into the truly dead and symbolic father. Until this work has been accomplished, the "murdered" and murdering father haunts the son, much as Pip's benefactors will later haunt him—the specter of Miss Havisham hanging; Abel Magwitch, the ghost made flesh. This haunting is based, as our ghostly metaphor implies, on a spectral resemblance of father and son—the mark of his father's crime inscribed on Barnaby's wrist—and can be ended only when the son has recognized the metaphorical relationship of himself to his father, has performed the work of symbolizing his debt, and so has entered himself into the structures that make him subject to himself in and through narrative.

The murdered father also returns because his figure is essential in the narrative structure of betrayal and revenge I identified in *Pickwick Papers* as linked to the fictional work of the father-son economic. At the end of *Barnaby Rudge,* the "murdered" father as ghost returns to the scene of his crime, murder, because he is haunted by the ghost of his victim. Throughout the novel, Rudge narratively asks to be punished by virtue of the spaces he haunts: he returns to the Warren sleeping and waking, visits his own grave, hears his secret spoken by the voices of nature, and so is drawn to the place of his earlier arrest by the "corpse" of Haredale (471-77). His murder, his "self-murder," is performed by the narrative structures of revenge. Haredale, brother of the master Rudge murdered, discovers Rudge haunting the burned-out Warren, and, recognizing Rudge, defines him as the murdered father. Sir John Chester has accused Haredale of himself killing his brother, and so Haredale inherits the narrative motivation for revenge. Indeed, he murders Rudge and narratively transforms him into the dead father. Once again, *Barnaby Rudge* displaces the work of the father-son economic — here, from the son onto a brother — but the text nevertheless performs its parricide, taking revenge not on a substitute or replacement for the father but on the father himself. In this way, the murdered father attains his symbolic place as the dead father, and the son begins to pay off his debt. Charles Dickens, the writing son, has only begun his recompense, but the wild displacement of the narrative structures of revenge and metaphorical parricide in *Barnaby Rudge* demonstrate that the father will indeed return to haunt him in later narratives.

Return from the dead in Dickens's novels, as in Freud's essay on the uncanny, is not limited to fathers. The motif finds its most symbolic expression in *A Tale of Two Cities*, where it first appears unrelated to fatherhood. Roger Cly, British spy and brother to Miss Pross, represents himself as dead, stages a grand funeral, yet is found out by Jerry Cruncher, the resurrection-man, who excavates Cly's coffin and finds it empty. The spy Barsad "feign[s] death and come[s] to life again" (289); likewise, the aristocrat Foulon "causes himself to be represented as dead," stages a grand mock-funeral, yet is found out by Mme Defarge, condemned to death by her husband's "deadly embrace," and hung and beheaded by Mme Defarge and the mob (212). Yet this motif, repeated in various guises throughout the novel, ultimately converges on the father. Dr. Manette, "recalled to life," is remembered by his daughter, summoned to return by Jarvis Lorry, and revived from a living death by the love of one and the attention of the other.

In *David Copperfield*, the dead father also returns. The "posthumous child" feels an "indefinable compassion" for his father's white gravestone "lying out alone" in the "dark night" with the doors to the warm parlor "bolted and locked against it."[33] The story of Lazarus, which David's mother reads him one night, frightens him, arousing his suspicions of that grave; Clara and Peggotty must take him out of bed and show him "the dead all lying in their graves at rest" (14). Yet when Peggotty tells David, "You have got a pa!" he associates his sudden fear with the "grave in the churchyard, and the raising of the dead" (42). Murdstone is David's father risen from the dead. When Murdstone takes David to the seashore in the "Brooks of Sheffield" incident, his two friends confirm this haunting: "Halloa, Murdstone," they yell; "we thought you were dead!" The new father responds, "Not yet" (22).[34] The adult narrator of this story thinks his "shadowy remembrances" of the earliest of these events even stranger than the uncanny fact that his father never saw himself (2).

In both *A Tale* and *David Copperfield,* the father rises from the dead to punish a son. David's sensitivity to his father's grave connects nighttime with bed and both with his mother; Murdstone punishes the boy for his oedipal desire. Dr. Manette returns not only because his daughter loves and "recalls" him, but narratively and structurally to punish his son-in-law, Charles Darnay, for the sins of *his* father. Yet in both narratives, sons set in motion the narrative structures of betrayal and revenge and so consign the fathers to inactivity. David, having run away to a figurative father who is "only a woman" and so nonpunishing and easily superseded,[35] takes his revenge against fathers in the act of writing: when Dora's father opposes David's proposal of marriage to the "child-wife" who will replace the mother in David's affections, Dora's father conveniently dies, as though the writing of the text had performed the parricide David intended in his "undisciplined" (and etymologically "incestuous") heart.[36] In *A Tale of Two Cities,* on the other hand, the narrative refuses to ascribe motivations of betrayal and revenge to individual characters, and so parricide is performed structurally, in the text but outside the intentions of the characters who passively fit Dickens's overdetermined symbolic (because serialized weekly) plot. The doubled figure of the father allows Charles Darnay to escape clear responsibility for the sins of his forefathers; the doubled figure of the son allows him to rise from the dead and redeem the intentions of the father. Sydney Carton, Darnay's twin, is also a son: as his death approaches, he discovers his sonly feelings for Jarvis Lorry, banker at "tell-son's," and becomes the figurative apotheosis of sonhood, Christ, the dying son who, choosing death, redeems the nearly dead to life in the name of the Father.[37] Carton remembers following his father to his grave, and structurally he "follows his father to *his* grave," speaking the words that were read at his father's death, "I am the resurrection and the life" (298).

This uncanny return of the apparently dead father to a primal scene of love and violence finds its fullest and most paradoxical expression in *Great Expectations.* Two systematic metaphors mediate the father-son economic in this novel: Pip as George Barnwell and Pip as viewer of *Hamlet.* Mr. Wopsle reads the "affecting tragedy" of *The London Merchant* to Pip and his supposed benefactor, Uncle Pumblechook. "What stung me," Pip reports, "was the identification of the whole affair with my unoffending self. . . . At once ferocious and maudlin, I was made to murder my uncle with no extenuating circumstances whatever; . . . it became sheer monomania in my master's daughter to care a button for me; and all I can say for my gasping and procrastinating conduct on the fatal morning, is, that it was worthy of the general feebleness of my character. . . . [It seemed] a well-known fact that I contemplated murdering a near relation, provided I could only induce one to have the weakness to become my benefactor."[38] Immediately following this "representation," Pip returns home to find Mrs. Joe beaten, and, with his "head full of George Barnwell," Pip believes himself responsible for the attack because he had "provided the weapon"—the leg iron he helped Magwitch file off in the novel's first scenes (113-14). When Pip leaves for London, Uncle Pumblechook regales him with a collation in the "Barnwell parlour" (144).

The Pip-Barnwell metaphor defines the structures of Pip's oedipal guilt and aggression, of the father-son economic.[39] Pip, like Barnwell, an apprentice, indeed desires to "murder" a benefactor or two: Miss Havisham, whom he imagines hanging and wishes burned; Mrs. Joe, against whom Orlick acts out Pip's aggressions; Clara's thumping father, whom he and Herbert Pocket wish dead; Uncle Pumblechook; and finally, Magwitch, whom for purposes of disguise, he and Herbert call "Uncle Provis." Pip's aggression against fathers, like that of Sim Tappertit and Hugh of the Maypole in another novel that mentions George Barnwell, takes the form of violence against surrogates, against "uncles," masters, and benefactors as well as sexual violence against a daughter, Estella.[40] In *Great Expectations*, however, Pip redeems the role of uncle-murdering apprentice and becomes the "London merchant," the uncle to himself, little Pip.

In the novel's second metaphor for the father-son economic, Pip watches *Hamlet* and resembles Hamlet, the son who tries but fails to "murder" an "uncle" to avenge a father's sexual supplanting in a primal scene of incest. Joe Gargery tells Pip their friend Wopsle has converted from preaching to "playacting," has performed *Hamlet* in the countryside, and will open it in London. "If the ghost of a man's own father cannot be allowed to claim his attention," Joe asks, "what can?" (208-9). Agreeing, Pip and Herbert depart—metaphorically—for Denmark. Pip represents Wopsle's performance of *Hamlet* as afflicted by foolishness out of place in such tragedy about the father-son economic: the King coughs in his tomb; the ghost forgets his lines; the Queen resembles a "kettle-drum"; Ophelia acts too slowly; Hamlet represents himself inconsistently as a seaman, an actor, a gravedigger, a clergyman, and a fencing match judge. Hamlet-Wopsle experiences his "greatest trials" in the "churchyard," whose scene is set with a turnpike gate and a washhouse. The audience throws nuts; shouts humiliating answers to Hamlet's metaphysical questions about being, doubt, and the place of man between heaven and earth; hoots through the struggle with Laertes and the King's final "tumble" off a "kitchen-table." Pip goes home following the performance and dreams of his expectations canceled, of marrying Clara (we are reminded of David's earlier incestuous desire for a "Clara"), of playing

Hamlet to Miss Havisham's ghost without knowing the drama's words (239-44).

Pip's dreams define the ridiculous drama as metaphorically significant. Figurative failure, incest, revenge, haunting, and self-representation ally Pip's experience to Hamlet's, despite Dickens's parody of the great procrastinator. Pip, like Barnaby and David, is haunted by his dead fathers. Pip assumes Magwitch, the fugitive who seems to rise from Pip's father's grave in the novel's opening scene, "dead" to Pip himself and wishes Magwitch "veritably dead into the bargain" (139). Yet, like Barnaby's father, the criminal Magwitch and his surrogates haunt Pip throughout the novel. The criminal who returns the two one-pound notes Pip gave Magwitch represents the "turning up" of Pip's "old misdeed and old acquaintance." He stirs his drink with the file that freed Magwitch and so caused Mrs. Joe eventually to be beaten with the leg iron: this file "haunts" Pip, waking and sleeping. This surrogate Magwitch, a kind of ghost made flesh, asks whether Pip is Joe's "son" or "nevvy" and so structures the scene as a haunting of a "son" by a criminal figurative father and defines the complex love and murder Pip experiences toward Joe, his other figurative father (72-73).

Guilty about his rejection of Joe after the announcement of his expectations, Pip finds this same mysterious convict seated behind himself on a coach Pip takes home for a visit. Pip awakes from a doze to find the convict-ghost telling another convict about Pip himself, with Pip's own dreamed words, "Two One-Pound notes," telling about Magwitch's sending Pip the money, about the marshes. Pip experiences a great fear, a "dread" of recognition which makes him tremble, which he identifies as a "revival" of the "terror of childhood" (215-17). As in *Barnaby Rudge*, in *Great Expectations* this uncanny haunting, Pip's revived childhood memories, the return of the repressed, define Magwitch's surrogate as a figurative father. This second haunting renders the first significant rather than accidental and identifies Magwitch as Pip's "second father," as his benefactor. Hearing the details of "Pip's story," however, the well-dressed "Handel," alienated from his repressed childhood memories, refuses to identify himself as subject of this narrative, refuses to admit the convict his benefactor, refuses to admit himself haunted by a figure for his second father.

Pip eventually finds himself, however, confronted with the original ghost made flesh. Experiencing a Hamletish "inability to settle to anything" (298), Pip reads a book one night, only to be visited by the convict who calls himself Pip's "second father." Pip feels an agony "of being so haunted"; doubts a real "ghost could have been more terrible" to him; imagines himself Frankenstein's monster pursued by the "creature who had made" him (303-7). The dead father returns from the grave because of the father-son economic, because the debt of son to father must be acknowledged: two one-pound notes. Magwitch owns, possesses Pip; the money that defines Pip's attempt to rise in life represents the debt he owes his figurative father, the debt he has denied. In this novel's haunting of son by father, Pip attempts to confront that debt, to acknowledge that he owes his second father love in return for his "fathering." Yet, as we see when Pip asks to be searched when he visits the dying Magwitch in prison, Pip acknowledges that his love for Magwitch, his second father, can be expressed only in a wish to consign him, finally, to death, to the realm of symbolic fatherhood.

This final attempt to murder the father allies Pip with another of the novel's ghosts, Compeyson. While viewing Wopsle acting in a doubly foolish double-bill musical and Christmas pantomime, Pip wonders why Wopsle stares at himself, Pip. After the performance, Wopsle reveals he stared at someone "sitting behind" Pip "like a ghost." That ghost behind Pip (who resembles the surrogate Magwitch ghost on the coach), Pip identifies as Compeyson, the other criminal arrested off the marshes with Magwitch on that significant Christmas. Yet this time Pip finds himself haunted not by a figurative father but by a figure for himself, a "compensating son," who will eventually kill his second father in order to alleviate his guilt, to "pay off" his debt. Compeyson's desire for revenge against Magwitch resembles Pip's own feeling toward his "second father." Indeed, Wopsle says he had "from the first vaguely associated him with [Pip], and known him as somehow belonging to [Pip] in the old village time." Pip describes the ghost of Compeyson behind him as a figure for his own unconscious: Pip forgets Compeyson, whom he fears will cause his second father to be "hanged," only while at the play, yet "it was in those very moments when he was closest to me." Pip metaphorically closes "a hundred doors to keep [Compeyson] out," then finds Compeyson at his "elbow" in a moment he is "unconscious and off my guard" (364-66). The ghost behind him this time represents not his father but Pip's own repressed murderous desires toward the criminal who fathered him, to whom he owes a symbolic debt he refuses to pay off. Yet the haunting of Pip by a figure for himself who quite literally causes the death of Magwitch betrays that despite guilt, the son must still perform in his text metaphorical parricide to liberate the love he should feel for that (and another) father.

Pip's hauntings by the "ghost of a man's own father" brings us back to *Hamlet*, which not only identifies Pip's desire to kill his "uncle," his "second father," but also calls into question the concept of performance, or representation. Dickens does not merely allude to *Hamlet* but represents Pip representing himself watching the drama. Wopsle, Pip's foolish Hamlet, appears structurally implicated in both hauntings and representations. Wopsle sees Magwitch and Compeyson apprehended at the beginning of the novel and so identifies Compeyson as the figure behind

Pip "like a ghost"; Wopsle reads *The London Merchant* to Pip and implies that Pip resembles George Barnwell; Wopsle "represents" a popular murder at the Three Jolly Bargemen the night Jaggers announces to Pip his "great expectations"; Wopsle performs *Hamlet;* Wopsle adumbrates Pip's "fall" from his expectations in his own "drop from preaching to playacting" and finally to voiceless mime. Wopsle, present at each important step of Pip's "great expectations," appears, like Orlick, as a figure for Pip himself. His role as performer in the drama of Pip's life identifies Wopsle as a figure of Pip figuring himself. Wopsle represents Pip's urge to represent himself, which is what Pip claims to do in writing this book we read, in reclaiming "Pip's story," in criticizing his "great expectations," his unconscious desires.

In *Great Expectations,* Dickens returns to a metaphor for representation, for performance, he had explored in *Nicholas Nickleby* and *The Old Curiosity Shop:* the theater. As a form of recreation and art, of course, Dickens's own "amateur theatricals" fulfilled a need to perform his fiction-writing failed to provide. The Reading Tours embodied a similar urge to act, to represent his characters directly and dramatically to a present audience. In *Nickleby,* the Crummles's theater appears as a metaphor for family capitalism, for the entrepreneurial manipulation of audience sympathy and finance. The father runs the company, blinded to the failures in mimesis of his infant phenomenon. The company performs any old drama, written around the props they have at hand, and the representation the narrator describes for us appears as a combination of *Antigone* gone wrong and a Jacobean drama: mistaken identity mixes with the unburied bones of a father. The patriarch appears most prominent in performing these dramas, as in directing the company. In *The Old Curiosity Shop,* however, Dickens questions not only the relationships among performance, patriarchy, and finance but also the relationship between art and reality. The Punch troupe fixes their puppets away from the scene of performance so as not to "destroy the delusion" (123). Codlin and Trotter describe the theater-on-their-backs as paradoxically a burden that names the hollowness of life and an entertainment to pass the time and make the best of everything (133). Mrs. Jarley's waxwork, in which the figures look "intensely nowhere" and stare "with extraordinary earnestness at nothing," appears "so like life, that if wax-work only spoke and walked about you'd hardly know the difference." Waxwork, Mrs. Jarley says, is not "quite like life," but some life "was exactly like wax-work" (214, 203). Waxwork's confusion of life and death makes it, according to Freud, uncanny, another version of haunting.[41] In both early novels, the theater houses the grotesque wanderers of the caricatured and caricaturing world. Mimesis appears farcical, absurd, and illusory. Representation and performance appear both as a betrayal and a deathly simulacrum of life.[42]

In *Great Expectations,* the theater remains farcical, yet bears a more metaphorical burden than it did in *Nicholas Nickleby* and *The Old Curiosity Shop.* All three novels figure the theater as a setting in which the self acts as other; despite its absurdity, the theater embodies a dark and symbolic mimesis. In Pip's narrative, Wopsle is that "other" acting Pip's need to represent himself. *Hamlet* assumes performance represents the structures of reality to which drama refers by virtue of the "play within a play"; *Great Expectations* questions representation and the structures to which it refers by virtue of Pip's narrative representation of Wopsle's performance. Pip's report focuses on Wopsle as actor, on the differences between the text of the drama and its performance. This discontinuity provides Pip's pleasure in reporting the drama as well as his interest in theater as metaphor. For Pip thinks texts, stories, and storytelling merely a version of "lying."[43] His childhood "inventions," for example, about Miss Havisham's black coach, about dogs that eat from silver baskets, about flags, swords, and pistols, create so much guilt he must confess his lying to Joe. Brotherly Joe warns Pip that "lies is lies" and originate with the "father of lies," the devil. Pip as a child realizes his inventions spring from wounded self-esteem, from Estella's insistence on the apprentice-boy's commonness: "the lies had come of it somehow, though I didn't know how," he reports (62-67). This guilt about "invention," this invention itself, defines storytelling as a "compensation," a criminal self-aggrandizement, a transgression of truthtelling. A story is a discourse of otherness which refuses to reveal its source as a son's guilty compensation for his symbolic paying off of a debt. A performed drama, in contrast, openly states its otherness and creates only farce when its performance differs from its text. Trabb's boy's remarkable mime of Pip's acting himself as a young gentleman demonstrates that Pip's own story revels in such confession of the self acting as other. Only by representing himself as a performer and actor can Pip expiate his guilt, recall himself to rightful love of his two figurative fathers, and relieve himself of the guilt of his inventions about himself, his benefactors, and his expectations.

Pip's narrative, which forces Pip himself to retell "Pip's story" as told by the convict on the coach, represents a performance. Pip writes his story to chastise himself but also to warn us, to indict us of having ourselves acted as others—just as he has. "Pause you who read this, and think for a moment," he adjures, about the consequences of your actions, which although you refuse to admit it, resemble mine. "It is the same with any life. . . . Think for a moment of the long chain of iron or gold, of thorns or flowers, that would never have bound you, but for the formation of the first link on one memorable day" (67). Making metaphors of performance, Pip's narrative aims to make us aware of ourselves as performers, as Pip is now aware of his own history. Pip associates—and intends us to associate—performance with acting, with self-delusion, with the inauthentic self acting as other. The drama portrays the actor as his own ghost; *Great Expectations* attempts to put to rest the ghosts of Pip, of fathers, and to encourage us to put to rest our own ghosts, our histories made flesh, our selves as other. The narrative inscribes the ghosts rising from the crypt to take revenge on the self for failing to see and hear the ghosts of itself behind it, to love the "ghost of a man's own father."

The storyteller Solomon Daisy of *Barnaby Rudge* retells his "ghost" story about fathers and murder each year on 19 March, the day the murder provided a source for the ghost story as well as for the narrative itself. Likewise, Dickens must repeat his narratives that perform textual parricide until the murdered father no longer haunts his texts. When his own father died in 1851, a year after *David Copperfield* was published, Charles Dickens's debt to his father was no longer economic, yet symbolically it still haunted him. Pip's relationship to Magwitch as figurative father to whom the son owes a literal as well as a symbolic debt springs most certainly from Dickens's feelings that he, like Pip, had refused to acknowledge and work through the debt to his father. This writing son, like the writing sons—the narrators, David and Pip—of Dickens's narratives, attempt to "compensate," to pay off, this debt. Pip, whose "compensation" occurs after his author's father's death, also attempts to make amends for what he defines as his guilt for desiring revenge against a figurative father. Yet while the text attempts to perform a parricide and so eliminate the ghostly "parasite," the metaphorical writer-as-son also attempts to give birth to himself in writing, to beget or engender himself without the help of fathers, to make himself subject to himself and subject in narrative—the "hero" of his own life.

Language Engenders

An Author feels as if he were dismissing some portion of himself into the shadowy world, when a crowd of the creatures of his brain are going from him forever. . . . Of all my books, I like this the best. It will be easily believed that I am a fond parent to every child of my fancy, and that no one can ever love that family as dearly as I love them. But, like many fond parents, I have in my heart of hearts a favourite child. And his name is DAVID COPPERFIELD —Charles Dickens, David Copperfield.

As this well-known prefatory remark to *David Copperfield* suggests, Dickens associated writing with figurative fatherhood, with parentage. Dickens spoke often of his young characters as his progeny—David, Oliver Twist, Little Nell. About Nell's written death, "Nellicide" as Dickens called it, he wrote to George Cattermole, the book's illustrator, that he was "nearly dead with work—and grief for the loss of my child"; to his friend John Forster, "nobody shall miss her like I shall" (*Letters*, 2: 257, 228, 184, 181). The author-as-father engenders his imagined progeny, his "family," provides them (and his texts) with legitimacy and himself with authority. For the concept of "authority," as Edward Said notes, invokes sexual, literary, and theological metaphors associated with masculinity and with the male author's power to engender. Said quotes the *OED*'s definitions of "authority," all of which describe power and the obedience it demands. Language creates and communicates authority: the author originates, begets, begins, fathers, and sets forth written statements; he produces, founds, invents, causes, and maintains a right of possession; finally, he maintains the continuity and controls the issue (whether textual or genealogical) of his action.[44] Dickens referred repeatedly to this set of paternal values and attributes in his letters, prefaces, and dedications. He decidedly objected, he grumbled early in his career, to "fathering anybody else's articles"; he refused in rage to "father" a bastard continuation of *Pickwick* (*Letters*, 1: 217, 433). Because his early offspring needed a double legitimacy, Dickens dedicated "The Village Coquettes" to J. P. Hartley, the metaphorical adoptive "father of Dickens's 'bantlings'"; Hartley would figuratively father "future scions of the same stock, no matter how numerous they may be or how quickly they follow in succession" (*Letters*, 1: 212). Dickens's fight for the international copyright itself proved to be a genealogical concern for the inheritance by authors' descendants of a permanent interest in the earnings their fathers' writings accrue (*Letters*, 1: 313).

In Dickens's retroactive structural search for the father as origin and in his thematics of parricide, the son discovers himself in the place of a father. Dickens's metaphor of the author-as-father identifies the writing son's way to become through writing a figurative father, to replace and become his own father. The narrative project serves to originate and engender the son himself. In *David Copperfield, Great Expectations,* and the "autobiographical fragment," Dickens's fictional sons—figures for himself, or parts of himself—attempt to confront or deny, to love and to accuse, their figurative fathers. In each narrative, a son tries to lay to rest "the ghost of a man's own father" by writing his life; in copying the act of fathering by authorship, the writing son fathers himself in language, in narrative. The text creates not only progeny but also the self as one's own progeny. David's, Pip's, and "Dickens's" autobiographical narratives all appear as a fictionalized version of Dickens's own struggle with fatherhood, his attempt through his "sons," his progeny, likewise to engender himself in narrative.[45]

David Copperfield celebrates, Pip Pirrip criticizes, retroactivity and self-engenderment. Both of Dickens's first-person male narrators attempt to account for their origins, recount their experiences, and make themselves subject to themselves in and through narrative. Yet both Pip and David are fatherless, and so their origins become enigmatic. David calls himself a "posthumous child," born after his father's death; Pip never sees his father or mother and has as proof of paternity only his sister's stories and the inscription on his father's gravestone. Metaphorically, then, David and Pip have no identifiable origin, no engendering father, and Pip has no mother as well: these two figures for Dickens owe their creations to no man. David's and Pip's fictions relate these births in which fathers clearly have no engendering function by representing themselves as reborn in narrative.

David's fiction of rebirth imagines a strangely lopsided family scene, whose fatherless structure facilitates and prophesies David's fathering of himself. This scenic structure makes sense only through its own deferral of signification and only in the context of the murdering, punishing father recalled from David's father's grave via David's own oedipal guilt. After feeling himself a "blank space" which "everybody overlooked" while on vacation from school with his new family, David parts from his mother and new baby brother in a mysterious scene of silence, gazing, and subsequent dream. As he rides away from Blunderstone Rookery, his mother calls after him; "I looked out," David tells us, "and she stood at the garden gate alone, holding her baby up in her arms for me to see. It was cold, still weather, and not a hair of her head or a fold of her dress was stirred, as she looked intently at me, holding up her child. So I lost her. So I saw her afterwards, in my sleep at school — a silent presence near my bed — looking at me with the same intent face — holding up her baby in her arms" (121). This triangular intersubjectivity defines Clara as lost to David by virtue of a new infant's arrival, as well as of a new husband's (father's) — who is conspicuously absent from this scene. Yet its uncanny disruption of the narrative, its excessive emotional charge, makes sense only when David's mother too dies, is literally rather than figuratively "lost" to him; this loss effaces his own origin and his last connection to an engendering father, to the Copperfields. After his mother's funeral, David associates himself with the infant who has also died, the child once held up for him to see when leaving home and so figuratively dies himself: "The mother who lay in the grave, was the mother of my infancy; the little creature in her arms, was myself, as I had once been, hushed for ever on her bosom" (133). This narrative moment banishes fathers, enshrines dead mothers, and kills that old young David, leaving him free to create himself.

Yet Murdstone prevents self-origination by putting David to work at Murdstone and Grinby's. To kill off this period of his life, to forget it as part of his self-engendered identity, David must be reborn at Aunt Betsey's cottage. Betsey bathes — purifies — and nourishes him, wraps him in figurative swaddling clothes, and puts him to bed an infant once more.

Aunt Betsey changes David's name, the name of his father, and—herself like a father—bestows her own name on him, marking it in his new clothes with "indelible marking-ink" in "her own handwriting." Deprived of his patrimony by Murdstone's hatred and Clara's childishness, David embarks on "another beginning," a "new life, in a new name, and with everything new about [him]" (215), ready again to engender himself.

Pip's fiction of rebirth begins not at the beginning of his narrative but at its end. It represents redemption, a second chance, Pip's desire to transcend his self-deluded "construction[s]" "repeated and thrown back" at him (289). After eleven years of self-imposed exile and penance as a workingman, Pip returns to Joe and Biddy to find, he says, "sitting on my own little stool . . . I again!" Yet this loving family scene, this reborn self who will redeem the past, must implicitly repeat the struggles of Pip himself. Pip takes little Pip to the churchyard, seats him on a tombstone, and listens to little Pip repeat his own childhood story of "Phillip Pirrip, late of this Parish, and Also Georgiana, Wife of the Above" (457). Pip's equivocal rebirth demands the retelling of the lost link between father-hood and origin. While the story initiates little Pip into the mysterious metaphysics of identity and self-naming, its status as repetition means rebirth as a figure for self-engendering remains problematic.[46]

The fictions the fatherless David and Pip write about themselves reborn become the books we read. David defines the power of this narrative to define its subject: "Whether I shall turn out to be the hero of my own life, or whether that station will be held by anybody else, these pages must show," he begins (1). In both novels, an adult man looks back on his life and attempts to give it shape, motivation, and causality by virtue of narrative strategies. As David's comment implies, the recounting of a life, the story told about past experiences, not only retells events but retroactively creates them as well. David cannot be sure at the beginning of his narrative project whether he will prove to be the "hero" of his own life; his narrative will create him as a hero to himself or will demonstrate his lack of heroism or seriousness as subject of the narrative. The writing of the narrative will create his life, not simply retell it; the account of David's past will cause that past, not simply recollect it. In writing the story of his life, David will thus create himself, give birth to himself, engender and so father himself in language.

The narrator who creates himself in the process of writing is the "autobiographer." If language gives birth, language about the self gives birth to the self. The writer of his own life story, his own "biography," makes himself his hero (or nonhero) in a narrative, creates himself in the process of writing his own narrative. Both *David Copperfield* and *Great Expectations* demonstrate the intense self-reflexive and -reflective mode of autobiography: each narrative structures the perceiving writer into the story itself. Pip's narrative circles back on itself through his self-reflection, his continual criticism of and declared distance from his earlier self as origin of his present writing self. His metaphors for his life in that early self figure his new difference: his "mazes," his "poor labyrinth" define that self as self-deceptive and lost (133, 219). David's narrative, however, nostalgic and immersed in its own self-origination, reflects on itself by virtue of David's occupation: writing. David writes about himself writing. We presumably read the story David writes "out of his experience" while in self-imposed exile in Switzerland after Dora's death. We read David's autobiography, which is also Charles Dickens's fictionalized autobiography.[47] The novel's hero, then, appears to resemble its narrator, who is also its writer, and who resembles its author—as Forster claims he pointed out to the surprised Dickens when he noted David's initials as reversals of Dickens's own. Dickens reflects on David, a part of himself, reflecting on himself; Dickens writes about David, who writes about himself writing. The novel takes as subject its writer in the act of his self-creation.

Yet Dickens's narrative about David, the boy who grows, like the author, into a novelist, surprisingly omits any reference to the process of writing fiction or to the contents of those fictions. David mentions almost as an aside that he writes his first novel; when it gets published, David demurs, "It is not my purpose, in this record, though in all other essentials it is my written memory, to pursue the history of my own fictions. They express themselves, and I leave them to themselves. When I refer to them, incidentally, it is only as a part of my progress" (690). David expunges his writing from his manuscript—which he claims he never intended to publish and which purports to tell only to himself the exact truth—because his writing is important only when it signifies his "progress." This truthful autobiography details not the writing of David's narratives but his career as a writer. Whenever David mentions his novels to, for example, Aunt Betsey, Agnes, Mrs. Steerforth, or Traddles, he or she remarks not on the significance or content of those novels but on their author's growing fame.

David admits his ambitiousness early in the novel, using terminology that unites worldly achievement with a rhetorical strategy for that advancement. Revisiting his old home, David wanders by the graves of his mother and father "by the hour"; his reflections, he confides, "were always associated with the figure I was to make in life, and the distinguished things I was to do. My echoing footsteps went to no other tune, but were as constant to that as if I had come home to build my castles in the air at a living mother's side" (320). Writing will make David a distinguished "figure" or worldly success, a "figure" in his autobiography, in language. The scene in which Dickens sets this admission also identifies David's figurative ambition with his oedipal desires and fears; David's success would please his mother and would demonstrate his ability to become successful without the mention of a father.

Pip, like David, views writing as a vehicle of worldly success. Both figures for Dickens understand that language makes the writer a figure in the world and to himself. David and Pip have in common their aversion to the "common," another terminology that associates language with class, with worldly success or lack of it. David works at Murdstone and Grinby's in a "common way, and with the same common companions, and with the same sense of unmerited degradation as at first" (166-67); Pip finds himself defined by Estella as "common and coarse," as a lower-class, unrefined, improper boy who calls the "knave" a "jack" (55). Because they want not to be "common," Pip and David dedicate themselves early to self-education, to autodidaction. Both assume that scholarship—mastering the skills and mysteries of language—will help them "rise" in the class structure. Joe unknowingly defines Pip and David's working-class self-hatred: Mrs. Joe dislikes scholarship, Joe explains, which makes men "rise . . . like a sort of rebel, don't you see?" (44). David desires to rise, as did Dickens, by going to school; with Aunt Betsey's blessing, he studies at Dr. Strong's. Yet David's autobiography mysteriously excludes from its narrative these apparently happy schooldays, just as it elided the process and content of his writing; this time in his life he relates as "A Retrospect"—a whirlwind rehearsal of events without attribution to them of any significance. Pip too decides education and knowing the correct language will cure his coarseness. The "best step" he could take "towards making [himself] uncommon was to get out of Biddy everything she knew"—"all her learning" (68). Pip, in fact, proves so apt and arrogant a pupil he presumes to teach Joe, his figurative father although literal brother-in-law and self-considered equal, the mysteries of language. Joe declares Pip an "oncommon scholar," even when Pip barely prints and totally fails to spell (66, 40). With Biddy's help, then, Pip learns language; with Miss Havisham's, he supposes, he learns socially appropriate terminology—a "knave" from a "jack"—and so appears to transcend his commonness: he becomes a young gentleman with great expectations, with money in his future.

Each of our autobiographers nevertheless reveals the difficulty of learning to read and write. Pip struggles through the "alphabet as if it had been a bramble-bush; getting considerably worried and scratched by every letter"; he falls "among those thieves, the nine figures" who "disguise themselves and baffle recognition" (40). David, who learned the "easy good-nature of O and Q and S" at his mother's knee, discovers at his punishing father's a "bog of nonsense." Later, when he perseverantly learns stenography, David rediscovers the mysteries of learning to write another language, the changes "rung upon dots," "vagaries . . .played by circles"; when he masters the alphabet, an "Egyptian Temple in itself," David moans, "there then appeared a procession of new horrors, called arbitrary characters; the most despotic characters I have ever known; who insisted, for instance, that a thing like the beginning of a cobweb, meant expectation, and that a pen-and-ink sky-rocket stood for disadvantageous" (53, 54, 545). The mystery of language resides in the arbitrary connections between inscription and significance. Both Pip and David personify the characters of alphabets, portray language and its mastery as figurative. Yet only by mastering this metaphorical language, only by assuming the connection between the "characters" and signification, can Pip and David "rise."

David and Pip value language-learning, then, precisely because it will initiate them into the bourgeois world of successful self-management. After Aunt Betsey's apparent financial ruin, David is once again reborn to a "new life" (537). He leaves the archaic profession of proctoring and becomes a successful parliamentary reporter—as did Dickens and Dickens's father before him. David's journalistic success, like Dickens's, depends on hard work and discipline, on "steady application," "perseverance," "patient and continuous energy," and "the habits of punctuality, order, and diligence." David reports, "Whatever I have tried to do in life, I have tried with all my heart to do well"; "whatever I have devoted myself to, I have devoted myself to completely"; "I have always been thoroughly in earnest, . . . and there is no substitute for thoroughgoing, ardent, and sincere earnestness" (665, 606-7). The bourgeois and more than slightly anal-retentive virtues that make David successful as a reporter also make him successful as a novelist. "I laboured hard at my book, without allowing it to interfere with the punctual discharge of my newspaper duties; and it came out and was very successful. I was not stunned by the praise which sounded in my ears, notwithstanding that I was keenly alive to it, and thought better of my own performance, I have little doubt, than anybody else did. . . . The more praise I got, the more I tried to deserve" (690). The lessons of learning to write, of writing shorthand or novels, David expounds faithfully: be earnest, work hard but punctually, become self-reliant, and you will be successful, famous, well-paid—in short, a self-made man.[48] David, the autodidact, fails in his autobiography to record the process of his writing because as a figure for his "progress" it signifies not self-knowledge but bourgeois success.

David's, Pip's—and Dickens's—theories of language as a vehicle for worldly success, as a vehicle for engendering the self without the help of fathers, however, is called into question by each autobiography. The subversive figures David chooses to represent language-users, writers, and himself hardly appear bourgeois, successful, or self-reliant. The stories Pip hears about fathers from his own figurative fathers hardly demonstrate that in narrative a son may create himself apart from fathers.

David refuses in his autobiography to confront the nostalgia of his paean to bourgeois success and self-creation; Pip criticizes throughout his narrative his earlier desire to originate himself in language. Although Dickens reread *Copperfield* before writing *Expectations* so as not to repeat himself, his second great fictional autobiography repeats with a self-critical perspective the psychoanalytic material about language and fatherhood of the first.

The doubleness, the dark side, of David's drive to become a figure in the world appears in two figures for himself. While David muses about becoming a figure in the world beside the graves of his mother and father, a madman watches David from David's old childhood window as he once watched his father's grave. This figure for David reappears whenever David goes home and demonstrates the lunacy of attempting to become a figure in the world, the figurative nature of bourgeois success. Uriah Heep also appears as a dark figure for David's desire for success and self-creation. Uriah, like David, wants to marry a father's daughter and rise to a higher class. Heep personifies to David greasy-palmed ambition, yet David finds himself curiously attracted to while nervously contemptful of Heep. The narrative in fact surreptitiously identifies their resemblance. Heep sleeps in David's old room at the Wickfields'; Heep sleeps on David's floor in front of the fire. Heep's ambition originates in a father's teaching, as David's originates in the lack or excess of it; Heep's "umbleness" mocks as it imitates David's arrogance. Heep recognizes his resemblance to David, if David does not. "You envy me my rise," he screams at David, who does. "You're quite a dangerous rival," he chuckles to David, who, although refusing to admit it, is (748, 573). The sexual triangle of David, Uriah, and Agnes finds its ironic biblical metaphor in that of David, Uriah, and Bathsheba—in which David appears as adulterous lover, Uriah as rightful husband.

David's figures for the writer also represent the lunacy of attempting to become a successful hero to oneself in narrative, to engender the self in language. Mr. Dick, Dr. Strong, and Micawber all identify through metaphor the doubleness of language, its insufficiency as a vehicle of the self-made man and the failure of the writer to father himself. Mr. Dick appears in the structural place of a father and represents the autobiographer.[49] Mr. Dick, once "Richard Babley," writes "a Memorial about his own history," as David calls it. This memorial literally petitions the Lord Chancellor for financial relief caused by Mr. Dick's family situation.[50] Like Mr. Dick, Dickens himself wrote a memorial-draft that associated financial relief with family distress and petitioned the Lords of Treasury for redress in his brother Frederick's fight for promotion at the Treasury Office (*Letters,* 2: 379-86). In *Copperfield,* however, Aunt Betsey explains to David the story the memorial tells of Mr. Dick's love for his favorite sister, his fear of her hateful husband, and his resulting fever. King

Charles the First's beheading, which Betsey and Mr. Dick try to keep out of the memorial but cannot, represents "his allegorical way of expressing it"; Betsey says Mr. Dick "connects his illness with great disturbance and agitation," and "that's the figure, or the simile, or whatever it's called, which he chooses to use" (200-206). Mr. Dick's memorial, then, connects family structures of desire and prohibition with the act of writing, particularly of writing a retrospective narrative about the self. King Charles the First's beheading is a metaphor for the madness of familial desire, for the prohibition that necessarily follows.[51] The Charles head that gets on Mr. Dick's frame, that appears and disappears from Mr. Dick's narrative, that gets cut off over and over, represents the double bind of attempting to write retrospective narrative about triangular and familial structures of desire. Mr. Dick's story is a metaphor for David's story of oedipal desire and the prohibitions visited upon a desiring boy. Mr. Dick with his Charles head beheaded represents Charles Dickens's continual obsession with narrating *his* memorial of family cruelty and desire. King Charles as a figure for the out-of-his-head Mr. Dick also signifies Mr. Dick's attempt to make himself a subject of his narrative, just as David makes himself the hero of his. Yet this writer—a lunatic full of literal common sense—cannot complete his memorial-narrative because he cannot keep that figure for himself, King Charles-Dick, out of the story. Like Mr. Dick, like David, Charles Dickens attempts to become a hero to himself in narrative and so engender himself, attempts to keep the dark and lunatic figures for himself out of narrative only to find them magically reappearing and hindering the completion of his retrospective autobiographical project.

Mr. Dick's failure to keep King Charles out of the memorial spawns a double narrative, just as Dickens's narratives create their double characters, motivations, and plots. Mr. Dick pastes "the old leaves of abortive Memorials"—those in which King Charles appears—on his marvelous kite. Whereas Mr. Dick understands nothing about where the completed memorial would go or what it would achieve, he understands perfectly where the kite will go and what it will achieve. "It flies high," he tells David, and "takes the facts a long way. That's my manner of diffusing 'em. I don't know where they may come down. It's according to circumstances, and the wind, and so forth; but I take my chance of that." While the kite flies, "disseminat[ing] the statements pasted on it," Mr. Dick's mind seems lifted out of its confusion, and his face appears serene; when it comes down, Mr. Dick looks about him "in a lost way" (203, 216-17). Kite-flying appears to be a metaphor for the process and function of writing, its uses and abuses, its rewards and losses. The kite narrative "diffuses" ("defuses") and "disseminates" the repressed but returned figures for the lunacy of the self in a story of family desire: it spreads about the wordy yet generative tale and provides a pleasant escape from the process of memorializing. Like Dickens's metaphors of his Broadstairs house as Gammon Lodge" with its "Gammon Aeronautical Balloon association," of the one-volume *Sketches by Boz* as a balloon on which to embark on his writing career, and of those "intrepid astronauts" of the *Curiosity Shop*, Don Zambullo and Asmodée (themselves figures for the narrator and reader who fly hand in hand), Mr. Dick's kite figures the pleasures and powers of narratizing (*Letters*, 1: 406-7, 116; *OCS*, 244).

Dr. Strong, fast friends with Mr. Dick, also links the powers of language with familial structures of desire. The doctor, figurative father to his young wife Annie, attempts to take language by its tail and get its meanings codified in his dictionary (Dick-tionary?). Annie's mother comments on a dictionary's usefulness, its necessity: "The meaning of words! Without Dr. Johnson, or somebody of that sort, we might have been at this present moment calling an Italian-iron a bedstead" (650). Exactly. Although she does not realize it, the "Old Soldier" identifies the tendency of language to shift, its failure to signify what its speaker intends, its refusal univocally to name its referents. Like Mr. Dick's memorial, Dr. Strong's dictionary demonstrates its failure to codify and complete language: because of his passion for "Greek roots," for retracing linguistic origins, Dr. Strong has gotten only to "D." We know he will get no farther: the head-boy, Adams, mathematically calculates the good doctor will complete the dictionary in 1,649 years! (237-38). Like Mr. Dick's memorial, then, Dr. Strong's dictionary gets tangled up with the number 1,649 and so metaphorically with the date of King Charles the First's beheading, with desire and prohibition, with the lunacy of fathering the self in language. Dr. Strong's dictionary, like Mr. Dick's memorial, appears as a metaphor for Dickens's obsession in *David Copperfield* with origins and so with fathering, his concentration on "D," his metaphorical association with the 1649 unrest, rebellion, and beheading of a figure for the narrating self.

Micawber as a figure for the writer openly contradicts Dickens's asserted metaphor of the author as father. Micawber, whose improvidence, imprisonment, and love of language Dickens bases on his own father's, announces unknowingly at the end of *Copperfield* the novel's narrative project. "The veil that has long been interposed between Mrs. Micawber and myself, is now withdrawn . . . and my children and the Author of their Being can once more come in contact on equal terms" (760). Micawber's confused metaphor of simultaneous paternity and equality merely points out, as do all his actions in the narrative, his irrepressible and irresponsible fatherhood. Yet this improvident father is an "Author," a figure for an engendering God, and, as all readers of the novel remember, a lover of language. He is, above all, a writer of letters. Micawber relishes his epistolary prose, rereads it "under pretence of having lost his place," "smack[s] his lips" over the tasty words, reads as though his letter were an Act of Parliament, or the text of a sermon, or a performance with which he were highly satisfied. Aunt Betsey declares Micawber would "write letters by the ream, if it was a capital offence"—shades of King Charles the First! (750-57). David, however, understands Micawber's passion for writing letters means he cannot leave any situation without adding a written postscript to real life. Micawber, in fact, enjoys his epistolary powers so fully because language compensates for reality.[52] In his first letter to David, Micawber forecasts his impending imprisonment for debt and likens it to death; David rushes to help but finds Mr. and Mrs. Micawber on the London coach, "the very picture of tranquil enjoyment," as tranquil as they had appeared the evening before the letter's writing and arrival (263-64). When Micawber exposes Heep as a fraud, he enjoys reading his document because "describing this unfortunate state of things, really seemed to outweigh any pain or anxiety that the reality could have caused him" (751). Language does not represent reality but instead compensates for its pain. This separation of language from its referent, Micawber's many letters imply, results from the generative power of metaphor, the figurative energy of language. Micawber's faith resides entirely in believing this metaphorical language literal: something will "turn up." Yet Micawber's experience demonstrates the considerable perils of living in the realm of language, of spurning the realities of life as father, provider, and husband. The father as "author" and "Author," the writer as engenderer, the autobiographer as self-engenderer, appear highly suspect.

David, however, fails to interpret Micawber's separation of language and life as associated with himself. Despite his perceptive commentary on Micawber, despite his own educational trials with the figurative energy of language, the separation of inscription and signification, David continues to believe his own theory of language as a form of discipline, earnestness, and self-reliance, as the engendering tools of the self-made, self-written man. Yet the scene in which Micawber exposes David's own dark double, Uriah Heep, as a fraud also causes David to muse on the duplicity of language:

> We talk about the tyranny of words, but we like to tyrannize over them too. We are fond of having a large superfluous establishment of words to wait upon us on great occasions; we think it looks important, and sounds well. As we are not particular about the meaning of our liveries on state occasions if they be but fine and numerous enough, so the meaning or necessity of our words is a secondary consideration, if there be but a great parade of them. And as individuals get into trouble by making too great a show of liveries, or as slaves when they are too numerous rise against their masters, so I think I could mention a nation that has got into many great difficulties, and will get into many greater, from maintaining too large a retinue of words. (754.)

David's metaphor of language and writer as servant (or slave) and master proves terribly unstable. Inherent in such metaphorical equivalencies, such ratios, is the slippage of signification brought about by the separation between inscription and signification, language and referent. As David meditates on Micawber's wordiness, on his lack of care about signification itself, David's metaphor undercuts his own linguistic theory of the autodidact, the writer who fathers himself through language. His meditation transforms his metaphor and radically alters his signification: the writer's control over language becomes language's service to the writer becomes language's rebellion against the writer. Language has a dangerous life of its own, generated by the energy of metaphor. David's insistence on engendering himself in self-referential narrative forces him to repress this dangerous slippage of signification. David goes on to Switzerland and writes his novel, which we read as Dickens's *David Copperfield;* David writes about himself as the hero of his life and ignores the lessons of duplicitous language, ignores the lunatic figures for the writer who call into question self-origination.

The novel's theory of language as a vehicle for making the self without the help of fathers finds its opposite in another of David's doubles, the "small Cain" of the autobiographical fragment. This small Cain, as psychoanalytic literary critics have demonstrated, appears obsessed by oral and anal imagery.[53] He cannot control his urge for stale pastries or puddings with currants, his interest in pineapples and in coffee shops. He cannot manage the economies of his small loaves and cheeses, despite dividing his money into "six little parcels," each containing the "same amount" of money and "labelled with a different day." This concern with the "scantiness of [his] resources," however, seems to me not primarily (although also necessarily) an indication of oral deprivation and the struggle for anal control but a concern with self-dependence and self-reliance which unites yet goes beyond the bodily imagery of Freud's two earliest developmental stages.

This small Cain's fear of self-dependence and self-reliance appears linked to his fears of paternal betrayal and replacement. Dickens, writing out the almost nostalgic grievances of his youth, writes of the small exile's experience at this time of his father's imprisonment and his own lonely working at Warren's Blacking: "I was so young and childish—how could I be otherwise?—to undertake the whole charge of my existence." He supposes his father pays for his lodging, since he pays for everything but that, yet writes with melancholy and repressed anger, "I certainly did not pay it myself; and I certainly had no other assistance whatever . . . from Monday morning until Saturday night. No advice, no counsel, no encouragement, no consolation, no support, from any one that I can call to mind, so help me God."[54] This rhetoric of negation, deprivation, and betrayal finds its way whole into *David Copperfield* and appears, although muted, in the *Pickwick* tale, "The Convict's Return" (*DC,* 159-60, *PP,* 80).

The small Cain, however, became David, who became Dickens. Both Cain and David are figures for Dickens's self, and both are fictional.[55] The fatherless exile, the wanderer, gives way to David: Dickens stopped writing the autobiographical fragment when he began *Copperfield*. Although Cain cannot manage his resources and so create himself without his father, David can and does and refuses to confront in his autobiographical narrative the clues that self-origination is at all problematic. Both Cain and David, however, give way to Pip, a later, more fictional, figure for Dickens himself. Pip writes his autobiography to criticize himself for assuming he could engender himself apart from fathers. Pip's story about fatherhood and language demonstrates that the son cannot father himself but must admit, in all his guilt, the father's precedence and origination.

Both Pip's figurative fathers in *Great Expectations* tell him stories about their fathers. Early in the novel, Joe tells Pip about the cruel and irresponsible father who sends him to work at his forge and prevents Joe from going to school. Joe eventually supports his father financially by working at his father's vocation in the forge. In this metaphorical story of father, son, and blacking warehouse, the son does not resent the father's betrayal; Joe's expectations, unlike the small Cain's and unlike Pip's, are not great. He accepts his father and writes a loving epitaph for his father's tombstone: "I made it . . . my own self," Joe tells Pip of the never-carved couplet that details the goodness of his father's heart despite paternal abandonment. Pip, who listens to a version of his own, of Dickens's own, story, doubts Joe's father's goodness of heart (40-42). Magwitch's story about his father, unlike Joe's, fails to name the father as betrayer of a son, although Magwitch's language clearly implies paternity: "Summun had run away from me—a man—a tinker—and he'd took the fire with him, and left me wery cold" (328). Magwitch's abandoning father originates and society corroborates his resulting poverty, criminality, and alienation. Magwitch, like Joe, is bitter, yet his story narrates the reality of his existence, of his need to father a young gentleman because he lacked a father, of his making himself in the only way a poor orphan can in a society in which Newgate appears at the center of the city, in which death runs the system—as Denis the hangman of *Barnaby Rudge* would say.

In both stories of fatherhood and engendering, sonhood appears linked with a "forge." Joe accepts his own place in his father's vocation at the forge, just as Pip apparently should but cannot accept his apprenticeship in the forge. Magwitch gets involved with Compeyson, whose business is swindling and "forging," whose companion, Arthur, is haunted by the ghost of his bridal-robed sister, Miss Havisham. Joe's forge and Magwitch's forgery link the metaphorical blacking warehouse with false writing. These two stories of fatherhood, taken together, represent the lesson Pip feels he must teach himself in writing his own narrative about figurative fatherhood. He must accept Joe as his figurative father and must love his second father as Joe loves *his* father. Although Pip punishes himself in the writing of his autobiography in order to find such love for his originating fathers in his heart, his logical doubt of Joe's clearly sentimentalized sonhood questions his final filial love of both Magwitch and Joe. Pip's love, his writing of himself into that love, springs from guilt. His criticism of self-engendering, of the son creating himself without fathers, appears qualified by that guilt.

Both Pip and David tell their stories about fatherhood and language, and Dickens tells his—the small Cain's—as well as theirs. Pip, David, Cain, and Dickens, despite the complex attitudes each portrays toward self-engendering, all tell stories in order to survive. All four read the classic novels to which their fathers provide them access. David "reads for his life" when Murdstone appears as his new father. Cain and David make "stories for [themselves] out of the streets" when father and family are imprisoned (*DC,* 168); David "impersonates" himself as the good characters and Murdstone, his punishing father, as the bad in the narratives he devours. David tells Steerforth stories at school so Steerforth will dispense to him wine and food: storytelling provides nourishment. The young Pip tells Joe—and the adult Pip, us readers—his "inventions," confesses guiltily his "lies," thinking storytelling a "criminal" activity.[56] Despite Pip's—and Dickens's—fears about the falsity of invention, however, despite the lunacy that threatens to disrupt David's glorification of himself as self-made man, Dickens's figures for himself survive on storytelling and narrate that survival. David ultimately realizes that the discipline that enables him to originate himself in narrative grows from that difficult time at Murdstone and Grinby's; Dickens must realize that the discipline that enables him to rewrite the story of fatherhood, language, and self-engendering sprouted in his survival of Warren's Blacking, in its testing and nourishing his imagination.

"The Golden Thread": The Daughter's Ministry

She was the ruling spirit of the house.... To find her, was to find love and sympathy. — Elizabeth Gaskell, Wives and Daughters

The "bride from heaven," Alexander Welsh argues convincingly, redeems the earthly city in Dickens's novels. She unites members of the family around the hearth, a spiritual center removed from the industrialized, capitalistic city, and brings the hero a healing message of love and truth. Welsh also demonstrates, however, this bride's dualistic nature as a figure of love, for marriage to her resembles death and usually coincides with the end of the narrative, a structural termination of its own.[57] This short synopsis of Welsh's sophisticated argument cannot, of course, render its emotional conviction or its ability to convince us. Yet I would like to emphasize here a fact about the "bride from heaven" Welsh discusses but on which he does not focus because the structure of his book not merely explores the doubleness of Dickens's moral attitudes but ultimately stresses transcendental structures as ways out of earthly dilemmas. This bride from heaven, this heroine, is always and primarily a daughter.

The daughter in Dickens's novels effaces origins, redeems temporality, and undoes genealogy through repetition. She represents the narrative escape, the loophole, that effaces the problematic of paternity, origin, the "symbolic debt," and self-engendering. Marriage to her appears to create an incestuous idyll in which such structural and thematic research into fatherhood no longer need exist. She transcends the worldly questions about orphanage and origin the hero-son so often asks. Like Agnes, she points upward; like Little Nell, she rises pictorially and symbolically into the clouds at her death. Like Agnes, she is changeless; like Little Dorrit, she is a "fountain of love."

Esther Summerson is the daughter who most clearly effaces origin. Esther's paternity defines her as originless; she is the daughter of "Nemo" and feels herself "no one." Esther feels herself "filling a place" in her godmother's house, which "ought to have been empty." She imagines her doll "staring at [her]—or not so much at [her] . . . as at nothing." This strange intersubjectivity in which the doll's stare as mirror of her own look makes Esther "nothing" represents Esther's only intimacy, and she in turn is "to no one upon earth what Dolly" is to her. This reflection of mirrored emptiness and intimacy induces Esther's first storytelling: she tells her doll all her shame and the story of her birth. Her one-sided and imaginary discourse with Dolly meets silence, as all intimacy initiates emptiness, creates "no one" (17-20). Yet Esther, as I have mentioned earlier, wants to know nothing about her origin. Once ensconced in John Jarndyce's Bleak House as Little Woman, Dame Durden, and Dame Trot, she happily sees her own name vanish among her nicknames, reposes her entire confidence in her "fatherly" guardian, and declines to ask him about her past. Esther appears the perfect Dickensian daughter who serves others, effaces herself, erases the riddle of origins which writing sons so clearly perceive as related to fatherhood.

Lucie Manette represents the daughter's ability to redeem time. Dickens's recurring metaphor in *A Tale of Two Cities* for daughterly redemption is the "golden thread," the phrase that provides Dickens the title for the novel's second book. Lucie Manette embodies "the golden thread that united [her father] to a Past beyond his misery, and to a Present beyond his misery" (74). Rhetorical repetition reinforces the daughter's symbolic role here: she redeems the discontinuity and suffering inherent in temporality by her presence in her father's restored life. Her love locates his misery in an indeterminate time, not forgotten but no longer constituting the line of his life, his continuing time. The daughter's memory creates this continuity and temporal redemption. Lucie's father, recalling his imprisonment, tells Lucie of the fancy he then had of his unknown child: was the child a son who, knowing his father's story, would avenge him; a son who would forget; a daughter who would remember; or one who would forget? Manette imagines the last alternative to be the worst: if the daughter forgets her father, he "perishe[s] from the remembrance of the living, and in the next generation [his] place was a blank" (180-81). Moreover, Dickens insists that Lucie "recalls" her father to life: she remembers, revives, and calls him to return to his fatherhood of her. In remembering him and in giving birth to his descendants, the daughter represents the generational principle of continuity, memory, and identity which gives the father life while at the same time giving a new generation life. As a result of Sydney Carton's sacrifice, Lucie gives birth to a line of redeeming daughters, of new Lucies, who will continue the daughterly work of redemption.

Lucie as daughter also "wind[s] the golden thread" that binds together father, daughter, and husband, "weav[es] the service of her happy influence through the tissue of all their lives" (200). As in so many Victorian novels and lives, the daughter's new husband, the new "son," simply moves into the home of father and daughter after the wedding. The same sweet daughter who recreated the father through her memory of him redeems the desiring structure of the family, represents devotion so complete her love never seems divided. Lucie's father finds her "more devoted to him married (if that could be) than single," and Darnay praises her for not allowing love of father to attenuate love for husband. Lucie embodies the "magic secret" of "being everything" to all, as though there were only one in the family demanding her love. The perfect love every child ever born desires is provided by Lucie and all Dickens's daughters.

Little Nell may be Dickens's most perfect daughter. She unites the ideals Lucie and Esther represent, yet the genealogical structure from which she originates makes her redemptive powers unique. In her family history, the elder brother's (Grandfather Trent's) wife dies young but gives birth to a daughter; this daughter marries, dies young, but gives birth to another daughter. In the wake of its many deaths, this genealogical structure contains only grandfather and granddaughter, Trent and Little Nell. The brother, Fred Trent, appears in this gapped structure only because sons, like gadflies, cause trouble for (grand)father and daughter and so provide impetus for the movement of plot. In telling this particular family history, the single gentleman recounts the blessing of begetting daughters:

> If you have seen the picture-gallery of any one old family, you will remember how the same face and figure—often the fairest and slightest of them all—comes upon you in different generations; and how you trace the same sweet girl through a long line of portraits—never growing old or changing—the Good Angel of the race—abiding by them in all reverses—redeeming all their sins—
>
> In this daughter, the mother lived again. . . . She died a widow of some three weeks' date, leaving to her father's care two orphans; one a son of ten or twelve years old; the other a girl—such another infant child—the same in helplessness, in age, in form, in feature—as she had been herself when her young mother died. (524-25.)

Dickens's metaphor of the "picture-gallery" creates his remarkable genealogy of daughters. In the line of family portraits, the same daughterly face repeats itself, never changing or growing old. She, the same, appears a representational copy of herself from one generation to the next. She represents the principle of repetition which undoes difference, temporality, and generation. The portraits of men change, father begetting son, who begets a son in his turn, but those of daughters remain ever the same. The daughter redeems the temporal difference inherent in the notion of generation, inherent in the implied conflict between father and son. Fathering a daughter, the father begets perfect repetition and so his own redemption.

This redemptive figure, of course, is familiar in Victorian literature, as well as in Dickens's novels. Yet Dickens does not term his daughter the "angel of the house," as Coventry Patmore does, although the home is her primary sphere.[58] Dickens's daughter represents the "good angel of the race." Her redemptive skills reach beyond the hearth to redeem the abstract concepts and structures of genealogy, lineage, and descent. The daughter who repeats herself, who in effect continually gives birth to herself, creates the convergence of generations upon herself, as the structures of genealogy collapse on her small figure.

The daughter performs these redemptive tasks primarily for a father. Lucie recalls her father to life; Nell attempts to restore her (grand)father to wholeness. Esther appears to be an exception, yet she too redeems by virtue of her connection to fathers as her narrative creates for herself figurative fathers: John Jarndyce and Allan Woodcourt. At the end of the novel, Jarndyce sheds his role as Esther's lover and declares himself once more her "guardian" and "father." He places her in a replica of Bleak House with Woodcourt as new lover and husband and so as repetition of Jarndyce himself. Yet Woodcourt appears in the narrative for the first time beside Nemo's deathbed and walks to the graveyard with Esther where her father lies buried. Jarndyce remarks, as I mentioned earlier, that Woodcourt "stood by your father" and so signifies Woodcourt's legitimacy as her husband by structural association with the father. The figurative father becomes lover, and lover replaces as well as becomes figurative father: Esther redeems by virtue of metaphorical fathers after all.

As my examples also indicate, the nature of this father-daughter connection appears incestuous. The daughter, as prophesied in the structures and thematics of *Barnaby Rudge,* substitutes in the oedipal triangle for the mother; she provides the father the perfect love a mother might provide a son. Like Little Nell, she never questions the father's authority and loves him without judgment. Yet the fulfilled love of daughter and father creates a community in which all members of the group—typically father, daughter, and lover—participate in this perfected love. Little Nell creates this community in heaven; Esther and Lucie create it on earth. When I use the term "incestuous" with regard to Dickens's fathers and daughters, I mean they create a community built on familial structures of desire yet also purified of desire and perfected through idealized love. The figure of the daughter draws to herself the father and lover—the father as lover, the lover as father—and also redeems the desire that calls this incestuous structure into being.

This double articulation obtains in Freud's various discussions of incest and the incest taboo. He identifies as incestuous fantasy and desire the oedipal structures of the family and the "nuclear complex" through which each individual must work his or her particular passage on the way to self-articulation. Freud also identifies cultural as opposed to personal structures of incest, especially in *Totem and Taboo,* as genealogical.[59] Paul Ricoeur describes this cultural incest as the "swallowing up" by the family of other social institutions and commitments. Society collapses onto the family as the family becomes the voracious devourer of wider human connection.[60] The incestuous communities that terminate Dickens's narratives represent this cultural structure in its transcendental, glorified form. The daughter's tasks of temporal and genealogical redemption, her effacing of origin, allow her to articulate this society of father, daughter, and husband in which the structures of genealogy collapse on herself. Within this society, she plays all roles available to her: wife, daughter, sister, mother. This incest matrix combines all familial functions and roles, as the family indeed devours all other human connection in Dickens's narratives. This devouring symbolizes Dickens's ideal of perfected, redeemed love; for Dickens the daughter represents the key to this structure, its turning point. She redeems in order to initiate this devouring, this genealogical collapse, this termination. Through her figure, narrative comes to an end, closing around the cultural structures of incest she has created. Through her figure, time, genealogy as a structure of difference, the problematic of origin, and narrative itself end.

Little Dorrit provides the most thorough example of this incestuous structure. Amy Dorrit nurses, ministers to, thinks of living always with, and occasionally sleeps in the same bed with her imprisoned father. Dickens's metaphor for the nurturing in deprivation with which the daughter serves the father is breast-feeding: "There was a classical daughter once—perhaps—who ministered to her father in his prison as her mother had ministered to her. Little Dorrit, though of the unheroic modern stock, and mere English, did much more, in comforting her father's wasted heart upon her innocent breast, and turning to it a fountain of love and fidelity that never ran dry or waned, through all his years of famine."[61] The metaphor of nursing sexualizes the father-daughter relationship, makes the father dependent on the daughter, and upsets the generations. Daughter becomes mother to her father. This figure for the daughter's "self-sacrifice" recurs when Clennam chooses to go to prison as a result of speculation and winds up in the same room Dorrit once inhabited. Amy "nursed him as lovingly, and GOD knows as innocently, as she had nursed her father in that room when she had been but a baby" (756). Dickens's metaphorical "fountain of love" defines the lover as a repetition of the father, defines sexual love as a version of symbolic father-daughter incest. In the scene in which Clennam tells Amy she will inherit money and her father will leave the Marshalsea with his debts paid, Amy swoons in Clennam's arms as he kisses her and cries "Father! Father! Father!" (415).[62]

At the novel's end, Clennam and Amy's marriage consolidates the now-familiar daughter-redeemed structure of incest. Their wedding accomplishes two narrative tasks: it attempts to cure the unnarrated paternal adultery at the novel's absent origin, and it metaphorically reunites a family split by adultery and illegitimacy. This narrative project is summarized in Clennam's guilty thoughts about paternity: "If my father had erred, it was my first duty to conceal the fault and to repair it" (721). Metaphorical incest at the novel's termination "repairs" or redeems the father's fault. The family genealogy (the space and time of engendering identity and difference) and the oedipal triangle (the structure of desire) collapse on this bride and groom. Mrs. Clennam's house collapses on itself, in the perfect metaphor for such incestuous desire. As I mentioned in the first section of this chapter, Amy and Arthur's marriage also "conceals" Clennam's father's fault. Amy Dorrit knows the secret of Arthur's birth but promises to protect him from knowledge of it. Amy effectively effaces the mystery of Arthur's origin and embraces her own disinheritance to lay to rest the entire question of origins.

Esther's, Lucie's, Nell's, and Amy's redemptive tasks as daughters, then, efface origin through the purified, redeemed structures of incest which unite father and lover in one metaphorical figure. The son who loves and marries a redeeming daughter need no longer seek his father as the figure of his own origin and initiator of his identity, and the narrative structure can now make origin both aim and end and so conclude. Darnay marries Lucie, for example, and so effaces his aristocratic origin and identity. The son who loves and marries a redeeming daughter need no longer commit textual parricide, or repay the "symbolic debt" he owes a father precisely because the daughter represents his paradoxical reward for and effacing of his sonhood. Good sons in *Barnaby Rudge* indeed marry daughters after bad sons burn out and beat up fathers; Pip marries Magwitch's daughter after wishing that "second father" dead. The son who loves and marries a redeeming daughter need no longer seek to engender himself, and so his narrative closes as he closes the question. Agnes will continue to point upward, redeeming David's striving to become a figure in the world; Estella will humbly submit to Pip's chastened love. Dickens's narrative project, then, to trace the father as a figure of origin, to murder him symbolically in the act of writing, and so to engender himself in narrative cures itself in the figure of the daughter. She heals the wounds these narratives open; she terminates their structures and paternal thematics. She allows Dickens to cover over the discoveries he makes about fatherhood in the act of writing narrative.

Yet Dickens's daughterly redemptions never quite convince us. Dickens's double attitudes attenuate his vision of the perfect originless, atemporal, nondifferentiated incestuous structure that fulfills and terminates his novels. The metaphorical father-daughter marriages of Lucie, Esther, and Amy, for example, appear overdetermined and unable to reconcile the antithetical narrative forces they intend to heal. In concealing Arthur's origin from himself, Amy ironically confirms it for herself and for Dickens's readers. In dismissing the question of her own origin, Esther writes a narrative that refuses to terminate and closes with her equivocal "even supposing—." In redeeming "their sins"—the sins of the father?—Nell causes the death of mothers. The strength as well as the tragedy of Little Nell resides in this dying out of a line of daughters who repeat one another: when Nell dies, repetitive redemption as a principle of the genealogy of daughters dies with her. The metaphor for daughterhood in this novel, in fact, identifies daughterly redemption as double: the "picture-gallery" represents a linear time and space because the viewer must walk from its beginning to its end to see the same face repeat itself from generation to generation; yet the space and time of genealogy is literally "branched," as in a "family tree." The figure of the daughter, then, dissimulates rather than heals the problematics of origin and genealogy. Her figure can never fully cover over a father who originates and so engenders temporal and generational difference; can never undo the symbolic debt of a son or his need retrospectively to rewrite himself in autobiography. Dickens's daughters give birth to a genealogy that not only repeats and undoes genealogy but also calls into question the structures they terminate, the thematics they fulfill and transcend. Two such daughters in particular demonstrate the danger and fragility of Dickens's equivocal way out of his paternal problematics: Esther Summerson and Florence Dombey. Both these daughters call into being the incestuous yet redeemed and purified structures of desire which terminate narrative; both heal fathers or the question of fatherhood. Yet Esther, a daughter who effaces origin, demonstrates the violent disfigurement that results from such erasure. Florence, a daughter who initiates incestuous idyll, identifies the structures of desire as dangerously triangular and reinstates through her figure the thematics of the primal scene. Each of these daughters, then, calls into question her own redemptive task.

Esther's attempt to efface the question of origin ironically intensifies rather than lessens her sense of herself as no one. When Esther reads the letter in which her mother explains the circumstances of her birth, Esther thinks, "how strangely did I hold my place in this world" (452). This fragile placement, this equivocal positionality as subject, reminds us of Esther's "place" in her godmother's house, which should have been "empty." To efface the question of her origin, Esther must efface herself as subject. Yet Esther writes her "portion of these pages"; she appears as a subject for her own narrative. This paradoxical inscription and effacement of the self structures Esther's narrative. She imagines herself a "destitute subject" not "worth the telling" (23); she recounts little of herself "which is not a story of goodness and generosity in others" (521). As her dolly mirrored to Esther her own sense of herself as no one, her fellow students at Greenleaf represent to her a "looking-glass" in which to view her inadequate self. Yet as Esther battles to efface herself from her story, she finds herself continually getting into it:

> I don't know how it is, I seem to be always writing about myself. I mean all the time to write about other people, and I try to think about myself as little as possible, and I am sure, when I find myself coming into the story again, I am really vexed and say, "Dear, dear, you tiresome little creature, I wish you wouldn't!" but it is all of no use. I hope any one who may read what I write, will understand that if these pages contain a great deal about me, I can only suppose it must be because I have really something to do with them, and can't be kept out. (102-3.)
> . . . .
>
> It seems so curious to me to be obliged to write all this about myself! As if this narrative were the narrative of *my* life! But my little body will soon fall into the background now. (27.)

The attempt to efface the self inscribes it as well and accounts for the fragile positionality of the self as subject in narrative.

The violence of Esther's last metaphor for writing about the self—the falling body—is metaphorically linked with narrative self-effacement as self-defacement. In fact, Esther's story relates among other topics her own disfigurement by smallpox. She falls ill twice, both times through contagion from her father's burial ground—first through Jo as intermediary, then through her own presence in Tom-all-Alone's. Before falling ill, Esther suddenly senses herself "as being something different from what I then was" (280); having fallen ill, Esther hallucinates her body falling. When she recovers, Esther's "poor face" is "quite gone" from her. She looks in a literal mirror after lifting the "veil" of her hair and sees the reflection, her face having become "strange" to her (443-44). In writing her story of self-effacement, Esther has violently defaced and disfigured herself until she has become "different" from herself. She assumes a literal veil and so resembles while now no longer resembling, her mother. In the final scene of *Bleak House*, Esther looks in the mirror of her husband's love and finds herself prettier than she ever was, metaphorically better than and redeemed through another who, like her fellow students at Greenleaf, reflects her effaced and redeemed self back to herself.

Esther, then, both is and is not the subject of her narrative. Recent critics find that her position as first-person participatory narrator, as storyteller, intensifies her nasty habit of being overly coy; she is, in short, a goody-goody.[63] Yet Dickens chooses Esther as his only first-person female narrator precisely because, being female and a daughter, she brings to her story a sense of her fragility as subject to herself and as subject of narrative. Whereas David writes to become a figure in the world, Esther writes to fall into the background. Whereas Pip writes to judge and punish his fathers and himself, Esther writes to equivocate about judgment and punishment. The son writes autobiography to engender the self; the daughter writes autobiography to efface the self. The first-daughter narrative openly expresses the fragility of the self's placement in narrative, in self-made fiction, the paradox of linguistic effacement and inscription.

This paradox of language structures not only Esther's narrative but the novel of which her story is part. Krook represents the central metaphor for writing: he inscribes then erases each letter of "JARNDYCE" until the signification comes clear but the letters do not appear together. The law-writing of a father, of "No one," initiates Lady Dedlock's search and so the novel's plot; the letters "LADY DEDLOCK" lead Bucket to track down the printed description of Chesney Wold with which Lady Dedlock's imitator, Hortense, loaded the weapon that killed Tulkinghorn. Personal letters identify birthright, carry proposals of marriage, and mystify origin. Letters burn; Caddy, Charley Neckett, Krook, and Esther all know the violence and unpredictability of the letter. Even Skimpole writes an autobiography that misrepresents his benefactor's generosity. Finally, the lifeblood of Jarndyce versus Jarndyce is paper covered with "wiglo-meration"; Miss Flite's law-named birds fly free when the case has come to an end—of sorts, for it has eaten itself up in costs. The narrator for half of this doubling narrative had to be Esther, a writer aware of the letter's cutting edge, the violence done to the fragile subject in her own story.

Although, unlike Esther, Florence Dombey does not tell her own story, the narrator's passionate sympathy with her point of view intensifies the problematic role of the daughter in *Dombey and Son,* a novel about a "daughter . . . after all."[64] Florence appears as another incarnation of Dickens's redemptive daughter. Like Lucie Manette, she represents to her dying brother Paul a "golden link between him and all his life's love and happiness" (200); like Little Nell, she redeems genealogy by giving birth to daughters—"the oftener we can repeat that most extraordinary woman," says Mr. Toots, "the better" (831). Florence's love for her abusive father, like Little Dorrit's, never changes. At the end of the novel, Florence magically appears to her despairing father, as Amy does to Clennam, and asks his forgiveness for having left him. She carries the message that genealogy binds and redeems because she herself has become a mother. Little Paul, her brother reborn, links her with her father; little Florence, herself (and her mother) reborn, redeems Dombey's love for Florence by initiating his love for herself as copy where was once hatred of the original. This structure of the daughter begetting repetition and redemption, however, cannot overcome the antithetical tensions the narrative creates. As Julian Moynahan points out, Florence reduces her father through love to a bumbling fool, a cripple.[65] She appears a dangerous daughter indeed.

The novel demonstrates, in contradistinction to the idyllic scene of incest at its conclusion, that structures of desire are triangular, that the primal scene recapitulates itself in the oedipal situation and in all loving intersubjectivity. This portrayal of oedipal love fits nicely into the structures René Girard defines in his essay on triangular desire, *Deceit, Desire, and the Novel.* The subject, according to Girard, does not generate desire spontaneously out of his or her subjectivity but always imitates the desire of some other person for an object. This third person, this mediator of desire, begets an imitated or double desire and so creates competition. Girard describes desire in the nineteenth century as "internally mediated": contact between subject and mediator becomes profound, and the primary scene in which this structure operates is the family. Girard's "triangular vices," jealousy and envy, result from such familial rivalry and desire.[66]

Dombey and Son—or daughter—represents Dickens's contribution to the literature of triangular vice and desire. Father and daughter in this novel live not in the hearths, pastorals, or romanticized idylls of *Little Dorrit, The Old Curiosity Shop, David Copperfield,* or *A Tale of Two Cities* but in a capitalistic city and "House" in which love and business breed hatred, in which the daughter's "thrill" (I use the term Dickens repeats throughout the narrative) for the father evokes or invites the presence of a third. Although Dickens takes great care to blame the failure of father-daughter love on Dombey's insensitivity and obsessive concern with the genealogical continuity of his business, he denies in the novel's preface his narrator's analysis of Florence as blameless and Dombey as hard-hearted. This contradiction exposes Dickens's ambivalence about the father's failure and allows us to explore Dombey's role as possible mediator of triangular desire.

The narrative structures triangular desire by repetition of a spatial metaphor: Florence's "nightly pilgrimages" to her father's rooms. Each approach of daughter to father identifies love as triangular. In a chapter entitled "Father and Daughter," Florence approaches but does not enter her father's rooms after Paul's death, wanting to console him, to "be allowed to show him some affection," to "win him over to the endurance of some tenderness from her" (244). On her second such pilgrimage, Florence enters her father's rooms and sees written on his face his belief that she was a "successful rival" for his "son's affections" (252). Florence later finds herself alone with her father in the drawing room, and he, watching her from under a handkerchief, begins to forgive her for having supplanted him in his son's affections. At this moment, Edith, Dombey's new wife, enters the drawing room and expresses love for Floy: Dombey sees himself once more supplanted by Florence in someone's affections (481-86). Florence makes a third "nightly pilgrimage" to Dombey's rooms after she witnesses a verbal duel between Edith and Dombey at dinner. The battle between stepmother and father, a metaphorical primal scene, thrills Florence, and on this visit she kisses her sleeping father (583). In a final pilgrimage, again invited by Edith's rejection of Dombey, Florence meets her father just outside the door to his rooms, finally speaks her love for him, and runs toward him as though to embrace him. In this well-known scene, Dombey verbally abuses and strikes Florence, who flees her father's house metaphorically "orphaned," with the mark of Cain "upon her breast" (636-37).

These recurring scenes of daughter approaching father always include the specter of the dead son or the figure of the self-assertive wife. Whomever Dombey loves, Florence loves and wins: she imitates his desire. Florence's movement toward her father intensifies his hatred, calls up the jealousy, envy, and rivalry of triangular desire. Narrative structure asserts Florence's innocence of such rivalry: she appears consciously to love the father who rejects her and thinks her his rival. Yet in a "nightly pilgrimage" taken while Dombey and Edith honeymoon away from the house, Florence expresses her unconscious feelings of hostility toward her father. The scene stands apart from the narrative, framed by reference to the personified house's Gorgonlike attempt to stare Florence into stone; its textures resemble the prose-poem's in condensation and intensity. The narrator recounts Florence's love for her now-absent father, her desire to learn from her new mother the "art" of expressing her love to her father. In this reveried scene, however, Florence expresses her daughterly love so passionately precisely because her father is absent. She creates a "pensive fiction" of paternal love for herself, watches an iconographic loving father with four daughters in the house across from her window, then "blooms" in solitude. This "blooming" represents a surreptitious narrative desire for the father's absence, when blooming is possible; it appears finally as a fear of (or wish for) his death. "In weeping for his alienated heart," Florence imagines, "she might stir the spirits of the dead against him" (311-18). Florence's unconscious recreation of triangular desire, her evocation or invitation of a third into the father-daughter dyad (here, revenging ghosts), signify her desire for the ultimate outcome of rivalry, the death of her father.

This wish appears dissembled throughout the narrative by Florence's conscious wish to die herself in order to win the love of her father. In another iconographic·father-daughter scene, Florence listens to an unnamed workingman talk lovingly of his peevish and ill daughter who he fears will die. Wondering why a spoiled daughter would win love when she cannot, Florence imagines if she herself "were dying, [Dombey] would relent"; if "she lay, serene and not willing to depart," the father would "take her into his embrace" and say, "'Dear Florence, live for me, and we will love each other'" (340). This metaphorically incestuous fantasy repeats the narratively reported embrace of love and death between mother and daughter, son and daughter. But Florence survives these embraces while the objects of her love expire. Indeed, at the end of the novel, Florence visits her stepmother, who truly loved her, and Edith metaphorically announces her own death, her status as pariah after her affair with Carker. Edith has become a "mere abstraction," a "ghost" who follows "the fate of all the rest about whom [Florence's] affections had entwined themselves" (623). Edith is spared literal death in the novel only because her distant cousin and dark double, Alice Marwood, stands in and dies for Edith. The last survivor of Florence's embrace, her father, pays the price for giving in to Florence: he is punished and maimed in a chapter titled "Retribution." Like Edith, Dombey loses his vitality in the tentacled grasp of Florence's love once mediation no longer exists, once the objects of his love all literally or metaphorically die.

Mrs. Wickham's story about her uncle's daughter, Betsey Jane, supports this reading of Florence's deathly embrace. "My uncle's wife," Mrs. Wickham relates, "died just like [Paul's] mama. My uncle's child took on just as Master Paul do. My uncle's child made people's blood run cold, sometimes she did! . . . She took fancies to people; whimsical fancies some of them; others, affections that one might expect to see—only stronger than common. They all died" (107-9). Although Mrs. Wickham likens Betsey Jane to Paul Dombey, Betsey Jane clearly resembles not Paul but Florence. Betsey Jane's story is of a daughter, of a survivor who kills those who dare love her. Betsey Jane's strong affections, her whimsical fancies, her implicitly deathly love, identify through metaphor Florence's surreptitious murderous wishes toward all who care for her or her rival-father. When Mrs. Wickham nurses Alice Marwood in her final illness—a metaphorically sexual disease—she alludes once more to Betsey Jane, the narrative metaphor for Florence's loving strangulation. While love appears won by death in *Dombey and Son,* love in fact kills. This deathly embrace, double of yet opposite to the daughter's long-suffering and changeless love, springs from triangular desire, its rivalries and jealousies.

As Julian Moynahan again points out, Walter Gay appears tailored for this enervated crew.[67] Walter calls Florence "sister," putting away sexual desire for the girl in a higher social class than himself. Of course, as Alexander Welsh wittily remarks, "To address a Victorian heroine as 'sister' is merely a prelude to a warmer theme."[68] In Dickens's novels, Pip and Estella, Tom and Louisa Gradgrind, Tom and Ruth Pinch, David and Agnes Wickfield appear to confirm Welsh's theory. Yet figurative brother-sister incest signifies not the fulfillment of desire but punishment of a rival in mediated desire. Agnes, whom David calls "sister" before he calls her "wife," represents the punishing woman who disciplines David's incestuous heart;[69] Estella punishes Pip throughout his story. Likewise, Florence punishes those who love her father by strangling their desire; she therefore appears at the end of the novel to redeem triangular desire itself. Only Mr. Toots escapes Florence. Unlike any other character in the novel, he loves without rivalry, wishing to be transformed into Florence's dog or to "hurt [him]self" as a "relief" to his feelings (524). As he tells Captain Cuttle, "I could be run over—or—trampled upon—or —or thrown off a very high place—or anything of that sort—for Miss Dombey's sake, it would be the most delightful thing that could happen to me" (448-49). Only a masochist escapes triangular desire.

Let me end this section where I began it, with Dickens's metaphors for the daughter. The "golden thread," the "angel of the race," clearly stand in opposition to the metaphors for daughterhood in *Dombey and Son.* "Girls," the jealous Susan Nipper informs Polly Toodles, "are thrown away in this house"; to the patriarchal and capitalistic father, the daughter is "no issue," merely "a piece of base coin that couldn't be invested—a bad Boy—nothing more" (28, 3). The metaphor of "base coin" signifies not only valueless currency but also illegitimate genealogical origin; "no issue" likewise signifies debased stock or money and makes ironic the daughter's redemption in giving birth to repetitions and copies of herself or the redeemed hero. Although Florence repeats herself and her brother in begetting "issue," we remember Esther's fragile and "empty" place, Nell's dying female ancestors, and her own death.

I do not mean to equate Florence with Dickens's other daughters. She appears clearly more dangerous than do Nell, Amy, Esther, Lucie, and others. Yet she exposes the dangers inherent in the figure of any daughter, as Esther exposes the fragility of the act of writing oneself as subject of autobiographical narrative. The daughters who follow Florence and Esther purify these daughterly dangers and fragilities, as Dickens represses the material he tapped in their figures. Bella Wilfer flirts with her Rumpty father but marries a Harmon son. Jenny Wren, the father-abused daughter in her golden bower of imagination, carries the scar of such repression: her crippled, grotesque form. In Florence's embrace, however, as in Esther's wanting to "win some love to herself," we see that the daughter desires as jealously as does the son. This jealousy springs from oedipal structures of love in the family. In *Dombey and Son*, triangular desire, oedipal desire, and primal scene are one. Florence, no less than David Copperfield or the "small Cain," looks on the love of a father or mother for someone else, feels betrayed, questions her own identity, and establishes it the only way she can. Dickens's narrative project plays and replays the thematics of the Oedipus complex and the primal scene: the metaphysics of origin and identity, the symbolic debt, and self-engendering. The daughter only appears to redeem this struggle.

2

George Eliot:
"A Sort of Father"

THE PATERNAL THEMATICS and narrative sequences of the self-engendering writer who fathers himself in language can only be metaphorically—perhaps literally—a masculine activity. The woman who writes encounters a different father, a different desire. Whereas the son banishes himself from the site at which the father's death and so meaning unites with himself, the daughter may become mired in the father's meaning and so herself never banish his shadow from her life. The asymmetry of the male and female Oedipus complexes makes the father's significance in the daughter's life an event from which banishment is at best problematic, at worst, impossible. The paternal metaphor fails a daughter, herself different from her father and like her mother, whom she perceives as lacking significance. The originating mastery inherent in linguistic and narrative structures fits readily the task of the self-fathering male writer. The writer who was once and is still a daughter, however, finds herself lacking the authority a son acquires in the structures of the male Oedipus complex. Mary Ann Evans became Marian Lewes by eloping to the Continent; Marian Lewes became George Eliot by writing as a man. At the beginning of her career as George Eliot, Marian Evans Lewes looked back at her relationships with fathers and wrote stories about fathers and daughters.

The Scene of Seduction

There was only one little drawback to this week of holiday and happy intercourse with her father. Everybody would ask them out to tea.

65

They were quite like bride and bridegroom. — Elizabeth Gaskell,
Wives and Daughters

The terminology of seduction reminds George Eliot's readers of Arthur Donnithorne and Hetty Sorrel, Anthony Wybrow and Tina Sarti, Tito Melema and Tessa, Stephen Guest and Maggie Tulliver. Yet when I speak of seduction, I mean not this invitation to sexual activity but the structural configuration in which father and daughter are linked by the daughter's emerging desire and the story that narrates it. In a remarkable essay on Eliot's social theory, Steven Marcus takes "Amos Barton" as example and explores how Eliot's first story obscures its sexual meaning. He deciphers the calendar in "Amos Barton," excavates Milly's miscarriage and unspoken second textual pregnancy, and determines that sexual rapport with her less-than-ordinary husband kills Milly Barton.[1] Marcus is clearly correct. His essay, however — in part a record of his own struggles with Eliot's recalcitrant text and so of the critical process itself — fails to complete its argument. He asks why Milly must die, yet he elides in his marvelous unriddling of "Amos Barton" the paradigmatic intersubjective structure with which Eliot worked throughout her career and toward which her attitudes became increasingly ironic: father-daughter seduction.[2]

"Amos Barton," Eliot's fictional point of departure, must be our own. This tale, as Marcus demonstrates, indeed obscures its meaning; it appears to describe only the love of Amos and Milly, the preacher and his hardworking wife. Into this happy although impoverished family moves the Countess Czerlaski, whose brother's marriage has forced her to leave his home. The Countess lingers at Shepperton Vicarage until members of the community begin to gossip about the sexual triangle her visit implies. "There's fine stories i' the village about her," says Mr. Tomms; "they say as Muster Barton's great wi' her, or else she'd niver stop here."[3] Amos, innocent of sexual transgression and ignorant of his neighbors' innuendoes, does nothing. Milly, however, understands both the implied sexual triangle and the rumors it creates. She falls ill — has a miscarriage — because of overwork and sexual knowledge. The Countess learns of the talk from the family's servant and belatedly moves out. She returns to her brother — the gossips assume her his mistress — despite his having married a member of the servant class. Milly, "fountain of love" (1: 30), pregnant once more, gives birth to a stillborn child, then dies herself.

Class status as well as sexuality appear at issue here. In this "family romance," as Freud describes such fantasies, the Countess as Milly's counterpart represents the mother imagined as aristocrat.[4] As the community gossips correctly assume, the Countess becomes in structural terms the literal wife and mother's sexual rival, and this rivalry (euphemistically, the visit) kills Milly. The Countess too then disappears from the narrative, which conveniently scapegoats both the mother and her aristocratic incarnation. After mothers die off or disappear, however, narrative structure defines the family romance: the daughter emerges from anonymity to replace the mother(s) in the father's life and love. Freud's structural definition of the "family romance" and its relation to the Oedipus complex, as we shall see later in this chapter, proves essential to Eliot's scenario of father-daughter seduction, both in its erotic and ambitious (or class) aims. In "Amos Barton," whose genesis and title Eliot dreamed while dozing, the family romance appears denied as content but affirmed by structure and so clearly wished.[5] The community gossip implies the father's faithlessness, yet the narrator denies such activity; the doubled mother enhances the father's image as a figure of sexuality; and the daughter reaps the structural rewards of familial desire.

The dying mother encourages her daughter to replace herself. She whispers, "Patty, I'm going away from you. Love your papa. Comfort him; and take care of your little brothers and sisters. . . . [to whom you must be] mama when I am gone" (1: 110). Patty passively and obediently fulfills this duty as daughter, substitute wife, and mother: "Patty's treat was to stay at home, or walk about with her papa; and when he sat by the fire in an evening, after the other children were gone to bed, she would bring a stool, and, placing it against his feet, would sit down upon it and lean her head against his knee. Then his hand would rest on that fair head, and he would feel that Milly's love was not quite gone out of his life" (1: 117-18). Yet immediately following this father-daughter scene, Amos Barton loses his curacy. His second loss appears textually unmotivated: hasn't Milly's death punished Amos enough? Apparently not, for the narrative structure must also punish Amos for his loving intimacy with his daughter. Ironically, banishment from Shepperton Vicarage also consolidates father-daughter love. In the tale's "Conclusion," the now white-haired Amos and an unnamed young woman of "about thirty" visit Milly's grave. The unnamed woman's expression "strongly recall[s]" Mrs. Barton's, although her face seems "less lovely in form and colour." Amos appears calm, even cheerful, and his "neat linen" tells of a "woman's care." This woman is Patty, who alone "remains by her father's side, and makes the evening sunshine of his life" (1: 123-24). The daughter, no longer substitute mother to her now-grown siblings, remains substitute wife to and housekeeper for her father.

"Amos Barton," my reader will demur, hardly appears to be a story in which a father "seduces" a daughter. Our associations with the term "seduction," however, bear little resemblance to the psychoanalytic terminology which according to Freud's earliest theories designates the causal links among sexuality, temporality, and repression. In addition, "seduction," like "incest," can signify activities ranging from caring and nurturing that gratify infant needs to overt child abuse; I intend "seduction" to signify paternal affection that may well be sexual in the broadest sense of the term but is not necessarily violent or overtly incestuous in nature. Moreover, although Freud's theory of seduction may be interpreted as serving to justify the aggressions and authority of fathers or to deny the occurrence of father-daughter incest, I view father-daughter seduction as a structural relationship within the mother-father-child triangle.[6] As Elaine Showalter demonstrates, the absent or estranged mother appears alongside the overbearing or supportive father in creating the nineteenth-century daughter's dependency on paternal approbation and her feeling of womanly reward in fulfilling filial duty.[7] The scene of seduction, then, portrays a relationship in which desiring fantasy and activity are enacted by both father and daughter in the context of the nuclear family. In the case of George Eliot's narrative project, however, the literary critic may interpret only the daughter's texts, for although we know little from Robert Evans's journals aside from the facts of his daily life, we do know about a daughter's struggle to narrate her own desire.

Freud developed his theory of seduction as the child's introduction to sexuality because in his earliest clinical experience his patients repeatedly reported instances from their childhoods in which they were passively sexual seduced by an adult. In the case of female patients, the part of seducer was invariably played by the father.[8] After undertaking his own self-analysis, however, Freud wrote a now-famous letter to his mentor, Fliess, in which he jettisoned his theory of seduction, partially because he could no longer accept that "perverse acts by the father" could be so widespread.[9] Yet as Jean Laplanche and J.-B. Pontalis demonstrate, Freud never totally abandoned the theory of seduction: Freud himself confessed, "It was only later that I was able to recognize in this phantasy of being seduced by the father the expression of the typical Oedipus complex in women."[10] In the intervening years, as this statement implies, Freud realized his female patients' stories of remembered paternal seduction did not necessarily report reality and may have reported fantasy.

Freud's later formulations posit seduction as one of the primal fantasies inherited by each individual from a historically recurring set of fantasies. Like the primal scene, which seeks to symbolize identity, the scene of paternal seduction retroactively seeks to represent and solve a major enigma confronting the daughter: the origin or upsurge of her sexuality. The scene of seduction, then, dramatizes the moment of emergence of desire; when related as story, it represents the beginning of a woman's history.[11] In his essay "A Child Is Being Beaten," Freud demonstrates the linguistic transformations that phrase undergoes while being narrated by a young girl *as a story;* Laplanche and Pontalis believe the phrase "a father seduces a daughter" may undergo similar linguistic transformation when a woman turns fantasy or screen memory of a real scene into narrative. This transformation locates the subject of the phrase and also defines the positionality of the desiring subject with regard to the structural intersubjectivity being narrated. The "subject" of the phrase and by linguistic analogy, the story, may be located as "daughter," or "father," or even the term "seduces."[12] The story of father-daughter seduction, a story told by a woman, then, narrates the origin and history of a daughter's desire and the complexities of placing herself as desiring subject of that story.

George Eliot's "Amos Barton" tells just such a story of paternal seduction and daughterly desire. The "smoke screens" Steven Marcus encounters in his attack on the self-obscuring text cover over the structural configuration of desire which emerges, as does the daughter, at the tale's end. Marcus's theory that Milly dies because she enjoys a rare sexual rapport with her husband does not disconfirm my theory about father-daughter seduction. That conjugal passion must be eliminated from the narrative along with the two incarnations of the mother so they can be repeated in the relationship of father and daughter. Although neither father nor daughter appears to attempt seduction — both seem sexually passive — the story's narrative structure defines its subject as the term itself, "seduces." The daughter is not yet the subject of Eliot's tale, although she soon will be.

The structures of desire in "Amos Barton" appear analogous to those in Eliot's experience. Ruby V. Redinger, Eliot's most recent and psychologically revealing biographer, begins her discussion of "Father and Brother" with a chapter that interprets as fictional John Cross's point of departure in his elegaic tribute to his wife — her first biography. Redinger reads Cross's picture of the happy Evans family as an invention: father, brother, and Mary Ann inhabit the intimate central space of this biographical scene, while the mother stands aside disapprovingly. This pattern of the displaced mother occurs throughout Eliot's novels and serves the story of father-daughter seduction. Mrs. Bede and Mrs. Tulliver, for example, are disapproving shrews; after these novels, mothers virtually disappear from Eliot's fictional world, leaving father and daughter to their mutual caring. Moreover, like Patty Barton, Mary Ann Evans found herself, after her mother's death and Chrissey's marriage, her father's housekeeper and caretaker. Robert Evans, like other Victorian fathers, disapproved of his daughter's flaunted and fragile independence and enforced her dependence upon him so laconically that he appeared inauthoritative and indecisive, as I will discuss in the next section of this chapter. Yet Mary Ann Evans clearly chose womanly and filial service as her young destiny; she spent her early life in the "offices of a daughter," as Elizabeth Gaskell terms them: love and duty.[13]

Eliot's biography, however, cannot fully account for the fact that or reasons why she wrote fiction. In my discussion of Freud's theory of seduction, I emphasize, as does he, that the daughter's fantasy is narrated *as a story*. Language, or the representation of the scene of seduction, transforms that scene into symbolic sequences and structures. As Freud asserted throughout his career, the manifest content of a dream or fantasy can never be known directly; all we know is the story that tells it, an image-laden narrative that demands to be translated—interpreted—into the latent content. Language taps unconscious representations in the dream or the fantasy of seduction when that tale is told, whether in the psychoanalyst's office or in a novel. Although the "talking cure," as Freud and Lacan called it, demonstrates the essential role of speech in the therapeutic act, writing can metaphorically "cure" precisely because its structures as story transform scenes of desire into an account of a subject's personal history, because the discourse of narrative allows the writer to represent and to question that history. In narrating the primal scene of seduction, however, language plays a more specialized role. In his resurrection of the theory of seduction, Sandor Ferenczi assigns language a causal function in the emergence of sexuality and therefore the fantasy of seduction. According to Ferenczi, the child when seduced is introduced to a new language, the language of adult passion, the language of desire necessarily marked by prohibition.[14] Ferenczi's theory implies that the woman who narrates the scene of seduction seeks perhaps at first unconsciously to incorporate this language into her own, thereby to confront through language the scene she represents and so to create her own personal history.

George Eliot's stories of seduction indeed incorporate the language of this desire. In "Janet's Repentance," for example, Reverend Tryan dies not only because of selfless hard work but because Janet's confessed story to him of her unhappiness and his respondent confession to her about his sexual profligacy create an attraction between them for which Eliot's metaphor is consumption. In *The Mill on the Floss*, Maggie's love for her father depends to a great extent on his loving language of tenderness. Maggie's father supports her willful activities, enjoys her tomboyish conduct, laughs at her antics, refuses to punish her, and soothes her with the language of love which signifies desire. When Tom rejoices in Maggie's self-inflicted haircut and resulting humiliation, Maggie runs sobbing to her father, who responds soothingly, "putting his arm round her," "Come, come, my wench . . . never mind; you was i' the right to cut it off if it plagued you; give over crying: father'll take your part." Maggie adores such "delicious words of tenderness" and "never forgot any of those moments when her father 'took her part.'"[15] When Maggie runs away to the gypsies, she wants nothing more than to be reunited with her father, or some hero out of books, for her father *is* her hero. Mr. Tulliver responds to her homecoming, "You mustn't think o' running away from father. What 'ud father do without his little wench?" (176).

In these recurring scenes, the daughter is identified as the desiring subject in the phrase and story, "a father seduces a daughter." The reciprocating father appears as a figure of wish-fulfillment: he is the loving, approving, rewarding father George Eliot never had. Mr. Tulliver soothes Maggie's passionate temper; Mary Ann Evans fought her own hard battle to restrain her "affections"—those "disturbing forces"—and to subdue her "passions" (*Letters,* 1: 142, 242). Mr. Tulliver thinks Maggie "'cute," smarter than the son who by privilege of gender ought to be the smarter child; the ambitious Mary Ann translated religion and philosophy only with the help and approbation of her figurative fathers, Reverend Francis Watts and Dr. Brabant. The fictional father, Mr. Tulliver's, "delicious words of tenderness" (1: 102) compensate for Mary Ann Evans's deprivation of loving language from her father. Only as he approached death did Robert Evans, as Mary Ann wrote Cara Bray, provide a "thousand little proofs that he understands my affection and responds to it." Cara wrote Sara Hennell that Evans "takes opportunities now of saying kind things to M.A., contrary to his wont. Poor girl, it shows how rare they are by the gratitude with which she repeats the commonest expressions of kindness" (*Letters,* 1: 283-84, 272). In her letters, Mary Ann Evans incorporates the language of tenderness into her own text, much as Ferenczi describes language before the scene of seduction. In *The Mill on the Floss,* however, George Eliot imagines a scene of father-daughter seduction which in fact inverts the desiring subject and the desired object of Eliot's incorporated language of love in these letters: Eliot's words after her father's death, "What shall I be without my Father?" become Tulliver's, "What'ud father do without his little wench?" (*Letters,* 1: 284). In fiction, a father speaks lovingly to his daughter.

In the middle of her career, Eliot wrote two more stories about the scene of seduction. Both insist on their fictionality, their nature as *stories: Silas Marner* is a fable, almost a fairy tale; *Felix Holt the Radical* begins with a parable. In the "Introduction" to *Felix Holt,* Sampson the coachman tells stories of the Transome family whom we will meet in the body of the novel; the narrator describes traveling rural England as a "modern Odyssey." The "Introduction" concludes with a metaphorical description of the fiction we have read: "The poets have told us of a dolorous enchanted forest in the under world. The thorn-bushes there, and the thick-barked stems, have human histories hidden in them; the power of unuttered cries dwells in the passionless-seeming branches, and the red warm blood is darkly feeding the quivering nerves of a sleepless memory that watches through all dreams. These things are a parable."[16] Both parable-initiated novel and fable tell two stories; their double narratives are linked by the revelation of paternity. The fairy tale of Silas and Eppie and the realistic tale of the Cass family seem wholly unrelated until the identification of Godfrey Cass as Eppie's father structurally conjoins them; the story of Esther and Rufus Lyon and the portrait of the upper-class Transomes likewise become linked by the identification of Maurice Bycliffe as Esther's father and Jermyn as Harold Transome's. The figure of the father structures these narratives. Yet parable and fable call attention to themselves as stories because Eliot no longer structures the scene of seduction while obscuring its content, or merely incorporates the language of father-daughter desire into her stories but uses narrative discourse to examine the origin and nature of that desire. The narrative identifies itself as a story of seduction, a romance about the family romance.

In *Silas Marner* and *Felix Holt*, as in the paradigmatic "Amos Barton," narrative structure kills off the mother and so sets the scene of father-daughter seduction. Yet both Eppie and Esther love and live alone with adoptive fathers, and both, when confronted with the identities of their "real" fathers, choose to stay with their "present" fathers. Eppie rejects Godfrey Cass, her "father by blood," in favor of her "foster father" because language defines Silas as her "old, long-loved father." Silas tells Godfrey, "Your coming now and saying 'I'm her father' doesn't alter the feelings inside us. It's me she's been calling her father ever since she could say the word"; Eppie's "feelings . . . vibrated to every word Silas had uttered."[17] Likewise, when Rufus Lyon tells Esther he is not her real father, she cries "Father, father! forgive me if I have not loved you enough." Her choice to stay with her adoptive father affirms the priority of his "great and strong feeling" over "circumstances [which] don't signify" (2: 26-28). Both fabled scenes of seduction, then, reject blood fathers and families because the authority of feeling, the language of love between foster-father and daughter, defines true fatherhood.

Eliot also demonstrates in both stories that the scene of (foster)-father-daughter seduction teaches as well as names love, and the controlling metaphor for the relationship of father and daughter in each story structures a redemption first of father, then of daughter. In *Silas Marner,* this metaphor is possession. The miserly Silas, lonely and alienated from his community, one night loses his hoarded gold coins and gains in their place a golden-haired little girl who restores love to his life and creates sympathy for him among his neighbors. Godfrey Cass decides on this same night that his daughter "would be just as happy in life without being owned by its father," and "the father would be much happier without owning the child" (183). "Owning" signifies both possession and recognition, and when the childless Cass later admits paternity, he offers a fatherhood based on material goods and social status, a fatherhood the redeeming golden-haired girl disowns. In *Felix Holt,* however, the central metaphor for father-daughter seduction is reform. Felix, a preacher rather than a politician, awakens Esther to a sense that her vanity has prevented her loving her father. In a recurring scene in which Esther combs her father's hair, her new love for her father grows, and the language of love begins to reform her character.

> "Let me lift your porridge from before the fire, and stay with you, father. You think I'm so naughty that I don't like doing anything for you," said Esther, smiling rather sadly at him.
>
> "Child, what has happened? You have become the image of your mother to-night," said the minister, in a loud whisper. . . .
>
> When Esther was lying down that night, she felt as if the little incidents between herself and her father on this Sunday had made it an epoch. Very slight words and deeds may have a sacramental efficacy, if we can cast our self-love behind us, in order to say or do them. (1: 231-32.)

The language of love between father and daughter becomes not only redemptive but sacred.

Both *Silas Marner* and *Felix Holt*, like "Amos Barton," incorporate into the scene of father-daughter seduction the family romance. Freud describes this family romance as a "work of fiction"; fiction performs psychic work for the child, who imagines his or her real parents to be of high social standing and him or herself as adopted by the parents of low social standing with whom he or she lives. This "romance" takes shape under the pressure exerted by the Oedipus complex and serves to liberate the child from the authority of her parents, whom she once thought irreproachable but of whom she now has a low opinion. Hand in hand with this denigration of the parents goes a feeling that the child's affection for her parents is not fully reciprocated, that the parents with whom she lives do not love her enough. The family romance, as I mentioned earlier, has two principal aims: one ambitious (based on desire for higher social class), the other erotic.[18] In addition, the term "family romance" includes both a psychoanalytic and a literary meaning: aroused by oedipal desire, this romance is also a story the child tells herself to wish-fulfill her desire for parental and primarily paternal love. In the middle of her career, Eliot turned from the social satire of *Scenes of Clerical Life* and the realism of *Adam Bede* to the fabulist fantasy of romance and ultimately to the historical romance of *Romola*.[19]

Eliot's work of fiction imagines the family romance of a daughter whose real father in fact enjoys a high social status and who has been adopted by a father of low social status. The family romance comes true; the father is an aristocrat, but the daughter rejects her inheritance in the name of adoptive paternal love and so liberates herself from the authority of a "real" but loveless or absent father. The adoptive father with whom she lives already reciprocates or creates her love, for Eliot's metaphor of redemption signifies desire in the story of seduction. Eliot's fictional family romances retaliate against a father who fails to return a daughter's love and replace him with one who does. They tell a tale whose structure fulfills the erotic aim of the story of seduction: Esther marries Felix, and Rufus "join[s] them where they dwelt" (2: 358); Eppie marries Aaron, who moves in with Silas and his daughter. Eppie tells Silas on her wedding day, "You won't be giving me away, father . . . you'll only be taking Aaron to be a son to you"; when father, daughter, and son arrive home after the ceremony, Eppie cries, "Oh, father . . . what a pretty home ours is! I think nobody could be happier than we are" (271-73). The romance of father-daughter seduction ends in both stories with the symbolic marriage of father and daughter through the linking figure of the "son."[20] At this point in her career, Eliot performed the work of fiction to expose as well as to represent Mary Ann Evans's need for the paternal love she never felt reciprocated by her own father.

Yet *Felix Holt* also chastises a daughter, Esther Lyon, for wishing her father aristocratic and so "better." Esther, unlike Eppie, manifests the ambitious aim of the story of seduction: she would like to be a lady. In *Middlemarch,* Eliot tells a caustic tale of father-daughter seduction because she now fully represents her heroine as the ambitious subject of the family romance. As the ironic, even satiric, tones of "poor Dorothea" echo throughout Books I and II of the novel, Eliot scoffs at this figure for the naive Mary Ann Evans who once yearned for fatherly love and approbation. Dorothea Brooke, unlike Maggie Tulliver, is a fatherless orphan with no narrative past, yet this fictional fatherless daughter, Dorothea, desires to overcome orphanage with a "really delightful marriage" in which the "husband was a sort of father."[21] The narrative repeatedly insists on Dorothea's husband as this "sort of father." Celia identifies Dorothea's attraction for the figurative father as a repeated syndrome in which "old Monsieur Liret" preceded the cramped and cold cleric (1: 23). Once Dorothea and Casaubon are married, Will's friend Naumann thinks the "sallow *Geistlicher*" Dorothea's "father"—until he notices the wedding ring on her left hand. Eliot invests great energy in portraying this relationship as neurotic, misguided, and inappropriate and blames Dorothea—as she once hinted at blaming Milly Barton—for being "shortsighted."

Dorothea's reason for marrying Casaubon appears quickly enough: literary servitude. This "sort of father" could "teach you even Hebrew, if you wished it." Dorothea imagines herself assisting Casaubon's "highest purposes of truth," though (because female) "only as a lamp-holder"; imagines herself a "neophyte about to enter on a higher grade of initiation." She will "throw . . . herself, metaphorically speaking, at Mr. Casaubon's feet" (1: 12, 23, 62, 73). The narrator puts tongue in cheek, metaphorically speaking, but Dorothea, poor Dorothea, is in deadly earnest. She believes Casaubon among the great thinkers: Hooker, Pascal, Locke (complete with mole, Celia sneers), and Milton.

> "Could I not be preparing myself now to be more useful?" said Dorothea to him, one morning, early in the time of courtship; "could I not learn to read Latin and Greek aloud to you, as Milton's daughters did to their father, without understanding what they read?"
>
> "I fear that would be wearisome to you," said Mr. Casaubon, smiling; "and, indeed, if I remember rightly, the young women you have mentioned regarded that exercise in unknown tongues as a ground for rebellion against the poet."
>
> "Yes; but . . . they were very naughty girls, else they would have been proud to minister to such a father. . . . I hope you don't expect me to be naughty and stupid?" (1: 92).

Dorothea knowingly compares her future husband and herself to father and daughter; she unknowingly, as Casaubon points out, compares him to the blind, misogynist poet and herself to the rightly rebellious daughter. Dorothea's inflated metaphor of Casaubon-as-Milton prophesies what the ironic narrator and the reader already know: the failure of the marriage, of Dorothea's literary servitude, of this scene of father-daughter seduction.

The language of desire in the scene of seduction becomes ironic in *Middlemarch*. Represented as attenuated story, this scene of "father" and daughter appears only as a sequence of tellingly juxtaposed literary scenes in which the narrator eschews commentary. The scene in which Dorothea compares Casaubon to Milton and herself to his daughters is framed by two conversations between the disappointed suitor, Sir James Chettam, and the town gossip, Mrs. Cadwallader.

> "[Casaubon] has got no good red blood in his body," said Sir James.
>
> "No. Somebody put a drop under a magnifying-glass, and it was all semi-colons and parentheses," said Mrs. Cadwallader. . . . "He dreams footnotes, and they run away with all his brains. They say, when he was a little boy, he made an abstract of 'Hop o' my Thumb,' and he has been making abstracts ever since. Ugh! And that is the man Humphrey goes on saying that a woman may be happy with." (1: 104.)

Mrs. Cadwallader's linguistic metaphors precede an explicit critique of Casaubon's sexual potency. Sir James remarks in the scene that follows Dorothea's offer to read Greek, Casaubon is "no better than a mummy," was never more than the "shadow of a man"—for proof, "look at his legs"! "Marriage to Casaubon is as good as going to a nunnery," sneers Mrs. Cadwallader in the earlier scene (1: 101, 84). Indeed, Middlemarch gossip proves correct. The figurative father's sexual drive has withered through excessive mythological research. Moreover, the narrator hints that this fictional marriage must never have been consummated. When Casaubon joins Dorothea after speaking to Lydgate about his impending death, his rigid arm refuses his wife's sympathy, and the narrator speaks metaphorically of the "wasted seed" of happiness (2: 231). After Casaubon's death,

Dorothea pointedly bears no heir. Casaubon fails sexually in this scene of figurative father-daughter seduction and fails as well to speak the language of love so important to Eliot's desiring daughters. Casaubon courts Dorothea with words but, once married, Casaubon gradually refuses to speak to his ardent wife and is himself disappointed in the "shallow rill" of his desire. Their two intimate conversations after the fiasco of their honeymoon in Rome take place in bed or in the bedroom, yet husband and wife never touch, remaining separate. The language of desire becomes Casaubon's word of chastisement to his wife in Rome, becomes Dorothea's silent frustration, becomes the narrator's metaphor of marriage as bondage.

Eliot's narrator proves the story of figurative father-daughter seduction, the language of desire, and the daughter's literary servitude ironic because all are fictional. In *Middlemarch*, Dorothea deceives herself with a fictive account of her future husband who will be a sort of father; Dorothea tells herself the story of father-daughter seduction while the reader constructs its scenic context. The reader knows at the novel's beginning that Casaubon will prove sexually, linguistically, and professionally inadequate. The ironic epigraphs to Chapters 2 and 5 demystify Dorothea's shining knight as a mere man; Casaubon convicts himself at the outset in conversation with Dorothea and in his written marriage proposal of intellectual and erotic narrowness (1: 23, 60-62). Like Milton, Casaubon needs a secretary, while Dorothea imagines herself his helpmate. Dorothea misinterprets the depths of Casaubon's caring by reading her own ardent ideals into his proposal of marriage; she creates a fiction of "passion" transfigured into an "ideal life" (1: 63) and so unconsciously hopes to achieve the erotic aim, as Freud calls it, of the family romance. The narrator comments on Dorothea's romantic misreading: "Signs are small measurable things, but interpretations are illimitable, and in girls of sweet, ardent nature, every sign is apt to conjure up wonder, hope, belief, vast as a sky, and coloured by a diffused thimbleful of matter in the shape of knowledge" (1: 34). The story of father-daughter seduction is now created by a daughter in a narrative, as she misinterprets signs in the world from her limited perspective.

Eliot's ironic narrator also demonstrates Dorothea's version of ambition in the family romance as fictional.

> But it was not entirely out of devotion to her future husband that she wished to know Latin and Greek. Those provinces of masculine knowledge seemed to her a standing-ground from which all truth could be seen more truly. As it was, she constantly doubted her own conclusions, because she felt her own ignorance. . . . Perhaps even Hebrew might be necessary — at least the alphabet and a few roots — in order to arrive at the core of things, and judge soundly on the social duties of the Christian. And she had not reached that point of re-

nunciation at which she would have been satisfied with having a wise husband: she wished, poor child, to be wise herself. (1: 93.)

Like Maggie Tulliver, who wants to be judged "cute" by her father, smart by Mr. Riley, and "quick" by Mr. Stelling, Dorothea Brooke, Milton's figurative daughter, truly longs not for literary servitude but masculine achievement. Thinking "truth" a "ground" upon which to stand, thinking the Christian life definable by centers ("cores") and knowable ends ("conclusions"), thinking necessary language merely the insufficiency of alphabets and a "few roots," Dorothea misinterprets not only what she must learn but that she may learn it. As Alan Mintz notes, a woman's vocation in pre-Reform England, the historical time of *Middlemarch*, expressed itself only through her husband's;[22] being female and defining herself as a daughter, Dorothea will remain a neophyte, will always dabble in charity. The narrative demonstrates that Dorothea must ultimately settle for an average life as wife and mother and so give up her romance, her literary ambition.

In creating Dorothea, Eliot criticizes her own youthful romances and defines them as fictions. The young evangelical Mary Ann Evans, after all, once confessed to Maria Lewis her own "besetting sin" of "Ambition, a desire insatiable for the esteem of [her] fellow creatures" — the "fruitful parent" of all other sins (*Letters*, 1: 19). In "misrepresenting" herself to Reverend Francis Watts and Dr. Brabant, whom she later satirized as Liret and Casaubon and excoriated in letters to her friends, George Eliot comprehended that Mary Ann demonstrated not only her oedipal desire for the figurative father but also her desire for worldly, especially literary, esteem. Watts was to be "foster father" to Eliot's translation of Vinet; Brabant acted as mentor during the translation of and designated Mary Ann — his "deutera" — the translator of Strauss's *Das Leben Jesu* when his own daughter, Rufa, dropped the project while on her honeymoon. Eliot repeats this story of father-daughter seduction to put her passionate and ambitious young self in her place — past, forgotten, and compromised.

Yet the woman who writes this story manifests her own ambition and achievement: she is no "silly lady novelist" but rather the lionized moralist of literary London. The joy Eliot makes the reader feel when Dorothea chooses Will Ladislaw and domestic love over ardent ambition is complicated by her understanding that Dorothea has given up what Eliot herself achieved. This author ironically invalidates her youthful ambition while validating her mature achievement. And Eliot's own retelling of the story of father-daughter seduction creates this irony. Eliot transforms the unrecognized scene of seduction in "Amos Barton" into a story that recognizes the daughter's desire for a father's love and approbation in *The Mill on the Floss*. She then portrays such daughterly desire as fabled fantasy in *Silas Marner* and *Felix Holt*. At the end of her career, Eliot fully demonstrates the self-deceptive nature of this romance. Setting the scene of seduction discovers to its teller the story's fictionality, its desire as ambitious, its original scene as fantasy. The heroine becomes the subject of the phrase and the story, "a father seduces a daughter," in *The Mill on the Floss*, only to become in *Middlemarch* the deceived destroyer of her own desire.

The Law and the Father

The struggle between Antigone and Creon represents that struggle between elemental tendencies and established laws by which the outer life of man is gradually and painfully being brought into harmony with his inward needs. — George Eliot, "The Antigone and Its Moral"

In *The Mill on the Floss*, Mrs. Glegg writes her will strictly on the "fundamental fact of blood"; despite what she regards as Mr. Tulliver's disreputable behavior to her sisters, her legacies "bear a direct ratio to degrees of kinship" (1: 201). In *Felix Holt the Radical*, Mrs. Transome takes pride in her genealogy and analyzes the world solely in terms of "blood and family" (2: 210). The Transome matriarch and the women of the Dodson clan—who store and hoard their belongings so as to will them to their survivors—believe all legal matters can be resolved on the basis of kinship and genealogy: the law is based on maternity and on the structures of the family.[23] *The Mill on the Floss* and *Felix Holt* also seem to define the law as a matter of paternal precedence. Mr. Tulliver owns Dorlcote Mill by virtue of one hundred years of family possession; Pivart, who has recently bought the farm upstream, therefore has no right to meddle with the Floss's water-flow. According to Tulliver, "water is water," and his right to the water is based on the genealogy of fathers who will the mill to sons: a son inherits land from his father, who inherited it from his father, and so he inherits the privilege and authority that go with ownership. Tulliver continually "goes to law" thinking patrimony guarantees him legal right to water, bridge crossings, and footpaths. In contrast, old Mr. Transome, the patriarchal figure of genealogy and property transmission in *Felix Holt*, appears foolish and mad. But Transome is not that patriarch. The novel seeks as it repeatedly invokes "the truth," and the narrative's "whole truth" resides in Jermyn's words to Harold Transome: *"I am your father"* (2: 241, 327). When Harold discovers his illegitimacy, he assumes he has no legal right to Transome Court and feels it his duty to offer the family's property to Esther, its rightful inheritor.

These two narratives link fatherhood with legal rights, inheritance, and authority. A father determines his progenies' privileges, duties, and properties; he empowers the structures of inheritance by virtue of having engendered offspring. Eliot's legal and genealogical metaphor enables the father to determine legitimacy and to wield authority based on precedence. In his theories about paternity and symbolism, Jacques Lacan also links the father, authority, and law: the signifier of the Father is "author of the Law." Lacan drew on Freud's *Totem and Taboo*, in which the symbolic murder by the sons of the precedent and authoritative father celebrates both their rebellion against him and their internalization of his prohibition against incest. Lacan's version of law is based less equivocally on prohibition: the law is constituted by the father's "no." When Lacan's sons metaphorically murder the father, they bind themselves as subjects "for life to the Law," to certain symbolic structures, to the cultural prohibition against incest, to a positionality in the chain of signifiers that is culture and language. Lacan sees as causal, then, the relationship between the father as signifer and the acquisition by the child of cultural prohibitions and symbolism. By "signifier," I think Lacan means that the "father" exists in a chain of desire and prohibition the structure of which, like that of language, can be understood to transform and codify itself according to certain laws—a notion that grows out of Freud's increasingly structural topologies not only of the unconscious and its functions but of the Oedipus complex as well. In contrast, the symbolic Father, the Father upon whose name religion teaches us to call, "signifies this Law."[24] Culturally authoritative and prohibitive paternity facilitates the real father's "no" and structures the symbolism to which the child must accede.

The authoritative and prohibitive father appears in Mary Ann Evans's first texts, her letters. Here she links fatherhood, authority, filial duty, and property (or domicile) just as George Eliot links them in her legal narratives. For Mary Ann Evans, these issues center on her role as her father's housekeeper. In 1837, she succeeded to the role of "mistress" of Griff (*Letters*, 1: 52). This official social and housekeeping role provided Mary Ann a sense of "usefulness" and autonomy which allowed her to welcome friends "independently" at her own home. It must also have facilitated her sense of personal authority; Dorothea Brooke, for example, who performed the same role for her bachelor uncle, "did not at all dislike her new authority, with the homage that belonged to it" (1: 13). In 1840, however, the possibility of her brother Isaac's marrying and so making his new wife mistress of Griff threatened Mary Ann's role as her father's housekeeper. For a period of nearly ten months, Mary Ann did not know either her future domicile or role. Would she live with her older sister at Meriden, or would her father take her with him as housekeeper to a new home? This uncertainty, she wrote her Aunt and Uncle Evans, "unhinge[d her] mind a little," although she wished to "imitate" her "father's calm endurance and humble gratitude and be quite free from anxiety respecting [her] destination" (*Letters,* 1: 73-74).

Mary Ann happily continued her role as her father's housekeeper at Foleshill once his decision was made. Yet within another ten months, Mary Ann refused to attend church with her father. In the "Holy Wars" that followed, as Mary Ann later called them, father and daughter struggled over filial obligation and paternal authority. This act of rebellion caused Mary Ann another period of uncertainty about her future domicile and role: Robert Evans threatened to leave Foleshill for Packington Cottage, blaming Mary Ann for the expenditure of money needed by married sisters and brothers. Mary Ann visited Griff while her father again refused to decide her destiny. When she agreed once more to attend church with him, Mary Ann's father reinstated her as mistress cf Foleshill, although she nevertheless reserved for herself the right not to listen to the church service. These two episodes define a father's complete authority over an unmarried daughter's destiny. He and he alone controls the domicile and role that create her sense of personal authority and daughterly duty.

Father and daughter struggle not only over authority but over symbolism and signification as well. The father's authority resides in his position of precedence and in his gender; his word, his prohibitive "no," constitutes the law to which his child must bind herself. The language of the father's authority, then, promulgates the law; his prohibitive word must be trustworthy, his promise acceptable. But although Robert Evans maintained total control over his daughter's future, he refused to speak clearly the language of paternal authority. Mary Ann noted to Cara Bray, "Unless I draw a circle round [my father] and require an answer within it, he will go on hesitating and hoping for weeks"; to Abigail Pears, "I must have a *home,* not a visiting place. I wish you would learn something from my Father, and send me word how he seems disposed" (*Letters,* 1: 138, 134). Lacan discusses this paradox of fatherhood in his essay on Judge Daniel Paul Schreber: the more completely the real father claims the function of legislator, the more opportunities he creates for himself of failing as the ideal promulgator of the law. His word, his authority, may therefore appear undeserved, inadequate, or fraudulent.[25] This gap between the language of authority and its representative speaker in the family makes the law itself suspect. In the "Holy Wars," Robert and Mary Ann Evans played out this struggle in a symbolic arena. As Ruby V. Redinger points out, the rebellion against a Heavenly Father's authority appears to be a displaced act of rage against an earthly father's authority.[26] Although her real father maintains authority over his daughter, that daughter refuses to allow the symbolic Heavenly Father to do the same. She declares His Word suspect, inadequate, and fraudulent; denies her obligations and duties to a symbolic Father; refuses to call on

His Name or to listen to the words of veneration and worship of Him. Yet the symbolic veneration of the Father which indeed calls on His Name structures the cultural and linguistic systems in which the child must situate herself. Mary Ann's eventual compromise recalls the totem meal of Freud's murdering sons: while rebelling against a father's law on one level, she fully accepts his authority on another and so binds herself to his word for life.

Eliot's legal narratives play out this ambivalent attitude toward paternal law. While *The Mill on the Floss* and *Felix Holt* assert the father's precedence as conferring authority, they also demonstrate the cultural decline of paternity as a legal and lawful category. Paternal precedence in fact no longer determines and defines ownership, its rights and duties. Each time Tulliver "goes to law," the lawyer Wakem outsmarts him. Wakem eventually owns Dorlcote Mill, and when Tulliver goes bankrupt, Wakem controls the right to its tenancy; Tulliver then remains on the land of his grandfathers only at Wakem's pleasure. *Felix Holt's* lawyer (and father), Matthew Jermyn, manipulates the law as skillfully if more corruptly than does Wakem. He controls the Transome land and timber by illegal use of the settlement laws; his past adultery with Mrs. Transome and resulting fatherhood of Harold Transome consolidate his power. In *The Mill*, the law as metaphor demonstrates the decline of legal rights and duties based on the concept of kinship and the simultaneous rise of monetary obligation based on business dealings. After the old-fashioned father Tulliver falls off his horse and into bankruptcy, his son rises into the professional management class. In *Felix Holt*, the law as metaphor demonstrates the decline of rights, duties, and ownership based on aristocratic paternal precedence and the concomitant rise of democracy. The novel's historical setting—just after the Reform Bill of 1832—enables Eliot to link the ownership of small parcels of land not inherited from fathers with the rights and duties of suffrage and participation in the political process. Whereas Eliot's nostalgic narrator in *The Mill* bemoans the loss of kinship as the basis of law and figuratively portrays this change in his histories of Rhine versus Rhone, his history of St. Oggs juxtaposed with the personal destiny of the business-minded Mr. Glegg, the narrator of *Felix Holt* understands fully the inevitability—if not the desirability—of this change. Both *The Mill* and *Felix Holt* represent social rights and privileges as no longer residing in lawful paternal precedence and authority, in patriarchal succession—although Eliot may well wish they still did.

In virtually all her early narratives, Eliot in fact questions the authority of her fictional fathers. Their competence appears problematic because they fail in the symbolic arena of language: they misinterpret the signs and symbols around themselves. Mr. Tulliver cannot read "the maze of this puzzling world" and so can only disentangle the threads of this complex web by pulling on one thread, by grabbing single-mindedly at one clue as that which unriddles the puzzle (*MF,* 1: 104). Tulliver's simplistic metaphors—the law as "cock-fight," for example—indicate not only his failure to interpret a complex world correctly but his failure to understand as well that it must be interpreted. Sir Christopher Cheverel, Tina's adoptive father in "Mr. Gilfil's Love-Story," misinterprets Tina's love for his son as love for the bungling Mr. Gilfil; "I thought I saw everything," he later moans, "and was stone-blind all the while" (*SCL,* 2: 6). Adam Bede, whose character Eliot based on her father's, fails to interpret Hetty's blush when he and she pick currants, thinking "the signs of love for [Arthur] . . . signs of love towards himself."[27] Like Tulliver, Adam misunderstands that "nature's language" needs interpretation. He assumes that Hetty's physical beauty is a sign of her character and that he as what the narrator calls a "great physiognomist" can read nature's writing in the "exquisite lines" of her face (1: 228). Amos Barton, whom Eliot's narrator ruthlessly satirizes as the "quintessential extract of mediocrity" (*SCL,* 1: 73), fails to recognize the signs of Milly's love or to interpret the stories about his supposed relationship with the Countess Czerlaski. In his professional life, Amos fails to understand that preaching must be tailored to suit his flock. He lectures poor people with exegetical "types and symbols" and refuses to bring his university-educated mind "to the pauper point of view." In contrast, the Reverend Cleves preaches sermons the "wheelwright and the blacksmith can understand" because he calls a "spade a spade" and moves freely among the people (1: 39, 84-88).

The fictional father's inability to interpret the world as different from or other than himself names him as Eliot's first egoist. Virtually all the fathers I have considered willfully misinterpret events because of paternal pride. Mr. Tulliver fails to realize that his pride drives him to "go to law" and so causes his eventual bankruptcy. Tulliver's obstinacy prevents him from interpreting his own behavior as self-indulgent; his debt to Mrs. Glegg, for example, need not have been paid off immediately but for his arrogance. In contrast, Sir Christopher Cheverel realizes he has "been too proud and obstinate" and should forgive his sister for marrying against his will (*SCL,* 2: 4). He reforms and takes his sister's son as his new heir. Likewise, Adam Bede eventually understands his pride and severity of character and vows never to be "hard" again. He bends his otherwise iron willfulness and recognizes he should have been generous with his now-dead father and with Hetty Sorrel. In each of these early narratives, the father's inability to interpret language and events around him as different from his wishes also creates a catastrophe that culminates in death, murder, or attempted murder. Amos Barton's ignorance inflicts death upon his long-loving wife as surely as does the Countess's selfishness; Sir Christopher's insistence that Tina marry Mr. Gilfil intensifies her passion for Wybrow and in turn helps cause her desperate theft of the dagger; Adam Bede's misreading of Hetty's love and resulting proposal of marriage drive her to murder her child as surely as does her illicit passion for Arthur Donnithorne. The fictional father's complicity in the crimes of passion makes him responsible for causal events in the "inexorable law of consequences" upon which Eliot's narratives insist so sternly.[28]

The fictional father's misinterpretation intensifies the suffering of others and so inflicts suffering and punishment upon himself. This severe and authoritative father must learn sympathy through suffering. In *Adam Bede*, Eliot articulates this moral fully: "Whenever Adam was strongly convinced of any proposition, it took the form of a principle in his mind. ... Perhaps here lay the secret of the hardness he had accused himself of: he had too little fellow-feeling with the weakness that errs in spite of foreseen consequences. ... And there is but one way in which a strong determined soul can learn it—by getting his heart-strings bound round the weak and erring, so that he must share not only the outward consequence of their error, but their inward suffering" (1: 316). Steven Marcus defines Eliot's doctrine of sympathy as the enabling social sentiment, as the power of communication among members of a community. Sympathy thus serves to control conflict and to expunge alienation and radical negativity from a community.[29] But it also serves to humiliate figures of authority: aristocrats, clerics, fathers. Adam Bede, as Eliot's brother Isaac recognized, is based on the author's memories of her father. In learning the lesson of sympathy through suffering, Adam learns what Robert Evans refused to contemplate. Adam binds himself to a law of a woman who preaches the authoritative doctrine of fellow-feeling; in writing *Adam Bede*, Eliot metaphorically binds her father to her own moral law of sympathy—a sympathy she was forced to learn when she lost the Holy Wars to her father. In *Adam Bede*, Adam's and Dinah's sympathy forgives a passionate woman, Hetty Sorrel, her transgressions and facilitates the mature love of Adam for Dinah. Eliot's doctrine of sympathy, moreover, accuses the fictional father of coldness. When Amos Barton leaves Shepperton after losing his curacy, he visits Milly's grave and speaks the words, "Milly, Milly, dost thou hear me? I didn't love thee enough—I wasn't tender enough to thee—but I think of it all now" (1: 122). Amos's misinterpretation, his refusal to see that the stories of the community demand interpretation, his arrogance, all come to this: he did not love his wife enough. And Amos's realization, the narrative implies, will increase his affection for and attention to his daughter. Eliot's morality of sympathy, then, serves her early narrative project: it humbles—dare we say humiliates?—the fictional father, demonstrates his authority inauthentic, and focuses his care on a daughter.

If Eliot declares the father arrogant and a failure in the realms of signification and authority, however, she also wishes him to be the law-giver. Mr. Tulliver speaks to his daughter the language of love in the scene of seduction, as we have seen, but he also fails to discipline her. When he buys Maggie back from the gypsies, Mr. Tulliver refuses to punish her and demands that Mrs. Tulliver not reproach and Tom not taunt Maggie. Yet Maggie's absolute hunger for love, her rage and vengeance when she is denied it, demonstrate her concomitant need for discipline.[30] Mr. Tulliver promulgates no law, utters no word of authority to his daughter. As a result, Tom provides Maggie the discipline and punishment her father refuses her. When she inadvertently kills his rabbits, cuts her hair, and pushes Lucy in the mud, Tom rebukes and taunts her. Yet Maggie continues to act in ways that encourage Tom's disapproval; narratively, Maggie appears to desire his rejection and punishment. Although Laura Comer Emery and David Smith describe Tom and Maggie's relationship as incestuous, Maggie's endearments to and caresses of Tom and her desire to live always with her brother repeatedly facilitate not fulfillment of her desire but punishment for what she herself considers her naughtiness.[31] When he grows up, Tom continues to punish Maggie for her desire: he refuses her the companionship of Philip Wakem and severely rebukes her for sexually desiring and running away with Stephen Guest—as her father failed to punish her for running away to the gypsies. Tom speaks the authoritative word of repudiation which defines Maggie's failure to bind herself to the laws of the community:

> Her brother was the human being of whom she had been most afraid, from her childhood upwards: afraid with that fear which springs in us when we love one who is inexorable, unbending, unmodifiable—with a mind that we can never mould ourselves upon, and yet that we cannot endure to alienate from us. . . . She almost desired to endure the severity of Tom's reproof, to submit in patient silence to that harsh disapproving judgment against which she had so often rebelled: it seemed no more than just to her now—who was weaker than she was? She craved that outward help to her better purpose which would come from complete, submissive confession—from being in the presence of those whose looks and words would be a reflection of her own conscience. . . . "You will find no home with me. . . . You have disgraced my father's name." (3: 340-41.)

The language of desire clearly names Maggie's urge to be punished in this passage; she "craves" harsh and severe judgment, desires discipline that will teach her society's law. Tom represents her conscience and so speaks the word that banishes Maggie from her home by invoking the name of a father. Tom resembles the willful and severe Adam Bede before Adam learns not to be "hard," yet this narrative shows the daughter needing the authoritative severity the earlier one repudiated. Tom's harsh judgment of Maggie appears narratively correct (although we sympathize with Maggie's exile), and he need not learn the lesson of sympathy through suffering as Adam Bede once did.

Tom's role as lawgiver establishes him as the figurative father whom Maggie desires will punish rather than love her. The narrative in fact insists metaphorically and structurally on the brother as figurative father. When Gritty Moss compares her relationship with her brother, Mr. Tulliver, to the relationship of Maggie and Tom, Tulliver recognizes the truth of her analogy. He treats Gritty with tenderness only because he fears if he is severe with his sister, Tom will be "hard and cruel" to *his* sister, Maggie. In addition, although the narrative appears to support the Dodson clan's belief that Tom resembles them rather than the Tullivers, Tom in fact resembles his father. He proves as "contrary as his father"; his "Rhadamantine" urge to deal "justice that desires to hurt culprits as they deserve to be hurt" merely exaggerates the "love of retributive justice" that continually drives his father to the law (1: 89, 76, 246). Tom is educated to business because Mr. Tulliver fears his son's desire to usurp the paternal property, and the narrative indeed proves this desire true. After his father's "downfall," Tom enters the peddling business, rises to join Mr. Glegg's firm, pays his father's debts, buys back the mill he now· rents from Wakem, and becomes the mill's "master" (2: 339). He fills the place a father vacated and fills it with more authority than did the father. *The Mill on the Floss* splits the father in two: one father desires the desiring daughter, the figurative other prohibits and punishes all her desire. No narrative conclusion can reconcile the opposition inherent in this narrative structure. As Eliot must have known when she researched inundations before beginning the novel, only the flood that paradoxically fulfills and sweeps away desire can overcome this motivational split.

The father who is taught sympathy and the figurative father who punishes exist as a dichotomy in Eliot's early narratives. These irreconcilable fictional fathers and the narrative structures they inhabit find their source in the dialectic of desire and prohibition which structures the female Oedipus complex. For Lacan's version of the child binding himself to the law and to the symbolic structures of culture and language through the father's prohibitive word pertains only to sons. How does a daughter bind herself to the law? I will discuss the female castration complex and the daughter's shifting her love from mother to father in my next chapter; here, I would like to characterize the problematic love between father and daughter. For at this difficult time, the daughter must confront her father as a figure of both desire and prohibition. To win his love, she must please him; she must express her love for him yet obey his law or risk his disapproval and punishment. Freud believes that because the daughter desires the figure of the law, she creates a weaker superego than does the son. I would say instead that she identifies with the father's authority less strongly than does the son; his role as model for conscience is tempered by her desire for him. Moreover, if she incorporates into herself even a modified version of the father's prohibition, must the daughter also deny her own desire? According to Nancy Chodorow, the daughter's desire for the father is less fundamental than the son's for the mother; a daughter's primary attachment to the preoedipal mother means a girl's desire for the father is always tempered by her first choice of love object.[32] Given that Victorian mothers (or their female surrogates) performed early infant child care and given the power of Victorian fathers, self-sacrifice in the realm of authority and self-mutilation in the realm of desire appear probable for this historical daughter.

Because of asymmetry in the male and female Oedipus complex, the daughter also enters the realm of culture problematically. What role, for example, does the daughter play in the symbolic murder of the father by the primal sons? Must she also metaphorically murder the father who was once her rival for the mother to accede to the structures of culture or to achieve the positionality required to define herself as subject? Clearly not. Indeed, the son entering the social order learns that he must renounce his mother because she belongs to his father, who has the power to punish his desire with the loss of his masculinity: the incest taboo. But the son also learns he will grow up to have his own woman, and he may also have a daughter. The girl receives no such compensation or reward for renouncing the Oedipus complex. The daughter entering the social order learns she may possess neither mother nor father, and she will one day be possessed by someone like her father. She will be exchanged by sons as confirmation of the pact that signifies the incest taboo. The daughter therefore has little incentive to give up the "haven" of the Oedipus complex, as Freud defines it; she need not give up the father, figure of approbation and discipline.[33] Desire and prohibition, authority and submission, law and dependency, then, structure the female Oedipus complex and make the father-daughter bond an ongoing issue for the Victorian daughter.

In her letters before and after Robert Evans's death, Eliot portrayed her relationship with her father as loving and disciplining. Despite her deprivation of loving words from her father, as I discussed in the first section of this chapter, Mary Ann wrote to Cara Bray while her father was dying: "The one deep strong love I have ever known has now its highest exercise and fullest reward — the worship of sorrow is *the* worship for mortals." This deep love for a father who failed to reciprocate feeling appears to have bred a concomitantly deep dependency. "What shall I be without my Father?" Mary Ann asked herself. "It will seem as if a part of my moral nature were gone. I had a horrid vision of myself last night becoming earthly sensual and devilish for want of that purifying restraining influence" (*Letters*, 1: 284). Without a father's authority and prohibition, without the strictures of duty, obligation, and self-discipline imposed upon her by that father and her role as his housekeeper, Mary Ann Evans feared regressing into the evangelical Mary Ann, ruled by religious rhetoric and evading with useless confession her passions and feelings, her raw desire. When she returned from Switzerland after her father's death, Mary Ann realized, "We are apt to complain of the weight of duty, but when it is taken from us, and we are left at liberty to choose for ourselves, we find that the old life is the easier one" (*Letters*, 1: 334). Having depended upon a father's authority for her own self-authority and upon a father's laconic expression of care for satisfaction of her desire, this daughter felt lost and without purpose without her father. That life with father, its deprivations and disciplines, now appeared preferable to the life in which she must define her desires apart from a father and discipline herself without his authoritative word. When with the help of George Henry Lewes, George Eliot was created, Mary Ann Evans began to work through this problematic father-daughter material about desire and authority.

Eliot's narrative dilemma in the early novels, then, comes to this: a fictional father is humbled and so binds himself to a daughter's moral law, or a daughter humbles herself in attempting to bind herself to a figurative father's and the community's law. When Amos Barton, Sir Christopher Cheverel, and Adam Bede lose their authority, they become Mr. Tulliver, the ineffective and bankrupt father. As Patty Barton emerges from anonymity, she becomes Maggie Tulliver, the daughter as subject of her story of desire and punishment. I treat Eliot's early narratives as one text to introduce two theories the remainder of this chapter will test. First, when the father loses his authority, the narrator acquires it; second, when the daughter becomes subject of the phrase and story, "a father seduces a daughter" ("a daughter seduces a father"), the narrative blames her for the structures of desire and punishes her accordingly. *Romola*, as I shall argue in the next section of this chapter, confronts this problematic prohibition and desire and attempts to put to rest father-daughter thematics: Savonarola and the narrator of *Romola* promulgate the moral law more severely than did the "hard" fictional father, Adam Bede; the daughter must learn willingly to accept chastisement for her desiring willfulness.

Romola was written between Eliot's two narratives about the family and law, *The Mill on the Floss* and *Felix Holt*. I would like to explore some differences between them which I deferred at the beginning of this discussion of law and the father. Whereas Maggie fluctuates between demonic desire and the self-humiliating need to be punished, Esther Lyon outgrows her desire—her "vanity"—and accepts the "law, and the love that gave strength to obey the law" (2: 45). Desire has been transmuted into sympathy, law into order. The later narrative daughter learns the sympathy and fellow-feeling a father once learned. "Father, . . . I have not loved thee enough," she tells Rufus Lyon, her adoptive father, and her words echo Amos Barton's, "Milly, I did not love thee enough." This daughter must also willingly choose to obey the doctrine of sympathy. Esther Lyon sets this morality against patrilineal law and chooses not to inherit the land that is rightfully hers but to marry Felix. When desire becomes sympathy and the father's prohibition becomes moral law, what does Eliot portray as a daughter's destiny? Esther tells her future husband she is weak and he "must be greater and nobler" than she (2: 356); Felix preaches against wealth, chooses to remain a member of the working class, and opens a night school to convert the rowdy workers to sobriety and family responsibility. Eliot's conjoining of love and law in the figure of Felix Holt appears to express standard Victorian morality both abstract and conservative.[34] It contains the potential challenges of uppity daughters and so plays into the hands of political conservatism; it adjures members of the working and lower classes to be content with their place in society without questioning the class structure that defines them as morally inferior. Eliot has not successfully resolved her narrative dilemma or put to rest her paternal thematics. Despite her efforts in *Romola*, law and desire continue to preoccupy George Eliot's narrative project.

Romola:
Trauma, Memory, and Repression

The languages of tenderness and passion have their initial encounter in childhood, and it is that clash which is at the origin of trauma. — Jean Laplanche, Life and Death in Psychoanalysis

Romola's composition appears to have been a unique process in Eliot's career.[35] At the same time, however, it is characteristic of a difficult period in that career, a period that began with the idea for the Florentine romance and ended with the completion of *The Spanish Gypsy*.[36] While researching the Florentine novel, Eliot suddenly experienced an overwhelming urge to write another story. Eliot described this interruption almost as a penetrating need: the desire to write this story "came *across* my other plans by a sudden inspiration" which "thrust itself between me and the other book I was meditating" (*Letters,* 3: 371, 360). Eliot's metaphors for the conception of *Silas Marner* indicate that planning and meditating the narrative material of *Romola* proved too painful for continuation. It demanded to be deferred, and the inspired interruption *Silas Marner* provided effectively put off beginning the historical romance. This dialectic of interruption and deferral, of course, appeared elsewhere in Eliot's career. Composition of "The Lifted Veil" interrupted the slow and painful initiation of *The Mill on the Floss;* work on *Felix Holt* followed the illness-ridden writing of *The Spanish Gypsy,* after Lewes took the poem's manuscript away from Eliot in February 1865. Yet Cross reports Eliot's own understanding of *Romola's* singular function in her career: "She could put her finger on it," he wrote, "as marking a well-defined transition in her life. In her own words, 'I began it a young woman—I finished it an old woman.'"[37] *Romola* marks a well-defined transition in a career as well as in a life, a transition for which the interruptions of writing *The Mill* prepared and the apparent ending of *The Spanish Gypsy* before its completion fulfilled. Like Felicia Bonaparte, I believe *Romola* occupies a "pivotal place in the evolution of Eliot's fiction";[38] Eliot herself accords that novel its place as turning point.

Eliot's letters and journal entries attest to the difficulty of beginning *Romola.* During the period of research in Florence, the author appears to have enjoyed visiting prospective narrative settings and reading old Florentine manuscripts. In London, however, Eliot later found herself unable to stop researching and begin writing. Lewes metaphorically described her state as a kind of death: she was "buried in old quartos and vellum bound literature" (*Letters,* 3: 430). Eliot admitted she suffered "greatly from despondency and distrust" of herself during this time; in her journal she wrote, "Got into a state of so much wretchedness in attempting to concentrate my thoughts on the construction of my story, that I became desperate, and suddenly burst my bonds, saying I will not think of writing!" (*Letters,* 3: 448). Eliot began the novel, then stopped writing. In her journal, Eliot wrote, "So utterly dejected that, in walking with G. in the Park, I almost resolved to give up my Italian novel."[39] Lewes described Eliot's "immovable . . . conviction that she *can't* write the romance because she has not knowledge enough. Now as a matter of fact I know that she has immensely more knowledge of the particular period than any other writer who has touched it; but her distressing diffidence paralyses her" (*Letters,* 3: 473-74). Eliot deferred writing by researching; the need to know everything about fifteenth-century Florence represented an exaggerated version of a writer's normal rituals for beginning a project. Given the great struggle with her material in *Romola* and immediately following it with *The Spanish Gypsy,* however, Eliot's deferring strategies appear reasonably self-protective. Yet Lewes identified "her singular diffidence" as "exaggerated in this case" (*Letters,* 3: 446). Eliot's despair over writing her historical romance eventually made her ill; in several journal entries she reported she had been ailing all week, with an "oppressive sense of the far-stretching task" of writing the narrative. "Will [the romance] ever be finished?—ever be worth anything?" she queried (*Letters,* 4: 17, 15, 17). The pain, suffering, even illness that appear characteristic of Eliot's writing process seem to have abated somewhat after she began *Felix Holt*. Lewes never again took a manuscript away from the genius he felt he must protect and nurture, and the dialectic of interruption and deferral became immensely fruitful in the composition of *Middlemarch*'s several plots. *Romola*, that "well-defined transition in her life," that "exaggerated" case of diffidence and paralysis, appears to have made a difference to its writer.

Despite suffering, interruption, and deferral, then, Eliot wrote *Romola*. In justifying to Sara Hennell her desire to write a novel she knew would not be popular, Eliot admitted how personal that historical romance had become to her: "If one is to have freedom to write out one's own varying unfolding self, and not be a machine always grinding out the same material or spinning the same sort of web, one cannot always write for the same public" (*Letters*, 4: 49). The distancing impersonal pronoun, like the historical setting and research for the novel, protected Eliot from what appears true of *Romola*: that it indeed unfolded herself. In Cross's quotation about its having aged his famous wife, he also reported the writing of *Romola* "ploughed into her"—provided the possibility of new growth as well as the harrowing of the ground of her self-esteem. Although critics usually consider *The Mill on the Floss* Eliot's most autobiographical novel, *Romola* is clearly more confessional than is the earlier narrative. The distance in time and setting of the romance allowed Eliot to include yet disguise her most painful personal memories and meditations.[40] The pain, the welcome, thrusting interruption of *Silas Marner*, and the deferral of *Romola*'s beginning suggest the difficulty of confronting those harrowing memories and suggest as well that writing *Romola* was nothing short of traumatic for its author. Eliot herself unconsciously figured that writing process as traumatic; it combined a sudden, thrusting inspiration with the pain of planning and meditation. As Jean Laplanche and J.-B. Pontalis point out, psychoanalysis adopts the term "trauma" from the Greek word for "wound," which itself derives from the Greek "to pierce."[41] The "exaggerated case" of interruption and deferral, of pain and piercing imagination, demands interpretation and makes most sense when read as a traumatic process of recollection and self-defense.

When I use the term "traumatic," I intend a particular psychoanalytic meaning. Freud defines trauma as an event that arouses psychical excitation too powerful to be dealt with or worked off in a normal way.[42] The psychical apparatus attempts to eliminate or bind these excitations by the principle of constancy, which achieves a balanced state of stimulation or a lowered level of tension. In his early theories, Freud formulated the essentially sexual nature of trauma and linked it in his theory of seduction with temporality and repression, as I mentioned in the first section of this chapter. Freud also postulates trauma as a double event, one with two scenes. The actual adult sexual advance takes place when the subject is a prepubertal child, and so she experiences no sexual excitation; after puberty, however, a second scene, often of a specifically nonsexual nature, evokes to the subject the first scene, and sexual excitation now associated with the first scene overwhelms the subject's ability to defend against it. This theory's mainspring is temporality: the discontinuous nature of human sexual development plus the function of retrospection make the memory itself rather than the adult sexual advance traumatic. Thus by deferral, or retroactivity, the postpubertal child must reconstruct events of the present in the light of a past event; to do so, she must defend against sexual excitation, bind the stimulus evoked by the deferred memory, or repress memory of the first scene. And just as Freud later disavowed the reality of the first scene of seduction, he also broadened his conception of trauma to include a variety of internal and external excitations as well as the larger events of a particular childhood history; he moved from a simple model of repression built on the two scenes of seduction to a complex model of primal repression, repression proper, and the return of the repressed. Yet Freud never totally abandoned the terms for temporality, repression, and sexuality he adopted in the early theory of seduction; I will generalize these terms and will also use them in discussing seduction, although not always in Freud's necessarily schematic early theoretical sense.[43] When I use the term "repression," I refer to the mechanism by which the mind banishes to the unconscious memories, images, and ideas — signifiers — that can arouse painful excitation. Repression, however, is only one of Freud's mechanisms of defense; when I use the terms "defense" or "binding," I refer to a general designation for the ways the mind controls excitation aroused by deferred memory or retroactivity.

When I identify Eliot's writing of *Romola* as traumatic, then, I refer to its ability to arouse in the author's conscious mind memories that by the mechanism of deferred action or retroactivity appear linked to the scene of seduction. I do not mean, however, to identify implicitly a first scene in which seduction actually occurred in Eliot's childhood; such biographical speculation would be purely conjectural. Freud's initial concept of "first scene" in fact became less schematic in his later speculation about seduction, primarily because his patients' originating scenes of seduction disappeared in analysis further backward into their childhoods. I intend here to articulate Freud's theory of trauma and temporal deferral with his later structural theory of oedipal desire; together, the two constitute a childhood history. In writing *Romola*, Eliot tapped the material of Mary Ann Evans's childhood history, material she had been unable fully to integrate into a conception of herself because it was linked to the scene of seduction, to issues of desire and prohibition. The traumatic memory of this first generalized childhood scene forced Eliot to reinterpret the events of her experience and to repress those memories or to control and bind them in order to go forward in her life and in her career. A psychoanalytic model, then, allows us to interpret Eliot's struggles with *Romola* as a traumatic confrontation with unassimilated material she must retroactively reinterpret in a "second scene" in which language symbolizes the memories of the "first."

In *Romola*, Eliot specifically confronts the complex memories of her struggles with father and brother. Every major male character in the novel represents a father or brother; Romola herself is a figure for the young Mary Ann Evans. Savonarola's triple message to the people of Florence stands as metaphor for the function of the narrative for its writer. Because of pestilence and moral corruption, God will scourge the city with His avenging wrath; He will purge of sin and so purify the people; this will happen in our days.[44] In the novel as a whole, Eliot scourges Romola and so a figure for herself for daring to have her own desires; she purges fathers and brothers from the narrative and so achieves a purified, virtually female society; this happens because Eliot retroactively reconstructs the events of her past as memory becomes traumatic. *Romola* demonstrates that for Eliot, the scene of seduction must be remembered with certain self-protection: the distance and artifice of historical romance, for example; the displacement of desire from its rightful subject, Romola; the invoking of extreme prohibition from within and without the subject; the binding of the subject to her own law or self-prohibition. *Romola* replays the Holy Wars (a generalized version of Freud's "first scene") in a fictional arena. *Romola* performs for its author the "work of recollection" and so can later be spoken of by her as a "well-defined transition" in her life.

In this transitional narrative, Romola binds herself to the law of fathers, discovers the inauthentic authority of each, and so proceeds to bind herself to her own law. Romola's relationship with her old scholarly father stands midway between Maggie's with Mr. Tulliver and Dorothea's with Casaubon. Bardo resembles Mr. Tulliver already fallen into paralysis at the beginning of the novel; Bardo prophesies what Casaubon will become when the daughter blindly devotes her life to the father as husband. According to the narrator, Romola lives a "self-repressing" life in which all her ardor and affection have been spent on sympathy with her father's "aged sorrows, aged ambition, aged pride and indignation" (1: 196). Her symbolically blind father fails to see his daughter's affection and pity, her passionate tenderness, just as will Dorothea's self-protective father-husband (1: 87-88). Like Dorothea's uncle and Miltonic husband, Romola's father belittles his daughter for her gender, her feminine imagination, and her failure to be a son (1: 104-5). Nonetheless, Romola devotes herself to this old patriarch simply because he is her father and promises to marry a scholar who will take her abandoning brother's place in the father's research project about antiquity: family ties indeed bind. Romola never questions her devotion to Bardo, but the narrator interprets the father-daughter scene and speaks Eliot's judgment of the patriarch. Eliot's portrait of Romola and Bardo represents her bitter resentment of the time she voluntarily spent as her father's house-keeper. This anger can be narrated only after the fact and only by a narrator clearly differentiated from either George Eliot or Mary Ann Evans. *Romola* retroactively reinterprets Mary Ann Evans's struggle with paternal law and incorporates into a figure for the young housekeeping daughter as subject a meaningful interpretation of that life with her father.

Although *Romola* explicitly represents the father's law, as I will discuss later, the narrative also symbolizes desire and, at its beginning, clearly displaces desire from its rightful subject, the daughter. Tito, the scholar Romola marries to replace the brother, calls forth Romola's first expression of desire. Yet as the novel's symbols prophesy, Romola's wedding is also a funeral, a nunlike renunciation of desire. For Tito, Romola's symbolic brother and figure for her own desires, immediately follows his impulses, obeys no law but his own "irresistible desire," and in a "lawless moment" marries Tessa at a carnival during the ironic Festival of the Nativity of the Virgin. This marriage, performed by a conjurer, parodies the lawful ceremony to which Romola binds herself and from which, soon enough, she wishes to escape (1: 223, 209). Romola soon desires voluntarily to leave her husband; this desire, Savonarola tells her, represents the urge to follow her "own blind choice," her "own will" (2: 105). In her well-known letter to her father during the "Holy Wars," Mary Ann Evans linked desire with choice and separation; she feared nothing but "voluntarily leaving" her father, but would do so, she wrote, should he prohibit her return to Foleshill (*Letters,* 1: 129).

Romola's narrative, however, refuses to allow her voluntarily to leave her husband. She returns to her loveless marriage in a state of "yearning passivity" (2: 112). Desire is then metonymically displaced onto brothers (or sons) real and symbolic in the narrative; Dino and Tito act out Romola's desire to abandon her closest tie and kinship, and this desire symbolizes the narrative desire voluntarily to leave fathers as Eliot displaces the struggles of filiation onto affiliation, descent onto consanguinity. Romola's brother, Dino, abandons his father for a "higher love" and counsels Romola to follow his example. Fra Luca accuses his father of "worldly ambitions and fleshly lusts"; he tells Romola of his new religious life of "perfect love and purity for the soul" in which he experiences "no uneasy hunger after pleasure, no tormenting questions, no fear of suffering." Yet Luca's rhetoric reveals this purified love as a traditional religious metaphor for desire: he understands the saints' "ecstasy," which truth "penetrates" even pagan philosophy; he understands the "bliss" of living with God; he feels "no affection, no hope . . . wed[s]" him to "that which passeth away" (1: 236-39). In pursuit of this life of purified or repressed desire, God calls upon Dino to flee his father, and the son obeys; only when commanded to abandon an earthly father by a heavenly Father can the son represent his flight from filial duty as a higher form of obedience. Eliot justifies this filial abandonment and represents it as a spiritual adherence, exonerating the desires of her young self.

If Fra Luca correctly abandons father for Father, however, Tito Melema does not. Tito's adoptive father, Baldassarre, chose through love to be his father rather than was destined through biological necessity, and as a result the narrative exaggerates Tito's crime as it exonerates Fra Luca's. After arriving in Florence, Tito chooses not to seek his adoptive father but to believe him dead, and by so choosing demonstrates his "desire" it "be the truth that his father was dead" (1: 152-53). Throughout the narrative, when confronted by his still-living father, Tito refuses to recognize him: he calls his father "mad" in a Florentine square; he renounces his father at a public dinner as Judas renounced Christ; he fails to heed the repeated and symbolic motif of the "hand on the shoulder" which brings him from Luca news of his father and finally brings his father to kill him. In fact, as Felicia Bonaparte points out, Tito Melema betrays all the novel's fathers: he refuses to save his adoptive father, Baldassarre; he denies Romola the opportunity to create Bardo's library; he conspires against Savonarola and later against Bernardo del Nero.[45] This lawless, desiring son enacts all the narrative's unjustified desires voluntarily to abandon fathers. Tito and Luca, the two abandoning sons, represent Eliot's narrative ambivalence about leaving fathers.

Such abandonment of fathers inevitably appears dangerous. Fra Luca conveniently wastes away after devoting his life to purifying the worldly desires of his earthly father. But another earthly father refuses to tolerate filial abandonment. Baldassarre enacts not the displaced rebellion of the son, as Carole Robinson suggests, but rather the punishment the father deals out for the child's abandonment.[46] Like his adoptive son, Baldassarre is passionate and lawless. Tito wears armor and buys a dagger because he understands his father will revenge a son's abandonment and will attempt to kill the son who metaphorically desires to kill him. When Tito attempts repentance, Baldassarre indeed tries to stab his son: "I saved you—I nurtured you—I loved you," he cries; "you forsook me—you robbed me—you denied me" (2: 29). The father's revenge, figured as a Christlike suffering, appears justifiable, even just.

If sons act out the narrative's desire to abandon filial ties, Romola must learn to act otherwise. She, like the narrator, comes to believe that the "sanctity attached to all close relations, and, therefore, pre-eminently to the closest, was but the expression in outward law of that result towards which all human goodness and nobleness must spontaneously tend; that the light abandonment of ties, whether inherited or voluntary, because they had ceased to be pleasant, was the uprooting of social and personal virtue" (2: 272). Romola learns this moral lesson from Savonarola, a figurative father. After the death of her father, Bardo, Romola is left "lawless," a worshiper of "beauty and joy" (2: 60). When she desires impulsively to abandon her closest tie, feels the "instinct to sever herself from the man she loved no longer" (2: 48), Savonarola waylays her outside the city gates and so replaces her dead father as the figure of law in her life. He demands absolute submission to the earthly law of marriage: Romola must not forsake her duty as wife, her place in the community for which the affiliated tie of marriage is metaphor. Savonarola teaches Romola to bind herself to his law, the "Divine law" for which he stands. Marriage, the father tells this daughter, is not "carnal only, made for selfish delight," but represents the "bond of a higher love." Romola must quench the "sense of suffering Self in the ardours of an ever-growing love" (2: 110-11). Accepting the divine law, binding herself to a higher love, signifies according to this father a repression of selfish desire and a devotion to fellow-feeling rather than personal happiness. In deciding not to abandon her closest tie, Romola dedicates herself to such self-repression; she binds her desire by the prohibitive word of a father and accepts his law as final.[47]

In psychoanalytic terminology, "binding" signifies a psychical operation that restricts the free flow of excitations, links ideas together, and constitutes and maintains relatively stable forms of energy. Freud often associated "binding" with the notion of trauma or memory as displeasure: the memories associated with trauma—excitations connected with the scene of seduction which have not been integrated into the subject's conception of herself—demand to be bound to previously established psychic structures. The energy associated with trauma must be related to or integrated with forms that have specific limits or boundaries, must therefore be fixed or controlled.[48] *Romola* performs this task for its heroine, binds her to social structures that compensate for or control the energy associated with desire in the scene of seduction: the marriage bond, the communal good. Desire must be controlled because it is unstable. The young Mary Ann Evans found her affections "disturbing forces"; she yearned for more love "than in sober reason and real humility" she thought she "ought to desire," until that yearning became her "curse" (*Letters*, 1: 142, 137, 70). The evangelical girl failed to understand her desire as a result of deprivation; instead, she believed it "egoistic," a sign of self-involvement and failure to relate well to others. Eliot's traumatic adult analysis of desire confirms and extends this definition. *Romola*'s narrator instructs: "It is in the nature of all human passion . . . that there is a point at which it ceases to be properly egoistic, and is like a fire kindled within our being to which everything else in us is mere fuel" (1: 413). The novel's characters destroy themselves because they desire: Baldassarre takes revenge against Tito with "a thirst . . . like that which makes men open their own veins to satisfy it" (1: 416), a "supreme emotion, which knows no terror, and asks no motive, which is itself an ever-burning motive, consuming all other desire" (2: 70); Tito "sacrifice[s] himself to his passion as if it were a deity to be worshipped with self-destruction" (1: 339). Such passion, revenge, and self-destruction clearly endanger other members of the community and so must be repressed.

Yet Eliot's ambivalence about such repression appears in the abstract terminology of the novel's morality. As Carole Robinson points out, Romola's duties to the community seem remarkably unpleasant to her: "She had no innate taste for tending the sick and clothing the ragged. . . . Her early training had kept her aloof from such womanly labours; and if she had not brought to them the inspiration of her deepest feelings, they would have been irksome to her"; "all that ardour of her nature which could no longer spend itself in the woman's tenderness for father and husband, had transformed itself into an enthusiasm of sympathy with the general life," despite its "miserabl[e] narrow[ness]" (2: 146-47). Romola commits her sympathy outward for lack of center at home. "Enthusiasm of sympathy" appears to be Eliot's euphemism for repression of love for father and husband.

Romola must free herself from her prohibitive fathers and husband-brother precisely because they fail to reciprocate affection. Yet she refuses "voluntarily to leave" either, and so the narrative machinery creaks as it casts off fathers for its passive heroine. The spiritual father, Savonarola, handily betrays Romola by refusing to save her godfather from execution and therefore provokes her rebellion against him. The struggle between the father and the woman he calls "my daughter" (2: 99-110) centers on authority and signification. In a chapter entitled "Pleading," Romola asks Savonarola to intercede politically so that her godfather, Bernardo del Nero, may be granted appeal against the death sentence for treason. Savonarola himself created the procedure for appeal which he now refuses to allow Bernardo and the other Mendiceans. Romola and Savonarola argue about "law and justice": Savonarola declares the city's welfare demands "severity" rather than "mercy" in this case.[49] The father's law resides, as this scene demonstrates, in his word, his promise of mercy. Romola begs Savonarola's lenience, saying, "You know that your word will be powerful" (2: 305). She believes the father gave his "word" that appeal would be granted any political prisoner regardless of his crime. Indeed, when Savonarola urges Romola not to flee Florence and her marriage, he identifies one's word as the basis of law: "Of what wrongs," he asks Romola, "will you complain, when you yourself are breaking the simplest law that lies at the foundation of the trust which binds man to man—faithfulness to the spoken word?" (2: 102). Savonarola binds Romola to his law by demanding she not break her word—her marriage vow—as

Tito has broken his word to create her father's library. In the case of Romola's godfather, however, Savonarola himself breaks his word and so the law that binds man to man. In this chapter, Romola speaks out against her father and defines her rebellion against his law as a verbal act. She senses her words in "painful dissonance" with her past relationship to him saying, "Forgive me, father; it is pain to me to have spoken those words—yet I cannot help speaking" (2: 301-9). When the father's word proves duplicitous and inauthentic, the daughter feels forced to speak against him. Although Romola waits at Savonarola's execution for his "last word" of self-justification, the father's silence implies and in fact confirms his guilt (2: 436-40).

Romola successfully rebels against one father only because in doing so she dedicates herself to another. Romola decides to walk to the scaffold in identification with her godfather's shame. Earlier in the novel, this godfather symbolically replaced and transformed Romola's unloving real father. This "second father" offers Romola a "father's home" and a "father's ear" for the words of her suffering; he tells her after Bardo's death, "I am your father" (2: 247-48). Romola's dedication to her "padricullo" reunites her with love for her dead father: her "affection and respect were clinging with new tenacity to her godfather, and with him to those memories of her father" (2: 235); Romola pledges to remember her godfather, "the man who alone in all the world had shared her pitying love for her father" (1: 318). Romola's public display of love for her godfather signifies her refusal to forsake fathers, despite her verbal rebellion against and ultimate forsaking of her spiritual father. This narrative trick justifies voluntarily leaving fathers while at the same time enforcing false and sentimental sympathy with them. This narrative justification, like so much of *Romola*, proves terribly contradictory. Romola identifies herself with Bernardo in an act of "sympathy with the individual lot" (2: 317). But Bernardo is guilty of treason against the government: Romola's sympathy with this individual father signifies a failure of sympathy with the community, a sympathy the novel elsewhere defines as its narrative ideal. This contradiction identifies Eliot's failure to resolve her feelings about paternal authority and daughterly desire.

Once Romola dedicates herself to the memory of her father, other fathers may be purged from the narrative. By the end of the novel, Lorenzo de' Medici, Bardo, Baldassarre, Savonarola, and Bernardo del Nero are dead. Lorenzo's death at the novel's opening and Bernardo's at its close represent the public death of fathers, the decline of paternal authority in fifteenth-century Florence, which initiates corruption, plague, and pestilence. Baldassarre dies while killing Tito. Savonarola, who fears to prove his innocence by walking through fire—symbol of his passion and his scourge—is executed. The apparently innocent daughter participates in this structural scapegoating of fathers. Romola's seemingly unmotivated guilt about her father's death and her desire to institutionalize Bardo's library spring from her unspoken wish to live happily alone with Tito—and therefore clearly without her father. Like Tito, Romola metaphorically wishes her father dead. Romola's rescue of her starving father-in-law from the streets of Florence enables his own and Tito's embracing deaths. Baldassarre identifies himself and tells Romola, "You would have been my daughter"; but, he confides, "we will have our revenge" (2: 239, 245). When Baldassarre kills Tito, and with his son himself, he acts out Romola's revenge as well as his own. Finally, the narrative also implies Romola's guilt for her godfather's death. Fearing she has hardened Savonarola against Bernardo by pleading for his life, Romola cries out to her padricullo, "If any harm comes to you, it will be as if I had done it!" (2: 249). The narrative surreptitiously attributes these deaths to its otherwise dutiful heroine and identifies the desire for parricide as belonging rightfully to her.

Romola decides at the end of the novel to obey only her own law, to "act on her own warrant." She decides voluntarily to leave her husband not only because he has taken another wife but because he has forsaken his father. The "demands of inner moral facts" now outweigh those of an "outward law." Although the marriage law is sacred, "rebellion might be sacred too" (2: 273-74). Romola's now rightful desire to leave her husband and fathers takes the metaphorical form of her deathlike drift to Spain and her dreamlike salvation of its people from the plague. Without fathers, without male relation, Romola becomes the desireless "Visible Madonna" and back in Florence the childless mother of Tessa and her children.[50] On the eve of the eleventh anniversary of Savonarola's death, Romola tells her little figurative family sentimental stories about the deaths of her father and spiritual father, moralistic fables about the lawless desire and necessary death of her husband. As "ideal" figure for the young writer, Romola's binding herself to her law facilitates Eliot's binding herself to her own law, her authoritative narrative word, her career as storyteller (*Letters*, 4: 104). When memory of desire and prohibition becomes traumatic, George Eliot retroactively interprets the first scenes of a history in the symbols of a second. *Romola* indeed marks a "well-defined transition" in the life of its writer.

As I intend to argue in this discussion of *Romola*, although Eliot's material forced her to confront her traumatic memories of father and brother, the concepts of retroactive reconstruction and of the "work of recollection" do not imply that the woman who remembers necessarily resolves the trauma memory creates. In symbolizing her memory, in binding and repressing desire and calling it "sympathy" or "fellow-feeling," Eliot controls her memory and so its traumatic effects. Yet she also ensures this repressed material will reappear in her later novels. Indeed, Eliot's final narratives, *Middlemarch* and *Daniel Deronda*, carry the trace of *Romola*'s bindings, its repressions. In both novels, the uncle replaces the scapegoated father as a figure of failed and apparently illegitimate authority, although the figurative "shadow of the father" nonetheless haunts both narratives.[51] The "ploughing up" and "scourging" of herself the writing of *Romola* performed enables Eliot to view Dorothea and Gwendolen with an irony that intends to declare the writer's difference from her two heroines, one blinded by her idealistic, the other her egoistic, ambition. Both narratives, however, place the daughter as desiring subject in a repressed scene of seduction, and both narratively blame that daughter for her desire. After having bound the daughter to her own law in *Romola*, Eliot nevertheless portrays her last heroines struggling to bind themselves to a community's law. Eliot condemns Dorothea and Gwendolen to learn sympathy through suffering, a fate once reserved for the "hard" fathers of the early novels.

The explicit and ironic figurative seduction by Miltonic father of daughter in *Middlemarch* gives way later in the narrative to a less explicit but no less figurative seduction of Dorothea by Will Ladislaw — "great aunt" and nephew (or "second cousin," as Naumann jokes) by marriage. As the gossips of Middlemarch know, if Dorothea had been a "nice woman" she would not have first married a man old enough to be her father, then the nephew the figurative father attempted by codicil to prohibit her from marrying (3: 464).[52] The suffering Dorothea endures in her first marriage teaches her the sympathy she expresses later when identifying herself with her apparent rival for Will, Rosamund Lydgate. In the emotionally climactic scene of the novel, Dorothea sacrifices her love for Will to help Rosamund and ironically learns from Rosamund that Will in fact loves Dorothea. In Eliot's most mature and finely crafted novel, sympathy facilitates a seduction so figurative it goes nearly unnoticed. *Daniel Deronda*'s story of seduction, in contrast, appears structurally clear although no less figurative. Gwendolen Harleth, unlike Dorothea, causes her own suffering because her love of ease and luxury causes her to break the word she gives Lydia Glasher not to marry Grandcourt. Yet Gwendolen, like Dorothea, suffers so excessively because she too identifies with her rival's lot. Gwendolen understands implicitly that "another woman's calamity" might some day be hers — and it is: exile at Gadsmere.[53] Yet unlike Dorothea, Gwendolen refuses to sacrifice her own desire in sympathy with her rival, and the narrative demands she pay a high price for her refusal.

Gwendolen's guilt and suffering, however, spring not wholly from her actions in this text. Despite the narrator's interpretation of her marriage as immoral, Gwendolen does no legal wrong. The narrative demonstrates that regardless of Lydia's belief Grandcourt will eventually marry her, he does not intend to do so. And to live with Grandcourt, Lydia herself deserted her husband and indirectly caused the death of her first son. Gwendolen suffers because she marries into a figurative scene of seduction. Indeed, Gwendolen not only excludes Lydia "from the place" as wife Gwendolen herself "was filling" (3: 92), she also wrongs a mother. Lydia wants to marry Grandcourt primarily to make her elder son Grandcourt's rightful heir and so to atone for the death of her first son (1: 395). When Lydia wants to terrify the impressionable Gwendolen, she appears to the Grandcourts one morning with two of her children, one the denied heir (3: 92); when Grandcourt visits Lydia at Gadsmere to tell her of his impending marriage to Gwendolen, Lydia sits nursing an infant (2: 196). The narrative explicitly identifies Lydia as a mother and Grandcourt a father in both scenes and in the Gadsmere scene implies as well their recent sexual involvement. Gwendolen, the "spoiled child," the fatherless daughter, marries a father. The scene of father-daughter seduction in *Daniel Deronda* appears figurative not, as in *Middlemarch*, by virtue of the metaphorical relationship between "Milton" and "St. Teresa," or between "great aunt" and nephew, but by the implied oedipal structures of desire among Gwendolen, Grandcourt, and Lydia Glasher. Eliot's analogue of the Creusa-Jason-Medea story makes metaphorical reference to triangular desire and transgression, rivalry, and murder.[54] Gwendolen wonders of Lydia's serpentine and poisoning revenge, "Why did you put your fangs into me and not into him?" (2: 261). The reader wonders the same. In Eliot's modern version of Medea's revenge, however, the figurative daughter is desiring subject and has knowingly married a father; she must therefore be punished. The scene of seduction no longer takes place within a narrative family, as it did in "Amos Barton," but in the repressed and figurative structures of oedipal desire.

Indeed, desire itself becomes figurative in *Middlemarch* and *Daniel Deronda*. The lawless desire bound by or purged from narrative structure in *Romola* makes desire in the last novels purely linguistic. Dorothea and Gwendolen are wooed by language, Dorothea in spite of the stilted verbiage of her Miltonic fiancé and later by the effusive if evasive talk of Will Ladislaw; Gwendolen by the penetrating and intoxicating words—each in its place—of Grandcourt (2: 39, 214). Maggie Tulliver's desire for her father's words of love and approbation has become Gwendolen Harleth's desire that words replace desire in the scene of courting. In Gwendolen's "fierce maidenhood," her hatred of physical contact, desire becomes *"tête à tête."* Although desire becomes a linguistic act, the heroine, however, must still hear the figurative father's prohibitive word. Dorothea's Milton banishes from their discussion subjects that make him vulnerable to her censure: the eventual publication of the Key to all Mythologies, Will Ladislaw's monetary claim on his kinship. The two sole occasions of intimacy between Dorothea and Casaubon occur at night, while Dorothea lights a candle for her husband: the chastising "conversations in the dark." Gwendolen, however, who desires more worldly ease than does the ardent and idealistic Dorothea, suffers not only Grandcourt's prohibitive word—his "words had the power of thumb-screws and the cold touch of the rack" (2: 206)—but Deronda's as well. Although they are peers—like Will and Dorothea cousins by marriage—Daniel and Gwendolen appear to be another although different figurative father and daughter. Henry James's acerbic Pulcheria identifies Deronda as Gwendolen's "lay father confessor."[55] Daniel indeed listens to Gwendolen's confessions of guilt, then speaks the word of rebuke, however sympathetic. Gwendolen, whose moral wrong consists in having "broken her word," having failed to bind herself to action through that word, finds herself driven to speak and listen to Deronda to "better herself." She welcomes Daniel's severity and thinks him "in some mysterious way . . . a part of her conscience" (2: 210). Indeed he is: Deronda speaks the prohibitive paternal "no," and his word creates Gwendolen's superego.

In Freud's definition of the superego, as I mentioned earlier in this chapter, that agency of the mind takes its shape and forms its contents from the father's prohibitive language.[56] Deronda's word of rebuke teaches the desiring and suffering Gwendolen a moral lesson much like that Savonarola preaches to Romola: he counsels Gwendolen to submit to the yoke of her wrongdoing, to scourge herself with her remorse, to seek elevation of feeling in the religious life, and to see beyond the "small drama of personal desire" by defining a "larger home" for passion (2: 263-70). Like the narrator of *Romola*, the narrator of *Deronda* supports the figurative father's morality. Tannhauser, Merlin, and Ulysses, the narrator explains, were victims not of the "enslaving excesses of . . . passion," but of a deficiency of "wider passion" (1: 359); the fatal desires of Daphnis, Tristan, and Romeo, the epigrapher proclaims, are merely textual and therefore fictional, but potent love and passion may have a "large scope" that allies itself "with every operation of the soul" (2: 125). In an early letter to Sara Hennell, Eliot metaphorically linked repression with the story of Daniel: "I am amusing myself," she wrote, "with thinking of the prophecy of Daniel as a sort of allegory. All those monstrous, rumbustical beasts with their horns—the horn with eyes and a mouth speaking proud things and the little horn that waxed rebellious and stamped on the stars seem like my passions and vain fancies which are to be knocked down one after the other—until all is subdued into a universal kingdom over which . . . presides—the spirit of love—the Catholicism of the Universe" (*Letters*, 1: 242). Mary Ann Evans's allegory of passion "subdued" becomes George Eliot's allegory of passion bound to and by a wide concern for the needs of others.

What do Eliot's final novels identify as their "wider passion"? Both *Middlemarch* and *Deronda* replace filiation with affiliation as the arena in which sympathy must work.[57] Dorothea's suffering creates a sympathy that finds a home in the life of "wife and mother," in the small and daily acts that prepare for the greatness of others, of future St. Teresas. In *Middlemarch* as in *Romola,* the heroine's marriage comes finally to stand for her devotion to the community at large. Gwendolen, however, must suffer more than does Dorothea in order to learn sympathy: her desires resolutely refuse repression. Her counterpart, Daniel, on the contrary, appears so sympathetic his friend Meyrick believes he experiences no desire. Daniel's story, the Jewish half of the narrative, subdues seduction or desire into human fellowship and fatherhood into "brotherhood." The single literal father, the thieving Lapidoth, makes his appearance solely to be cast off by the idealized hero, his son Mordecai. Having "broken his bond," the father—which "word" Mordecai declares a "reproach"—falls out of the narrative, and the prefigured Judaic brotherhood replaces filiation with affiliation as the closest tie in the human community (3: 353-55).

Eliot's transcendental brotherhood attempts to short-cut genealogy and so undo filiation, yet her metaphors for spiritual friendship all take as source an abstracted scene of seduction. When Daniel discovers his origin and identity as a Jew, he resembles Mordecai "even as my brother that fed at the breasts of my mother." This racial brotherhood represents a "marriage of . . . souls" in which the spirits of Daniel and Mordecai, the "betrothed," will "unite in a stricter bond" after Mordecai's impending death (3: 316). Brother-marriage gives birth, then, to Daniel as Mordecai's "expanded, prolonged self" (1: 299). The successor-soul, Mordecai explains, purifies and fulfills its "maternal," birth-giving counterpart: "Souls are born again and again in new bodies till they are perfected and purified, and a soul liberated from a worn-out body may join the fellowsoul that needs it, that they may be perfected together, and their earthly work accomplished" (2: 332, 398). Thus although Deronda marries Mirah in the flesh at the end of his story, he marries Mordecai in the spirit and so engenders the Judaic brotherhood Eliot envisions as a new, higher form of passion and sympathy.

In this brother-marriage, soul impregnation occurs not through sexual intercourse but with the word. Mordecai believes himself the reborn soul of a Sephardic visionary poet. Because of his father's treachery and abandonment, Mordecai no longer writes his Hebrew psalms of exile; Deronda must carry on the work of representing and so creating the Jewish homeland. Daniel's new "inheritance," no longer the patrimony of an English gentleman but the transcendent word of a Jewish exile, demands he too inseminate with the word. The transmission of manuscripts replaces genealogical inheritance in this metaphorical cross-generational brotherinsemination. When Deronda discovers his father was a Jew, he claims the "kindred and heritage" of Judaism and declares his vocation to restore or perfect the "common life" of his people (3: 258-66). His father's manuscripts represent the sign of Daniel's vocation and racial origin—family papers that record the fellowship of a long line of Sephardic Jews. These manuscripts represent the inseminating word of communion among disciples; they enshrine a genealogy of patriarchs and ensure the new generation of Judaic devotion. Daniel and Mordecai will work together with these manuscripts and so become among the "great Transmitters" who preserve and enlarge the "heritage of memory" and save "the soul of Israel alive as a seed among the tombs" (2: 370).

While replacing filiation with affiliation, then, Eliot's book of Daniel surreptitiously confirms the authority of the Judaic patriarchs. Mirah's attachment to her father evokes Eliot's metaphorical yearning for filial ties: Mirah's father was "like something that had grown in her flesh with pain, but that she could never have cut away without worse pain" (3: 354). The pain of cutting away the father inscribes metaphorical patriarchs back into the text: despite his mother's attempt to undo his Judaic gene-alogy, Daniel's dead grandfather eventually wins his descendant back to the faith of the fathers. In fact, Eliot's moral rhetoric of brotherhood and discipleship in *Daniel Deronda* takes the same figurative language as did the daughter's submission to the father in *Romola:* "Let us bind love with duty; for duty is the love of law, and law is the nature of the Eternal" (3: 270). The vow of brotherhood resembles Savonarola's demand that law bind desire; it displaces the father's word of prohibition onto the soul-brother and abstracts it into a transcendent word or law. Eliot binds familial desire into transmissible form, into sympathy with a race of exiles seeking a homeland.[58]

The Jews become Eliot's ideal because, as Daniel discovers in a syna-gogue, their heritage as rendered in Hebrew prayers, psalms, and liturgies invokes and glorifies a "binding history, tragic and yet glorious" (2: 137). Ishmaelites, wanderers and exiles all, the Jews are nonetheless bound to their suffering by genealogy, by race, by destiny. Mirah tells Mrs. Meyrick, "It comforted me to believe that my suffering was part of the affliction of my people, my part in the long song of mourning that has been going on through ages and ages" (1: 321). Jewish artistic trans-mission remembers and retells this history: "If there are ranks in suf-fering, Israel takes precedence of all the nations. . . . What shall we say to a National Tragedy lasting for fifteen hundred years, in which the poets and the actors were also the heroes?" (2: 363). In *Daniel Deronda,* the Jews make an art of exile and declare their kinship despite dispersion; the artists are all Jews who struggle with the English middle-class philistines as their forefathers once fought the biblical Philistines. This dialectic of kinship and exile as rendered in literature and art recalls Mary Ann Evans's feelings of exile after the death of her father, when she identified herself in a letter to Cara Bray as a metaphorical Melchisedec (*Letters,* 1: 336). This historical destiny of the Jews to suffer recalls the words Mary Ann Evans wrote of her loving response to her father's impending death: "The worship of sorrow is *the* worship for mortals" (*Letters*, 1: 284). The Jewish search for a national homeland recalls Mary Ann Evans's desire for a domicile; a Jew's search for his patrimony and vocation echoes a duty to which she is called. Eliot's idealization of the Jews in her final novel bears the trace of the repressed scene of seduction, the fathers as figures of law, and the desiring daughter as failing to bind her desire into that idealized, historicized "wider passion" the Jews represent. When Eliot chooses to bind memory's traumatic excitation in the symbolic and symbolizing second scene of *Romola,* she consigns the images, the signifiers that represent that material, to the unconscious, the place from which repressed desire eventually returns.

"George Eliot": Gender and Narrative Authority

. . . a tub to throw to the whale in case of curious inquiries. . . . — The George Eliot Letters, *ed. Gordon S. Haight*

Freud's theory of father-daughter seduction, as I have emphasized, depends upon narration. The story the daughter relates about this scene, this moment in her history, symbolizes the emergence of her sexuality expressed as desire for her father and represents her attempt to solve this enigma of childhood history. Throughout this chapter, I have identified the writer as female and the father as the figure that links the narrative scene of seduction with the daughter's binding to the law. Yet "George Eliot," as critics now recognize, signifies a persona distinct from the woman Mary Ann Evans or the wife Marian Lewes. "George Eliot" is a man, although he writes anonymously—dissembles his identity but not his gender. Recognizing the significance of a name, Ruby V. Redinger bases her recent biography on a paradigmatic theory of Mary Ann Evans's "transmutation of self" into "George Eliot"[59]—a terminology Redinger takes from Eliot's early letter to John Sibree (*Letters*, 1: 251). Redinger identifies a singular and unique discontinuity between personal and public identity necessitated not solely by a publisher's (and author's) desire to sell books. Eliot's pen name allowed her to perform in writing the task she told Sara Hennell she undertook in a "quiet meditative journey among fresh scenes": "Removed to a distance from myself," she noted, "I can take myself up by the ears and inspect myself, like any other queer monster on a small scale" (*Letters*, 1: 239-40). Gender difference, like geographical distance, allowed the male author, George Eliot, to take up by the ears the girl, Mary Ann Evans. More important, this pen name represents a transformation of gender which granted the author male authority and placed her in a patriarchal tradition of story-telling.

The concept of "authority," as I discussed in the chapter on Dickens, invokes sexual, literary, and theological metaphors associated with masculinity and the male's power to engender.[60] As Sandra M. Gilbert points out, however, this theory of authority defines literary power not only figuratively but literally as partaking of male sexuality: the "poet's pen," she writes, "is in some sense (even more than figuratively) a penis." Gilbert quotes various male authors who invoke the trope of male sexual prowess to define the power of creativity, of writing; she defines this masculine sexual aesthetic as one which excludes women from the realm of authorship, and she proposes to substitute for this phallocentric male aesthetic a female one based on the power of woman's sexuality and on motherhood.[61] Gilbert's theory merely replaces one gender-based metaphor for writing with another although different one; more important, however, it ignores nineteenth-century female complicity in the metaphor of the pen-as-penis. For rather than rebel against that metaphor, George Eliot positioned herself within the patriarchal tradition of writing and so assumed to herself the public authority of male authorship, the power to engender implied by the phallocentric aesthetic. George Eliot's pen name provided her the power of the penis, the power to engender in writing, and so the power of the phallogos, the authority of the male word.

Eliot implicitly confessed her delight in the critical reviewers' assumptions that she was male. In her journal entry, "How I came to Write Fiction," she recorded the literary gossip about the new author of "Amos Barton" and *Adam Bede;* she enjoyed the speculation that George Eliot was a clergyman, a Cambridge man, the "father of a family," a man "who had seen a great deal of society" and might "overhear his own praises at the club" (*Letters,* 2: 408). Eliot's incognito created the brouhaha over the new and unknown author's identity that eventually led to an imposter's claim to have authored *Adam Bede.* Indeed, Marian Evans Lewes promoted "George Eliot." She asked Blackwood to send copies of *Scenes of Clerical Life* and *Adam Bede* to prominent literary figures; when *Adam Bede* became a popular success, she asked him to reissue *Scenes* so George Eliot would not appear to have written only one book. Eliot's later anger over the resulting literary curiosity appears directly linked to her incognito, to her paradoxical desire to conceal and reveal her identity, to be both anonymous and well-known. When Sara Hennell dared assume George Eliot the author of Mrs. Oliphant's *Chronicles of Carlingford,* Marian Lewes testily defended George Eliot's identity and integrity: "When a *name* is precisely the highest-priced thing in literature, any one who has a name will not, except when there is some strong motive for mystification, throw away the advantages of that name. I wrote anonymously while I was an unknown author, but I shall never, I believe, write anonymously again. . . . And in general, you may be sure that whenever a fiction is mine it will bear the name of George Eliot, or at least be formally and officially announced as written by George Eliot" (*Letters*, 4: 28). Although her identity had by this time become known, Eliot maintained her literary and masculine name.

Eliot not only identified herself as author as masculine but her narrators as well.[62] In *Middlemarch*, the narrator refers to himself as "he" one abstract and theoretical yet significant time (2: 102). In Eliot's early and late writings, the narrator discusses his attitudes and experiences as having been shaped by his boyish childhood. The narrator of "Janet's Repentance" remembers the first time he appeared in "coat-tails," when he blushed and fancied Miss Landor laughing at him when he appeared as a candidate for communion and failed to understand that the ceremony signified the male "assumption of new responsibilities," when he went home and imitated the bishop's sermon until his sister cried (2: 55, 198, 116). The significant detail of coattails appears in each of Eliot's narrators' meditations upon boyhood, as memory links itself to the initiation into manhood. The narrator of *The Mill on the Floss* remembers his mother's refusal to allow him a "tailed coat," although "every other boy of his age had gone into tails already" (1: 98). The bachelor speaker who "looks backward" in *Theophrastus Such* remembers himself as a boy and wonders whether his memory links him by synecdoche to the memories of the other men he elbows each day in London drawing rooms; did each "mere species of white cravat and swallow-tail" once lean in "dubious embryonic form" against "a cottage-lintel, in small corduroys" before assuming coattails?[63] In these passages, memory appears to be a purely male faculty, one that may bind one man to another through shared experience.

Male memory, looking backward, also provides a narrator his authority. Each of Eliot's narratives, with the exception of *Daniel Deronda*, takes as its point of departure a figure for the narrator or the narrator himself mediating between the reader's present time and the narrative's historical time. The central term of this mediation is "memory." The narrator of *The Mill on the Floss* returns to Dorlcote Mill, views its landscape from the stone bridge, falls in love with moistness, and enters his memory of Maggie Tulliver's life. The spirit of Florence in the "Proem" of *Romola* overlooks modern Florence from the hill of San Miniato and compares what he sees with his memory of fifteenth-century Florence. The coachman, Mr. Sampson, who introduces *Felix Holt*, specifically links this male memory with storytelling. He provides the "happy outside passenger" with a journey through the complexities of English history, landscape, and class structure. He comments on the scenery, reveals the names of persons, explains the meaning of communities, and tells stories about families. He knows who owns the land and remembers the "fathers of actual baronets." Mr. Sampson's memory of the past, his ability to tell stories and to relate the details of past family history, his knowledge and presumed wisdom, provide him a "position of easy, undisputed authority" — despite the threat of industrial, fast-paced life after the railroads and the Reform Bill (1: 1-13). Male memory enables the activity by which narrative is made: looking back, knowing one's neighbors, and so endowing the details of a community's life with structure.

The authority of narration belongs to male narrators because Eliot envisions the traditions of storytelling as patriarchal and genealogical. The narrator of "Looking Backward" specifically identifies boyish memories with his father, with the country parson born "about the same time as Scott and Wordsworth" and popular among the people to whom he ministered. After his mother's death, this narrator became his "father's constant companion in his out-door business"; he remembers his own shadow riding by the side of a larger shadow on horseback, listening to his father's stories and absorbing his father's Tory philosophies. He recounts how this much honored and graying father related his own memories to his son. The England of the father's youth seems "lovable, laudable, full of good men, and having good rulers"; things in his father's prime had more chance than do the narrator's fancies of "being real." He tells his reader, "That parental time, the time of my father's youth, never seemed prosaic, for it came to my imagination first through his memories, which made a wondrous perspective to my little daily world of discovery" (25-39). Paternal stories and memories initiate the son's powers as a storyteller. They allow him access to a time earlier than his own memory and experience, a past beyond his own knowledge and more "real" than his own fantasy. Like this narrator, George Eliot recounts *his* father's memories and stories. When Sara Hennell wrote to say she had heard Isaac Evans assumed his sister the author of *Adam Bede* because he recognized details about his father only she would have known, Eliot replied, "I should think Sara's version of my brother's words concerning Adam Bede is the correct one — 'that there are *things in it about my father*' i.e., being interpreted, things my father told us about his early life" (*Letters,* 3: 99). A storyteller thinks back through his father and through his father's memories.

In recounting the father's memories, the male narrator also constitutes himself as subject. In his essay "A Case of Paranoia," Freud mentions primal fantasy for the first time and accords sound — the signifier in the aural sphere — a privileged role in the primal fantasy scenario. Freud interprets the "noise" his female subject heard while making illicit love as fantasied and rooted in the primal scene. As Laplanche and Pontalis point out in their essay on the origin of fantasy, Freud's earliest theoretical documents about the scene of seduction demonstrate that the child constitutes primal fantasy from what he or she has heard about and "*sub-*

sequently turned to account." Sound, the aural signifier, or the "word," articulates the structure of primal fantasy out of the child's larger experiential data, which in turn subsequently gets narrated as story. These originating "words" may also represent or include "the history of the legends of parents, grandparents and the ancestors: the family *sounds* or *sayings,* this spoken or secret discourse, going on prior to the subject's arrival, within which he must find his way."[64] In recounting the father's memories as well as his own memories of his father, Eliot's narrator speaks this spoken discourse and so positions himself within the father's history. Yet he also defines his own linguistic position as subject and so constitutes his own history, his own story. Thus in speaking the sayings of the father, the narrator assumes the authority of paternal discourse and exposes to himself the secret discourse that surrounds him and within which he as son must "find his way."

In *Silas Marner,* Mr. Macey represents the fully authoritative teller of stories. He demonstrates that identity in a community depends upon its members' knowledge of paternal genealogy:

"Ay, you remember when first Mr. Lammeter's father came into these parts, don't you, Mr. Macey?" said the landlord.

"I should think I did," said the old man, who had now gone through that complimentary process necessary to bring him up to the point of narration. . . . "We heard tell as he'd sold his own land to come and take the Warrens' and that seemed odd for a man as had land of his own, to come and rent a farm in a strange place. But they said it was along of his wife's dying; though there's reasons in things as nobody knows on. . . . [Folks] pretend this young lass is like [the Miss Osgood Mr. Lammeter married], but that's the way wi' people as don't know what come before 'em." . . .

Here Mr. Macey paused; he always gave his narrative in installments, expecting to be questioned according to precedent.

"Ay, and a partic'lar thing happened, didn't it, Mr. Macey, so as you were likely to remember that marriage?" said the landlord, in a congratulatory tone. . . . "Mr. Drumlow . . . when he come to put the questions, he put 'em by the rule o' contrairy like, and he says, 'Wilt thou have this man to thy wedded wife?' . . . and I says to myself, 'Is't the meanin' or the words as makes folks fast i' wedlock?' . . . [Rev. Drumlow] says, 'Pooh, pooh, Macey, . . . it's neither the meaning nor the words—it's the re*ges*ter does it—that's the glue.'" . . .

Everyone of Mr. Macey's audience had heard this story many times, but it was listened to as if it had been a favourite tune. . . .

"Ay, and there's few folks know so well as you how [the Warrens] come to be Charity Land, eh, Mr. Macey?" said the butcher. . . .

"Why, . . . Mr. Cliff as came and built the big stables at the Warrens . . . couldn't ride, lor bless you! . . . My grandfather heared old Squire Cass say so many and many a time. But ride he would, as if Old Harry had been a'driving him; and he'd a son, a lad o' sixteen; and nothing would his father have him do, but he must ride and ride. . . . It was a common saying as the father wanted to ride the tailor out o' the lad, and make a gentleman on him.

. . . Howsomever, the poor lad got sickly and died, and the father . . . died raving . . . and that's how the Warrens come to be Charity Land. . . . That's what my father told me, and he was a reasonable man, though there's folks nowadays know what happened afore they were born better nor they know their own business." (74-79.)

Macey's narrative links story, storytelling, and storyteller with paternal precedence and authority. This paradigmatic story recounts the doings of fathers and forefathers: their marriages, their sons and heirs, their properties. The authority of a story resides in its command of lineage, in how far back it traces fathers. This genealogical structure corresponds to the structure of narrative: father and son stand in the same metonymical relationship on a family tree as do chapters, scenes, and words in a narrative. In a thematics of paternal precedence, fathers engender families and acquire property; the storyteller engenders the story of their engendering. Macey acquires his authority as teller of these tales because he repeats what his father told him and what his grandfather told him he heard old Squire Cass say. A storytelling based on such paternal thematics and genealogical structures renders its authority, its control of its own signification, a male prerogative: to tell a story, one must be a son recounting the events of fathering. Storytelling depends upon masculine memory, upon remembering when Nancy Lammeter's father came to Raveloe, yet it also depends upon the genealogical privileges of the storyteller, the privilege of repeating the memories of those who came before the teller, of knowing what happened before the teller was born because his father and grandfather told him so.

George Eliot's pen name and her masculine narrators imitate this genealogical structure that renders storytelling its authority. Her male narrators, like Mr. Macey, relate events about forefathers and sons, about, for example, Thias Bede dying and Adam Bede originating and fathering a new familial community. Adam's name signifies such paternal initiation, combining the names of the biblical first father and the earliest chronicler of English history. The narrator of Adam's story relates events he has heard from Adam himself; he tells us he had "gathered from Adam Bede" the differences between Reverend Irwine and Mr. Ryde and commences to relate *in toto* a conversation between himself and Adam about religious doctrine. Adam speaks, and the narrator responds in his own voice: "Adam said," "I said," the writer reports, identifying his speakers. Here too the storyteller depends upon masculine memory for the substance of his recounting this conversation and acknowledges he knew the participants in his story when he was young and they in their old age. Adam Bede presumably tells the narrator of *Adam Bede* the stories of his youth, which the narrator in turn tells us. This structure imitates the structure of the storytelling event in which Mr. Macey tells his listeners the stories he heard from his father and grandfather about

Mr. Cliff, the Lammeters, and the Warren. The narrator of *Adam Bede* hears the story of passion and murder from a man based on Eliot's father who becomes himself a father; by virtue of this direct knowledge of Adam as well as by prerogative of masculine memory, the narrator metaphorically participates in the genealogy of storytellers, appearing a metaphorical son to Adam as "father." This narrator acquires the authority of storytellers because he heard this story from a father, just as Mr. Macey heard his story from his father.

In the genealogy of storytellers, "George Eliot," like her narrator, stands in metaphorical relationship to Mr. Macey's forebears. Macey tells a story of Mr. Lammeter told him by his father, as well as an earlier story of Mr. Cliff told his father by his grandfather—and by implication repeated by his father to himself. "George Eliot" authors the story a male narrator tells of Adam Bede as he heard it from Adam Bede, now dead along with "Old Leisure," the narrator's nostalgic figure for past ease. In the genealogy of storytellers, three male figures enable the story's thematics, structure, and authority: the grandfather, the father, and the storyteller, who appears by virtue of lineage a "son." Eliot's retention of her pen name ensures her place as the "son" in this genealogy of storytellers, as it renders her male narrator *his* place as "son." In this way, Eliot not only acquires the authority a male author immediately enjoys with his publisher and his public, she also creates for herself a position in a patriarchal structure of storytellers which enables her to "father" her own writing. For the generative principle of this genealogical structure renders listening sons future storytelling fathers as well. Imagining herself a male author, then, George Eliot usurps the figurative and generative authority of the "pen as penis."[65]

George Eliot also acquires the power to promulgate the word of paternal authority. Macey's story of the Cliffs and Lammeters invokes the metaphors I examined earlier in discussing the law in Eliot's fiction: fatherhood, property, the authority of the word. Like Dickens, Eliot imagines authorship linked to fatherhood and the symbolic name of the Father. The Evangelical Mary Ann Evans aims at "the attainment of that perfect ideal, the true Logos that dwells in the bosom of the One Father"; she praises Carlyle for his "devotion to the Author of all things" (*Letters*, 1: 126, 123). As a "male" author, Eliot acquires the authority of such culturally symbolic fatherhood, of the logos, and can promulgate the law in the figure of herself as father. As Macey relates in his story, Mr. Drumlow maintains that neither the meaning nor the words "glue" people together in marriage, but "the re*ges*ter does it." The church's register records in the name of the Father the names of the townspeople and in so inscribing them legalizes their possessors' familial relationships to one another over time—their weddings, births, and deaths. Eliot's narrative register similarly binds characters to the named events that define their filial privileges and duties. In this sense, by imagining herself a male author Eliot can effectively carry out the narrative project I discussed in my second section of this chapter: the reform or humbling of the fictional father. The woman writer can bind the father to a law promulgated by daughters, but the male writer can promulgate and bind the fictional father to his register, to the symbolic and authoritative logos of the "Author of all things."

The male writer accomplishes this binding through the male narrator, who in constituting himself accedes to the authority of paternal discourse. Eliot's narrator in fact assumes the authority the humbled fictional father lacks with regard to the law. To simplify analysis, I will refer to Eliot's narrator as though he were one identifiable—and of course fictional—character. This narrator interprets a complex world, recognizes the ineluctibility of otherness, and expresses sympathy for others while teaching the reader to feel sympathy as well. Unlike his fictional fathers—Mr. Tulliver, Sir Christopher Cheverel, and Adam Bede, among others—Eliot's narrator uses the tools of language to interpret a puzzling world. He understands the difficulty of reading rightly, the discrepancy between sign and referent, signifier and signified. He assures us in *Middlemarch* that "signs are small measurable things, but interpretations are illimitable" (34); in *Adam Bede,* that "the sign is so slight, it is scarcely perceptible to the eye or ear." He speaks here of love's signs and excuses both Dorothea and Adam for misreading those signs of passion which yield such immeasurable interpretations, which often fail to correspond to a referent in "reality." In *Adam Bede,* he constructs an elaborate grammatical structure in order to interpret a world in which the arbitrary nature of the sign creates such slippage between signifier and signified, sign and correct interpretation. He assures us that "nature . . . has a language of her own, which she uses with strict veracity," yet nonetheless "we don't know all the intricacies of her syntax just yet, and in hasty reading we may happen to extract the very opposite of her real meaning." When Adam reads the language of Hetty's physiognomy, for example, he assumes "nature has written out his bride's character for him in those exquisite lines of cheek and lip and chin, in those eyelids delicate as petals, in those long lashes curled like the stamen of a flower, in the dark liquid depths of those wonderful eyes." Whereas Adam misreads the language of physiognomy, the narrator believes he does not; he understands the wisest of us must sometimes be "beguiled" by nature's signs, and he—through falling victim to beguiling passion himself—has come to "suspect at length that there is no direct correlation between eyelashes and morals" (1: 228-39). This lack of correlation between eyelash and moral, between nature's language and signification, means nature, like a text, must be read or interpreted.

Eliot's narrator reads his characters as texts, characters themselves involved in the mystery of interpretation: Lydgate attempting to trace the structures of primary tissue; Casaubon, to archaeologize the Key to all Mythologies; Mrs. Garth, to teach her children the correct meaning and usage of words. The narrator, unlike his characters, knows interpretation must account for broader causes than origin, for more discontinuous relations than correspondence. His well-known passages of interpretation in *Middlemarch* speak to the problematic act of interpreting: his parable of the pier-glass; his description of Rome as the "spiritual centre and interpreter" of the world; his monologue about the "stealthy convergence of human lots," the "double change of self and beholder," the "movement and mixture" of Herodotus, old England, and Middlemarch (1: 403, 142, 295-97, 70-71). His metaphors identify the act of interpretation as necessarily attempting yet failing to account for causality's complexity and lack of singularity as emanating from an origin without or a center with too much fixity. In fact, this narrator's metaphors for causality and narrative shape—webs, flowing water, scientific microscopy—derive from, as J. Hillis Miller points out, the medieval Latin word for "text."[66] His metaphors refer not only to the world he interprets but to his own act of fictionalizing. Late in *Adam Bede*, this narrator calls attention to the metaphorical systems of his discourse: "Those slight words and looks and touches are part of the soul's language; and the finest language, I believe, is chiefly made up of unimposing words, such as 'light,' 'sound,' 'stars,' 'music'—words really not worth looking at, or hearing, in themselves, any more than 'chips' or 'sawdust': it is only that they happen to be the signs of something unspeakably great and beautiful" (2: 310-11). A sign is a sign, the narrator says, and despite the value of its referent, it remains a sign related diacritically to other signs. Yet "light," "sound," "stars," and "music" all refer to both a literal and a transcendental realm, whereas "chips" and "sawdust" refer to literal, material things only.[67] The narrator's theory of figurative language identifies signs as duplicitous and unstable and implies that any linguistic structure must question its own systems of grammar and metaphor so as to represent the act of interpretation with all its puzzling complexity.

Our narrator also, however, understands the tricks of metaphor. The urge to see difference in terms of resemblance beguiles and deceives us. He says of Casaubon—and of himself and us—"for we all of us, grave or light, get our thoughts entangled in metaphors, and act fatally on the strength of them" (*Mid*, 63). In *The Mill on the Floss*, he derides metaphor as delusory.

> It is astonishing what a different result one gets by changing the metaphor! Once call the brain an intellectual stomach, and one's ingenious conception of the classics and geometry as ploughs and harrows seems to settle nothing.

But then it is open to someone else to follow great authorities, and call the mind a sheet of white paper or a mirror, in which case one's knowledge of the digestive process becomes quite irrelevant. It was doubtless an ingenious idea to call the camel the ship of the desert, but it would hardly lead one far in training that useful beast. O Aristotle! if you had had the advantage of being "the freshest modern" instead of the greatest ancient, would you not have mingled your praise of metaphorical speech, as a sign of high intelligence, with a lamentation that intelligence so rarely shows itself in speech without metaphor,—that we can so seldom declare what a thing is, except by saying it is something else? (216.)

As Cynthia Chase notes, the narrator here satirizes Mr. Stelling's tutorial authority over Tom Tulliver and implies that delusory metaphor bespeaks the effort to exert control or authority over the incomprehensible and puzzling signs and facts of the material world.[68] He constitutes his narratorial authority by demonstrating the limits of interpretational authority. His task demands that, unlike Eliot's fictional fathers, he eschew pride, hardness, and narcissism; he must expunge egoism from his broad and complex perspective. He therefore attempts to sympathize with all points of view and seeks to teach his reader to imitate himself. He preaches sensitivity by admitting his own youthful lack of sympathy: "It is the way with us men in other crises," he continues; "the golden moments in the stream of life rush past us, and we see nothing but sand" (*SCL*, 2: 109). He believes memory of our own lives and childhood pasts can teach us sympathy with others unlike ourselves:

We have all of us sobbed so piteously, standing with tiny bare legs above our little socks, when we lost sight of our mother or nurse in some strange place; . . . Every one of those keen moments has left its trace, and lives in us still, but such traces have blent themselves irrecoverably with the firmer texture of our youth and manhood; and so it comes that we can look on the troubles of our children with a smiling disbelief in the reality of their pain. Is there anyone who can recover the experience of his childhood, not merely with a memory of what he did and what happened to him, of what he liked and disliked when he was in frock and trousers, but with an intimate penetration, a revived consciousness of what he felt then—when it was so long from one Midsummer to another? (*MF*, 97-98.)

The narrator's theory of sympathy depends on an implicit topology of memory in which revival of the forgotten memory-trace reminds us that we too are ineluctibly other to ourselves simply by virtue of duration. If we can feel sympathy with our young and "other" selves, we can therefore feel sympathy with other young selves and, by analogy, with any other self. As the narrator tells us in "Janet's Repentance," "sympathy is but a living again through our own past in a new form" (2: 226). Sympathy for otherness exists only in retroactivity.

This memory-trace must be inscribed and so retained, yet must also allow for freshness of perception and so be forgotten. Sympathy likewise demands freshness of perception. When the narrator asks, "—but why always Dorothea? Was her point of view the only possible one with regard to this marriage?" (2: 9), he reminds us always to question our habitual perspective on a complex issue. He cautions his reader against a "too hasty judgment" of, an "absolute conclusion" about, a "prejudice" against, the mole-faced scholar. If Casaubon tends to forget his own ineluctible otherness to himself and to those around him, we too own the same frailty. The narrator's praxis of sympathy in his storytelling, then, provides him the power of loving reciprocity which the fictional father lacks in Eliot's narratives. Whereas the fictional father appears hard, prideful, and punishing, the narrator appears sympathetic, caring, and tolerant. His authority as narrator resides at least in part in his ability to use the word, the vehicle of the law, not only as a tool of prohibition but also as an instrument of fellow-feeling. In repeating the "sayings of the father," Eliot's narrator redefines paternal authority and speaks the ideal, loving, yet properly authoritative narrative discourse the patriarchs ought to have spoken.

This narrator's paternal discourse appears to be Eliot's goal in her narrative enterprise. Yet if sympathy works through retroactivity and by analogy, it too is metaphoric. Indeed, at the end of her career, Eliot demystified her doctrine of fellow-feeling. She admitted the cost of such idealization, of having constituted her writing self as masculine in order to "take up by the ears" her younger, female self, that ineluctible other. "Looking Inward," the bachelor narrator of *Theophrastus Such* confesses, one finds that otherness in one's present, one's presence. Narrational authority, he ruefully admits, is itself born of the consolations of egoism, of blindness as well as insight, of the "*naive* veracity of self-presentation." Like the characters about whom he has written, Eliot's narrator has after all misread a puzzling world, has spoken tolerantly only because he himself longed for "approbation, sympathy, and love." Being a bachelor —a son but never a father—he has found in his experience none of the moral intersubjectivities that lie at the heart of Eliot's idealized fictions about sympathy. In his limited and solitary relationships, the bachelor finds he listens to "all kinds of personal outpouring, without the least disposition to become communicative in the same way." He discovers, in fact, his interlocutors dislike hearing his complaints, preferring to confess intimate details of their lives while he plays the role of "dummy" (7-8). Like Daniel Deronda, whose "activity of imagination on behalf of others" (1: 266) those others assume signifies a lack of desire and ambition on his part, the eccentric and disgruntled old bachelor of *Theophrastus Such* finds himself counted out of desire and intersubjectivity. As a result, he understands the ironic consequences of his hitherto highly touted doctrine of self-sacrifice. Sympathy disallows reciprocity; sympathy annihilates the self. The cost to the sympathetic self is emptiness, repression of desire, and moral deadness. This narrator, who physically resembles George Eliot's worst impressions of her own appearance, who lives alone as she lived ostracized for ten years, betrays her own dissatisfactions with idealized empathy. She too confesses late in her career in the persona of this isolated man the consequences of sympathy.

Deronda, who resembles Eliot's narrator because he preaches both self-prohibition and fellow-feeling, portrays another aspect of Eliot's uncertainty about her doctrine of sympathy. Deronda cultivates his "subdued fervour of sympathy" (2: 266) because not to be sympathetic signifies a desire to punish. Daniel's "imaginative lenience towards others" expresses his disposition "to check that rashness of indignation or resentment which has an unpleasant likeness to the love of punishing" (3: 259). If Daniel fails to express sympathy, then, he might well resemble Tom Tulliver—angry, spiteful, and retributive. Eliot's narrator too represses his desire to punish by virtue of his sympathetic tolerance for otherness. In *Middlemarch*, although he asks us, "but why always Dorothea?" and demands we tolerate Casaubon, he nonetheless portrays Dorothea sympathetically because she expresses sympathy, portrays Casaubon punitively because he does not.[69] As a result, the reader feels little compassion for the cold-hearted scholar; the narrator's demand that we withhold judgment of this "Milton" appears to be merely a rhetorical exercise. While his interpretational discourse expounds the moral value of sympathy, the writer's narrative structures punish those who fail to live up to this doctrine: Hetty Sorrel, Godfrey Cass, Mrs. Transome, and—most clearly of all perhaps—Gwendolen Harleth. Gwendolen, whom Daniel counself never to gain from another's loss, loses all human consolation and relation at the end of *Daniel Deronda*, while Deronda ironically gains his own and presumably Israel's future. The narrator's assumption of tolerant yet authoritative paternal discourse, then, contradicts George Eliot's punitive narrative structures.

By the end of her narrative project, Eliot has controlled her memories and material fully enough to question that control. With regard to memories of her father, however, repression continues. Let me juxtapose Adam Bede with Caleb Garth, both of whom Eliot based on the character of her father. Eliot nonetheless insisted on the fictionality of the narrative fathers whose originals are Robert Evans. In her journal entry, "History of 'Adam Bede,'" she maintains that Adam "is not my father any more than Dinah is my aunt" and that "not a single *portrait*" exists in *Adam Bede*. The germ for that novel combines "recollections" of Eliot's Aunt Samuel with "points in my father's life and character" (*Letters*, 2: 502-4). When C. H. Bracebridge announced he had discovered the originals of *Adam Bede*'s characters among Eliot's relatives at Wirksworth, Eliot wrote Charles Bray, "I could never have written Adam Bede if I had not learned something of my father's early experience: but no one who knew my father could call Adam a portrait of him" (*Letters,* 3: 155). Eliot fictionalized her memories of her father and insisted on her refusal simply to copy her characters from life not only because she felt under attack by Bracebridge, but also—as in the well-known chapter 17 of *Adam Bede*—because she rendered complex the artistic grounds of realistic narrative. "The course of Adam's life is entirely different from my father's," Eliot wrote Bray; "the whole course of the story in Adam Bede" differed from that of Eliot's own experience (*Letters,* 3: 155). Eliot's terminology of "courses" implies that narrative structure, the particular succession of fictional events and actions, the diacritical mode of linguistic and fictional signification, transformed Marian Evans Lewes's personal memories of her father into the authoritative and public morality of George Eliot. As "George Eliot," Marian Evans Lewes fathered her own father in his fictional incarnations and engendered him to serve her particular needs.

At the end of this remarkable career, George Eliot fictionalized Marian Evans Lewes's father into an idealized patriarchal figure who performs the acts of sympathy and reciprocity his original never enacted. Caleb Garth, as critics have long recognized, represents Eliot's final memorial to Robert Evans. Unlike Adam Bede, the father's earlier fictionalization, Caleb devotes himself to work without judging harshly those who do not. The narrator figures Caleb's work as religious: his "virtual divinities were good practical schemes, accurate work, and the faithful completion of undertakings: his prince of darkness was a slack workman" (1: 383). This mystified father has no need of word or discourse: Caleb often fails to find "speech for his thought" but need not worry because Mrs. Garth teaches the novel's "grammar lesson." The "original" of Caleb Garth appears in a chastising letter Marian Evans Lewes wrote Charles Bray in response to Bracebridge's letter naming Robert Evans as Adam Bede's "original."

> There is one phrase which I am prompted to notice by my feeling towards my Father's memory. He speaks of my Father as a "farmer." Now my Father did not raise himself from being an artizan to be a farmer: he raised himself from being an artizan to be a man whose extensive knowledge in very varied practical departments made his services valued through several counties. . . . I mention this subject to you, because I have some reason to believe that in using the phrase "self-educated farmer's daughter" Mr. Bracebridge was borrowing from you. My reason is, that long ago George Combe told me you had spoken of my father to him as a "mere farmer," and I had to explain to George Combe what my father really was.
>
> So far as I am personally concerned, I should not write a stroke to prevent any one, in the zeal of antithetic eloquence, from calling me a tinker's daughter; but if my Father is to be mentioned at all—if he is to be identified with an imaginary character, my piety towards his memory calls on me to point out

to those who are supposed to speak with information, what he really achieved in life. (*Letters*, 3: 168-69.)

This pious "memory" of the father appears a remarkable reconstruction prompted by the deceptions of memory itself. Marian's attack on her friend, based not only on hearsay evidence but on the one word "farmer," demonstrates her insecure and contradictory feelings about her father's "memory."

The father as fictionalized in this letter—the man of the land who is no simple farmer but a valued and knowledgeable land agent—becomes in *Middlemarch* the heroic Caleb Garth.[70] In his metaphors for the noble father, Eliot compares Caleb to the Roman king, captain, farmer, and equivocal tyrant, Cincinnatus:

> "Come here and tell me the story I told you on Wednesday, about Cincinnatus" [Mrs. Garth requests of her children].
>
> "I know! he was a farmer," said Ben.
>
> "Now, Ben, he was a Roman—let *me* tell," said Letty. . . .
>
> "You silly thing, he was a Roman farmer, and he was ploughing."
>
> "Yes, but before that—that didn't come first—people wanted him," said Letty.
>
> "Well, but you say what sort of a man he was first," insisted Ben. "He was a wise man, like my father, and that made the people want his advice. And he was a brave man, and could fight. And so could my father—couldn't he, mother?"
>
> "Now, Ben, let me tell the story straight on, as mother told it to us," said Letty, frowning. . . .
>
> "Letty, I am ashamed of you," said her mother. . . . "When your brother began, you ought to have waited to see if he could not tell the story. . . . Cincinnatus, I am sure, would have been sorry to see his daughter behave so. . . . Now, Ben."
>
> "Well—oh—well—why, there was a great deal of fighting, and they were all blockheads, and—I can't tell it just how you told it—but they wanted a man to be captain and king and everything—"
>
> "Dictator, now," said Letty. . . .
>
> "Very well, dictator!" said Ben, contemptuously. "But that isn't a good word: he didn't tell them to write on slates." (1: 374-75.)

Ben's metaphorical story concludes very late in the novel; when Mr. Brooke and Sir James Chettam rehire Caleb as land agent for the two estates, Ben yells, "like Cincinnatus—hooray!" But Ben's early attempt to tell the story of Cincinnatus makes the father as hero a questionable metaphor: his misinterpretation of the term "dictator" is a comic confusion of paternal authority and appropriate language. Indeed, Ben's story is interrupted by Fred Vincy's visit before the punch line that confirms paternal metaphor; the reader knows before Ben begins his story that Fred will álmost immediately announce Caleb's failure to manage his finances by having signed for Fred's debts. Rather than appear the hero of his metaphorical story, Ben's father resembles the girl-imagined paternal "hero" of Eliot's earlier story, *The Mill on the Floss.* Despite his moral disregard for mammon, Caleb Garth's religious dedication to work cannot make him the "hero" of this complex and multiple-plotted story, *Middlemarch.* This idealized memorial to the father carries little emotional conviction in a novel filled with the moving and involving failures of Lydgate's and Dorothea's vocations and marriages. Eliot's sentimental fictionalizing of her father appears undercut not only by her equivocal comparison of him with an equally—if not more—equivocal father-king-farmer but also by narrative context and structure. Caleb is indeed a fictional father.

The novel I have discussed as disclosing yet displacing traumatic memory demonstrates that Eliot created this final fictional father out of guilt. Romola wishes to preserve her father's library intact and to inscribe the collection with his name, wishes to "rescue her father's name from oblivion." She feels a sense of "love and duty to her father's memory" and conceives of the library as a "sacramental" monument to his scholarship. Romola's memorial, however, exposes the double nature of the urge to memorialize: "The sense of something like guilt towards her father in a hope that grew out of his death, gave all the more force to the anxiety with which she dwelt on the means of fulfilling his supreme wish. That piety towards his memory was all the atonement she could make now for a thought that seemed akin to joy at his loss" (1: 374). The daughter creates a memorial to her father because of guilty joy at his death. The memorial inscribes the father's name in a public register and so alleviates the daughter's private guilt. This memorial not only immortalizes the father but defines him as dead; Romola's wished-for library reveals her desire to "bury" the father, to declare him dead and herself as joyfully living without him. George Eliot's male narrator can view this problem with a certain sympathetic detachment, can declare Caleb Garth a heroic father-farmer. But George Eliot's urge early to humble and late to sentimentalize the fictional father resembles Romola's paradoxical urge to bury and to memorialize her father. This "burial" recalls the terminology of defense: binding, repression, scapegoating. Eliot's final memorial to her father, her fictional father as heroic farmer, appears to have been created by her own fictionalizing memory, by repression of the memories rendered traumatic in the writing of *Romola.* For despite the public authority of George Eliot, the paternal discourse of the male narrator, Marian Evans Lewes is a woman and still a daughter. The discontinuity between her masculine personae and her female self becomes visible in the conflicts, repressions, and discourses of her late work.

Charlotte Bronte:
Masters and Mastery

A MASTER has power, control, or authority over another. He is the head of a house, an employer, the owner of an animal or a slave, a male schoolteacher or tutor. Charlotte Bronte's imagination entwines itself around all these masters. Her heroes are all authoritative, all desirable yet somehow unavailable, all desired yet kept at bay. The dialectic of master and slave threads its way through Bronte's texts; she is thrilled and repulsed by it. The faculty of masters is mastery: control, rule, victory in a struggle or competition, expert skill in an arena of knowledge. The master conquers; he possesses. He is a proprietor, and the force of his actions must find their object in the world: he conquers or owns someone or something. The dialectic of mastery and submission likewise weaves its way through Bronte's texts.

The question of gender becomes immediately apparent in such oppositions. Master/slave or master/mistress, male/female, father/mother, active/passive, all play out the same cultural binarisms in different realms. Charlotte Bronte desires to challenge such differential thinking yet fears the consequences of questioning dominant ideologies of masculine and feminine. She seeks to redefine the terms of mastery, to invert male and female, always finding subversion and female mastery at the last minute too risky for completion. Bronte's mastery of masters when not wishful is equivocal, her heroines' female skill or knowledgeability tentative and provisional. Despite desire, difference survives and thrives in her doubly committed narratives.

Language and Desire

> Writing aloud *is not phonological but phonetic; its aim is not the clarity of messages. . . . It searches for . . . the language lined with flesh, . . . the articulation of the body, of the tongue, not that of meaning.* — Roland Barthes, The Pleasure of the Text

Charlotte Bronte's creative process has been described by her biographer, Winifred Gérin, as "trance-like," as "exclud[ing] all possibility of self-criticism and almost, one is tempted to think, suspend[ing] consciousness."[1] In her novelettes, for example, Bronte rushes into language, pouring out her creations on the page, not stopping long enough to use punctuation, capital letters, or quotation marks. Her pages resemble nothing so much as a prose-writing Emily Dickinson's, riddled with dashes; in manuscript the lines occasionally run into and over one another because Bronte composed with her eyes shut, better to receive and perceive her visions. These visions, in commonplace critical parlance, appear primarily sexual, governed by gender and fantasy. Bronte described her visionary process in her Roe's Head journal: "The [pupils] went into the school-room to do their exercises & I crept up to the bed-room to be alone for the first time that day. Delicious was the sensation I experienced as I laid down on the spare bed and resigned myself to the luxury of twilight and solitude. The stream of thought, checked all day, came flowing free & calm along its channel. . . . The toil of the day, succeeded by this moment of divine leisure had acted on me like opium & was coiling about me a disturbed but fascinating spell such as I never felt before."[2] Bronte's figurative linking of bed with creativity, her metaphors of flowing and coiling, her reference to spells, opium, delicious sensations, and loss of consciousness, represent the ecstasy of release. Bronte's imaginative world, as she explained to her brother Branwell, tapped as "fanatically as ever" when she was alone in her Brussels bedroom, the "old scene in the world below," the world of childhood sexual wishes "below" the public body and the conscious mind.[3]

Sandra M. Gilbert and Susan Gubar identify this trancelike fantasizing as particularly female, these visions as an escape from the confines of a gender-based Victorian sexual destiny. They set Bronte's "trance-writing" against her early habit of "male mimicry" and "male impersonation" in language and narrative. Both gender modes of writing allay the "anxieties of female authorship," and trance-writing defines Bronte's "simultaneous enactment and evasion of her own rebellious impulses."[4] Gilbert and Gubar clearly identify the double gender-based motivation in Bronte's early narratives and define it more carefully than have other feminist critics as bisexual rather than androgynous.[5] Let me defer, however, the larger questions of gender and authorship; I would like to begin here by examining the ways in which narrative represents unconscious desire at the level of language.

In psychoanalytic theory, language inscribes desire by virtue of its role in constituting the subject. The unconscious, according to Stephen Heath, is "forged on the trace of what operates to constitute the subject," which is language.[6] Traces, representations, or signifiers, once repressed into the unconscious, become available to consciousness only by entering the language of the subject's personal and therapeutic discourse. The unconscious works by structures and laws analogous—identical—to those of language. Language that speaks from the unconscious and so represents desire takes as its tropes the figures that correspond to unconscious work: displacement and condensation, which structure the dream-text, become in the language of desire metonymy and metaphor.[7] Bronte's early narratives indulge both desiring tropes in the language of their texts. The novelettes create narrative structure purely as metonymic contiguity and so refuse—or fail—to define the linguistic positions of speakers as fixed; the text's subject is constantly constructed and represented in the fluid and associative language of unconscious desire. Moreover, as the writer who speaks in the voice of Charles Townshend as easily as she speaks in her own voice, Bronte identifies with both male and female desire and so partakes of the pleasures of both libidinal economies. The language of desire takes as its metaphors for such gender difference, for crossing the bar between the sexes, the woman's voice, the man's gaze.

Each of the five novelettes begins with a reference to the process of its writing: "The last scene in my last book concluded within the walls of Alnwick House—and the first scene in my present volume opens in the same place" (125). Bronte's reference to "last" and "last," to "first" and "present," define writing as a process that attempts to efface difference, as an ongoing event that is continually present to itself and through which she, as narrator of this novelette, hallucinates herself. Time may change —moving as it will into the future, the present moment vanishing and becoming past—but writing makes that change somehow bearable; even as present becomes past, Alnwick House remains itself, always and eternally present to the writer who recreates it. Yet beginning initiates difference. Townshend admits as he begins *Julia* that he does not know where writing will lead him; he must follow it, as we must follow him. Not knowing his subject matter, he takes as subject the writing he wishes to begin. This lack of subject for narrative Townshend represents as enjoyable:

> There is, reader, a sort of pleasure, in sitting down to write, wholly unprovided with a subject. There now lie before me a quire of blank sheets which it is my intention to cover with manuscript, and not a word have I prepared for the occasion, not a scene, not an incident—yet somehow my feelings, far from

being uneasy, are similar to those I have often experienced, when with a carpet bag containing two shirts, four pocket-handkerchiefs, a pair of stockings & a suit, I have mounted the Edwardston Mail . . . — & without aim or end allowed myself to be rattled away in the dawn of a June morning, East, West, North or South, as Fate & the Presiding Jehu determined. (87.)

Lack of subject for narrative serves the primary process because writing without "aim or end," the pure process of writing, is a pleasure in itself. Writing writes itself, and the writer, following where it leads without conscious plan, lets the writing write him. Such freely associative discourse initiates the language of unconscious desire.

Bronte's primary metaphor for such writing is "gazing." Charles Townshend represents "flashback" literally: he sees a "mental vision" of past domestic scenes (94). During a "silent spell" in one of the novelettes' many drawing rooms, Townshend looks around himself, and the "tout-ensemble," he says, "of what I saw recalled to me another picture." This flashback, this "picture" as the narrator "gazed at it" suggests yet another, a scene represented in an earlier novelette. As experience becomes a picture that calls up another, retrospective, picture, Townshend gazes his way into language, his presence as participatory narrator a variety of voyeurism. Yet if writing takes gazing as its metaphor, reading becomes viewing as well. Townshend reminds us that "while you gaze, reader," the character you watch hurries on. "Where is he?" Townshend imagines us quizzing him; "follow me & we shall see," he promises (198). Reading a story, like narrating one, appears a paradoxical act of watching and following, of picturing scenes and attempting to link them one to another.

How do we arrive at the scenes of this dreamlike discourse? Bronte sets "another scene"—Freud's pictorial and spatial terminology for the unconscious—with metaphors of entry, of crossing thresholds. She pictures this other scene as a landscape rendered in language by the principle of the gaze, the connecting links the haphazard order in which the viewing writer notices them. These landscapes open or are opened; the Cross of Rivaulx, Zamorna's lodge, which Bronte sketched as well as wrote about, has doors "constantly open," with "no decided grounds laid out around it" (42). Entry to these spaces appears fortuitous yet recurrent, leisurely and pleasant. Charles Townshend begins narrating *Julia* with a humorous metaphor for the process of entering the other scene: following a cow through a meadow. "Follow me still, reader," he invites us, "and I will trace further, though generally, the lines in which [those idle days] have lapsed with me. We are now among the straight stems of a young plantation, skirting the field we have just crossed, it is bounded by a high wall, too-high to overleap—but there is a door, shut fastened—try to open it, you cannot—but I know the secret—press the spring so, it flies apart—What a pleasant landscape!" (87). The scene revealed opens onto limitless horizon, has patchwork field and room to wander in. The narrator schools us in the pleasures of entering the unconscious, locating its secretly opening doors demanding to be crossed.

Bronte also hallucinates a second kind of "other scene" in the novelettes: the drawing rooms of aristocratic houses. The metaphors for entry of these scenes combine gazing with the crossing of thresholds. Henry Hastings and Charles Townshend will enter Massinger Hall through the shutterless, screenless window that opens on the turf outside and throws warm light upon the surrounding night. As Hastings looks into the bright interior, he "could see into the very penetralia of the grim house as distinctly as if he had been actually within its walls" (199). Looking becomes itself a version of entry; thresholds between inside and outside function as visual doors, as "windows." The narrator's gaze penetrates inward and opens inner space outward; he enters the "very penetralia" of manor houses, their secrets and narrative spaces. Townshend invites the reader to enter these spaces just as he and his characters do: "You must now, Reader, step into this library where you shall see a big man sitting at a table. . . . The scene is a silent one—. . . it reminds you of the wise allegories shewn by the Interpreter to Christian" (257). The reader looks and enters, sees and interprets.

This narrative penetration, enacted by a male narrator, we may identify as figuratively masculine; the gaze enters as does the phallus the unconscious scene of desire. This trope for male sexuality appears not only in Bronte's discourse but in that of psychoanalysis as well, where it serves to interpret desire and gender. In his discussion of the gaze, Jacques Lacan associates these terms for desire at the scopic level: the perceiving subject, the phallus, and castration.[8] Although Lacan refuses to assign gender to this structure of desire, it is clearly masculine, as Stephen Heath demonstrates in his critique of Lacan's 1972 seminar on female sexuality. Lacan bases his discussion of the constitution of the subject in desire and the phallus as its signifier on the visual drive. The gaze represents, for example, the "subject sustaining himself in a function of desire," and desire is established "in the domain of seeing." Moreover, the "gaze is [the] underside of consciousness"; it becomes "symbolic of the function of the lack, of the appearance of the phallic ghost."[9] This subject who gazes himself into desire and who fears the phallic ghost is male, as Charlotte Bronte intuited.

Lacan's gaze merely elaborates Freud's. In "The Uncanny," Freud identifies the "substitutive relation between the eye and the male organ"; in "The Psycho-analytic View of Psychogenic Disturbance of Vision," the eye is phallus in the story of Lady Godiva and the Peeping Tom.[10] Freud's late essays on the Oedipus complex and on femininity employ tropes for seeing to represent the group of ideas associated with the problematic of sexual difference, with castration, the phallus, and penis envy. Freud defines libido before the phallic phase as "masculine," or more correctly as "active," although its passive component coexists with this activity: "A desire to see the organs peculiar to each sex exposed is one of the original components of our libido. . . . The libido for looking . . . is present in everyone in two forms, active or passive, male and female; and, according to the preponderance of the sexual character, one form or the other predominates."[11] At this point, a child's desires are innately bisexual—active as well as passive—and as yet undifferentiated by gender. In the phallic stage, however, the scopic drive becomes linked with the phallus. When the little boy "first catches sight of a girl's genital region, [he] begins by showing irresolution and lack of interest. . . . He sees nothing or disavows what he has seen."[12] Reconsideration, though, provides the little boy the understanding that he, like the girl, might be without the phallus, might be castrated or passive, might lose his maleness. After this gaze, the boy retroactively reinterprets his sights of the female body, and the fear of castration initiates the taboo against incest. The little girl, however, "behaves differently" from the boy. She "notice[s] the penis of a brother or playmate, strikingly visible and of large proportions, at once recognize[s] it as the superior counterpart of [her] own small and inconspicuous organ. . . . She has seen it and knows that she is without it and wants to have it."[13] Whereas the boy fears he will be castrated, or maleless and so powerless, the girl understands that she is castrated, or not male and so powerless.

Julia Kristeva and Luce Irigaray criticized Freud's phallocentric theory of the scopic drive and sexual difference. The gaze in Irigaray's female-based psychoanalytic theory is secondary in woman's gender identification. "Investment in the look is not privileged in women as in men. More than the other senses, the eye objectifies and masters. It sets at a distance, maintains the distance. In our culture, the predominance of the look over smell, taste, touch, hearing has brought an impoverishment of bodily relations."[14] Kristeva and Irigaray identify the voice as a primary trope in what they call "feminine writing" and associate it with the "flesh of language." This metaphor for desire links the feminine in writing with the primitive and undifferentiated, with the child's tie to the mother, with, in narrative terminology, the romance. Irigaray associates the voice with the speech of women which refuses linearity and teleology. She differentiates this trope for female desire from that for the male in positing for the woman a different libidinal economy: "The prevalence of the gaze, discrimination of form, and individualization of forms is particularly foreign to female eroticism. Woman finds pleasure more in touch than in sight and her entrance into a dominant scopic economy signifies, once again, her relegation to passivity: she will be the beautiful object." Irigaray interprets the gaze as the male fear that the "female sex organ represents the horror of having nothing to see"; differentiates the phallic urge to discriminate form and structure from the apparent formlessness of the sex which is not phallic; and associates the individualization of form with linguistic univocal signification, the proper name, and literal meaning.[15] A narrative form and language, then, that represents female desire speaks from and in formlessness and privileges touch—or contiguity—over teleology and voice over the gaze.

In Charlotte Bronte's novelettes, the voice exists alongside the gaze as metaphor for desire. In drawing rooms the reader and narrator enter over thresholds, characters speak about sexual, social, or military strategy. Yet this dialogue is also no dialogue. It does not pass between those who speak it across the blank spaces of a page or fictional drawing room but emerges simultaneously in typographic blocks, as a presence in a room. Dialogue in Bronte's novelettes sounds like a limitless, placeless buzz, a hum filling the space it inhabits in the "very penetralia" of manor houses. The characters who speak it often lack coherent identities, motivations, and relationships, lack the linguistic positionality necessary to define themselves as subjects. Bronte's dialogue-as-voice attenuates the metaphysics of identity and philosophical categories of the "proper name," undercuts narrative cause and effect, and fragments temporal sequence. Voices speak themselves, run from word to word and mouth to mouth without logical shapes, structures, or breaks.

These scenes of continuous speech or voice in the early novelettes structure themselves next to one another without narrative link. In *Passing Events,* for example, events simply pass. Language exists without any signifying chain: whatever comes next comes next. Speaking of political fervor in Angria, Townshend metaphorically identifies narrative structure as well: "What a queer disjointed world this is," he muses of the political world while we consider the "world" of the novelette. "No man can say how things will turn"; "[I] turned my attention to the pulpit. Lo! the scene was changed or at least the actor, two men now filled the little pulpit, and seemed as if they would split its sides" (49, 53). This sudden shift of scenes appropriately describes Bronte's narrative structure and discourse; scene and character shift as the novelettes' settings break and other actors fill their space and moment. The links between these shifting scenes simply get the reader from here to there. The Edwardston Mail coach becomes Bronte's structural link between and among fragments and novelettes, since narrative end refuses to serve as conclusion: Townshend packs his bags and boards the coach for a different city (80-83); a carriage speeds in the direction of Zamorna (152); a hackney coach drives off "the d — — —l knows where" (193). Narrative has no teleology, no structured outcome. It appears purely associative; its principle of production and generation is contiguity. Indeed, the reader reading Bronte's early narratives which privilege metonymy finds they all but overturn the philosophical and linguistic concepts of signification, frustrating all his or her readerly expectations that narrative "mean" something.

This fragmented, gapped, discontinuous narrative, which overtly ruptures or traverses traditional narrative stances, structures, and categories, Irigaray would identify as characteristic of "feminine" language.

> In her statements—at least when she dares to speak out—woman retouches herself constantly. She just barely separates from herself some chatter, an exclamation, a half-secret, a sentence left in suspense—When she returns to it, it is only to set out again from another point of pleasure or pain. One must listen to her differently in order to hear an *"other meaning" which is constantly in the process of weaving itself, at the same time ceaselessly embracing words and yet casting them off to avoid becoming fixed, immobilized.* For when "she" says something, it is already no longer identical to what she means. Moreover, her statements are never identical to anything. Their distinguishing feature is one of contiguity. They touch (*upon*).[16]

This female speaker refuses to assume a place as speaking subject in which mastery of linguistic structures and submission to the law define herself. She does not speak in the logical linguistic structures characteristic of the phallocentric cultural system; her fragmentation of language in her texts calls into question the concept of such mastery.[17] The language of this speaker is close to the body, to unconscious desire, and to a "geography of pleasure" not fixed, symbolic, and phallic but multiple, plural, and diffuse.

At the end of Bronte's novelettes, an emerging narrative teleology links this structure, language, and voice with female eroticism. Bronte sets the scene of a woman's desire in symbolic female spaces and defines its subject matter as intimate conversation. In two parallel narrative scenes, one of parting, one of reunion, a woman desires her father. Caroline Vernon discovers she loves Zamorna, her guardian and legal father, after she has left him to live with her blood father, Northangerland. Montmorency, one of Northangerland's henchmen, tells Caroline about Zamorna's many mistresses; Caroline feels "an electrical stunning surprise," a thrill, and admits to herself—shocked yet pleased—that she loves Zamorna. When Zamorna journeys near Northangerland's hideaway, Caroline's desire for her guardian drives her to join him. The scene of Zamorna and Caroline's reunion confirms their mutual desire, just as the scene of their parting, whose overtly incestuous desire Bronte cut from the narrative, suggested yet deferred it. Both scenes take place in spaces which are silent yet filled with intimate dialogue; in both, Caroline fears yet desires her demonic, powerful legal father. In the first scene, Caroline will soon leave Zamorna but wants to be told he cares for her. Zamorna's reassurances satisfy her; she realizes "it was not the Duke's words but his voice that produced this happy change" (318). In the second scene, Caroline fears parting from Zamorna and wishes to exchange places with his wife, her own half-sister. Zamorna tells Caroline he must leave the next day and asks, "Will you go with me to-morrow, Caroline?" She answers and the scene ends with the word, "Yes" (349-54). In the penultimate scene of Bronte's novelettes, their true "climax," female desire quietly voices its future consummation in that woman's intimate word.

This woman's word, however, is inscribed by Charles Townshend, who gazes his way into language. Jacques Lacan's theory of the gaze—its articulation of perceiving subject, the phallus as signifier of desire, and castration—helps to account for Bronte's "male impersonation." For although in the novelettes Bronte usually inscribes female desire with the phallic pen, her narrative geography of pleasure ignores neither male nor female libidinal economy and simultaneously cherishes both the gaze and the voice. In terms of subject matter, Bronte indulges and identifies with both the female's erotic attraction for the dominant male and the swashbuckling male's for the subordinate female. When she bids "farewell to Angria," however, quitting the "burning clime" for the "study of real life," Bronte's masculine narrator enters a libidinal economy of gender-based dominance and submission.[18] As speaker-narrator, William Crimsworth purposively defines his identity by mastery of linguistic structures and of human intersubjectivity. For only by dominating a succession of women can Crimsworth become the master, patriarch, and father he imagines himself. Moreover, the gaze serves as metaphor for this masterful and dominating male sexuality by virtue of the third term in Lacan's (and Freud's) intersubjective structure of masculine desire: castration. Freud and Lacan center their terminology of sexual difference, the scopic drive, and the constitution of the subject on castration, on presence and absence in the symbolic realm: who has the phallus and who lacks it. According to Lacan, the gaze posits for the male this (female) lack yet also eludes it. The male gaze substitutes for castration and thereby achieves the potency, mastery, and dominance which castration threatens. Voyeurism becomes specifically male and exhibitionism female; the man spectates, the woman is spectacle. Lacan's discourse assigns to the female both narcissism and false consciousness. In exhibiting herself, the woman receives the satisfaction of knowing "she is being looked at, on condition that one does not show her that one knows that she knows." This necessarily narcissistic female who takes pleasure in being spectacle is unable to constitute herself as subject. For Lacan identifies the consciousness of self and other in the Cartesian *cogito* as illusory and replaces these concepts with those of misunderstanding and vision.[19] When a woman "sees herself seeing herself," she suffers the illusion of self-consciousness the gazing man never encounters and becomes as well a specular reflection of the gaze that beholds her. For the male, on the contrary, the figure of the gaze assures the gazer of female castration and male possession of the phallus: he has the phallus, she lacks it. The male gaze eroticizes, represents, and empowers the phallus.[20] The body of a woman being gazed at is a fetish for the gazer, who asserts his own position as subject, hers as spec(tac)ular object.

In Crimsworth's masterful and self-mastering autobiography, the gaze is metaphor for such dominant masculine desire. Moreover, Bronte ultimately submits to this sexual ideology of the female-as-fetish by virtue of her first-person male narrative stance, even while she implicitly criticizes it in Crimsworth's unbearable and priggish arrogance. As professor to young Belgian girls, Crimsworth combines intimidation with a "steady and somewhat stern gaze"; he takes "pleasure in answering [their] glance of vanity with the gaze of stoicism."[21] As he dominates in the classroom, so does he in the "closet." He masters Mlle Zoraide—he supposes—and increases her desire for him with his steely gaze: "Arresting, fixing her glance, I shot into her eyes, from my own, a look, where there was no respect, no love, no tenderness, no gallantry; where the strictest analysis could detect nothing but scorn, hardihood, irony. . . . She approached me as if fascinated" (117). In his desire for his pupil, Frances Henri, however, Crimsworth proves himself the voyeur whose authority covers his impotence. In a scene that associates the figures for male mastery, William provokes Frances's embarrassment with his gaze and so assumes an "authoritative tone" that calms and pleases her; he demands she read from *Paradise Lost* so he can be near her, hear the sound of her voice, and watch her: "As long as I dogmatized, I might also gaze," he asserts (184).

Crimsworth's voyeurism and fetishization of the female first appears when he arrives in Belgium. He is shown to his room at M. Pelet's school for boys and finds the window that overlooks the garden to the neighboring girls' school boarded up, as "propriety" demands. Propriety aside, however, the disappointed Crimsworth fancies himself "peep[ing] at the consecrated ground," watching the "demoiselles at their play," studying "female character in a variety of phases, myself the while sheltered from view by a modest muslin curtain" (65). Ironically enough, when Crimsworth has the window unboarded and may let his "eye roam" over the girls at their sports, over the "allée défendue," he inadvertently watches Mlle Zoraide and M. Pelet discuss their imminent marriage and so his own rejection. As the gaze figures male desire, Crimsworth clearly lacks potency; his arrogant voyeurism identifies him as a desiring male behind whose mastery and power lurks the continuing threat of the woman who gazes back, who threatens castration. Throughout the narrative, in fact, Crimsworth confesses his own "shortsightedness"; he must put on his spectacles to view the spectacle of his pretty pupils, his watchful mistress, his pupil-wife.

When a woman gazes, the threat of castration indeed hovers over the text. This gaze portrays Bronte's profound ambivalence about female power, mastery, and self-mastery. For the gaze penetrates and inscribes desire with the urge for dominance. As Freud interprets the female gaze, its thirst for otherwise "male" mastery identifies it as a trope for castration threat by the female and anxiety by the male. The Medusa's head, Freud believes, represents the woman with the multiple phallus; her possessing the symbol of masculine potency identifies her as both masculinized and castrating. The gaze of this Gorgon sister—or the male glance upon this figure of female potency—turns the beholder to stone.[22] In *The Professor,* Crimsworth's student Adèle gazes at him to provoke his returned gaze; the anxious and threatened professor pronounces her "gorgon-like" (100-101). In *Shirley,* the curate Malone thinks Hortense Moore's head like a Gorgon's; the significantly named old maid, Miss Mann, who owns a "formidable eye for one of the softer sex," turns upon Robert Moore a "gaze" "equal to . . . Medusa['s]" and upon Caroline Helstone a dread "Gorgon gaze."[23] Although Mlle Zoraide apparently finds Crimsworth's gaze fascinating, she gazes back at the professor in *The Professor* with what he thinks is a clear desire for mastery. Early in the novel, Crimsworth fears the gazing directress seeks to "find some chink, some niche, where she could put in her little firm foot and stand upon my neck" (89). Bronte's male narrator fears the power of women and interprets that power as castrating, just as Freud later feared and interpreted.

The female voyeur surreptitiously usurps masculine power when she is spectator instead of spectacle. Mme Beck demands her teachers maintain no private desires: she searches Lucy's drawers for telltale signs of her love for Dr. John; she reads Lucy's letters to see if they signify desire. Lucy laughs bitterly after secretly watching Mme Beck look through her locked drawers and workboxes, her symbolic female spaces. Lucy knows herself "loverless and inexpectant of love" and therefore "safe from spies in [her] heart-poverty."[24] She refuses in this scene of peeper spying on voyeur to instigate the reciprocating look between herself and Mme Beck which would sweep away disguise between the two women. When Mme "borrows" her letters from Dr. John, Lucy ignores Mme's surveillance; she finds the "steady contemplative gaze" not "at all malevolent," for she has mutilated her own powerful desires and cannot be found out. The French word Bronte quotes and then assimilates into her own language, "surveillance," perfectly defines spying in *Villette:* it disciplines while watching desire, makes a fetish of the letter that ironically signifies not desire but its lack (250-53).

Lucy and Mme Beck identify a problem Charlotte Bronte poses throughout her narrative project. How does a woman's desire inscribe power? How does she achieve mastery or self-mastery? How does a woman write the story that recounts such desire and its various masteries?

To begin an answer to these questions, I would like to look at Bronte's repeated subject matter: a woman's desire and its object, the figurative father.

Presence, Absence, and the Punishing Father

"You fear in the presence of a man and a brother—or father, or master, or what you will—to smile too gaily, speak too freely, or move too quickly: but in time, I think you will learn to be natural with me, as I find it impossible to be conventional with you."
—*Charlotte Bronte,* Jane Eyre

Rochester's words to Jane Eyre define their relationship literally as master and servant, metaphorically as father and daughter. Like Caroline Vernon, who desires her legal father, Jane—and other Brontean heroines—desire figurative fathers. Shirley Keeldar hopes to marry a man capable of mastering her; the otherwise passive Caroline Helstone flirts with the fatherly Mr. Hall. In *Villette,* however, Bronte represents the literal father-daughter relationship as implicitly seductive. In a scene paradigmatic to Bronte's narrative career, Polly Home serves her father tea; she, like so many Victorian literary daughters, sits at her papa's feet. "Be near me, as if we were at home, papa," Polly pleads, intercepting his teacup so she can herself add sugar and cream to his liking. Polly later sits by her father's elbow and hems a handkerchief for him to take on his travels; her daughterly sewing metaphorically defines the desire between father and daughter. Polly "bored perseveringly [at the hem] with a needle, that in her fingers seemed almost a skewer, pricking herself ever and anon, marking the cambric with a track of minute red dots; occasionally starting when the perverse weapon—swerving from her control—inflicted a deeper stab than usual; but still silent, diligent, absorbed, womanly" (14). The "perverse weapon," the pricking masculine needle, injures the child, who, little-womanly, submits with silent satisfaction.

Lucy Snowe, the novel's as yet unnamed narrator, observes both these iconographic scenes of desire and comments upon them with condescension. She thinks Polly Home a "little busybody"; she reports the narrative action but coldly watches and judges and so distances the reader from the rather raw desire these scenes present. When Polly asks Mr. Home to kiss her, Lucy writes, "He kissed her. I wished she would utter some hysterical cry, so that I might get relief and be at ease. . . . She seemed to have got what she wanted—*all* she wanted, and to be in a trance of content. . . . She nestled against him, and though neither looked at nor spoke to the other for an hour following, I suppose both were satisfied" (13). By virtue of her spectating, snowy-cold narrator, Bronte both admits and denies desire between father and daughter. Lucy's disapproving yet metaphorically orgasmic language demonstrates both Bronte's conventional representation and complex transgression of that representation of love between father and daughter. If Polly cries out in her progress toward her satisfied trance of content, Lucy Snowe—the surprising subject of this emotional grammar—will obtain relief; the spectator, despite her disapproval of this intense desire, experiences a vicarious joy and release in the witness of it.

Figurative versions of this scene appear throughout Bronte's narratives. Jane Eyre's master pronounces himself "old enough to be [her] father";[25] when Jane announces her engagement to Rochester to the housekeeper, Mrs. Fairfax acts, like Lucy Snowe, as the disapproving observer. Her displeasure rests firmly on her perception of the differences between Rochester's and Jane's positions, fortunes, and ages: "He might almost be your father," she observes with bewilderment, as Jane denies the resemblance between Rochester and her own father and so misreads as literal Mrs. Fairfax's metaphor for the master-as-father (233). Jane desires this figurative father because his authority thrills her: "My master's colourless, olive face, square, massive brow, broad and jetty eyebrows, deep eyes, strong features, firm, grim mouth,—all energy, decision, will—were not beautiful, according to rule; but they were more than beautiful to me: they were full of an interest, an influence that quite mastered me,—that took my feelings from my own power and fettered them in his" (218). The master who is a figurative father owns the power to dominate and fetter, to approve and punish Jane with his presence at Thornfield or his absence. Jane Eyre, like Caroline Vernon, finds this alluring combination impossible to resist: her master masters her.[26]

Shirley Keeldar, like Jane Eyre, desires to marry an authoritative man who, like Rochester, unites the approving and chastising roles of a master who resembles a father: "Did I not say I prefer a *master*? One in whose presence I shall feel obliged and disposed to be good. One whose control my impatient temper must acknowledge. A man whose approbation can reward—whose displeasure punish me. A man I shall feel it impossible not to love, and very possible to fear" (627). Whereas *Jane Eyre* defines the figurative father as the governess's "master," *Shirley* defines him as teaching "master" and "master" of the factory hands. In fact, when Shirley Keeldar first appears in the narrative, the reader assumes with Caroline Helstone that Shirley loves Robert Moore, master of the mill in the hollow. But Shirley Keeldsar, Esq., owns the mill and so is *his* "master." Accordingly, the narrative later reveals that Shirley loves Robert's brother, look-alike, and narrative double, "like and unlike,—Robert, and no Robert" (465). Louis Moore, Shirley's cousin Henry's "master," was also once her tutor and schoolroom "master." The strong-willed and masculine-named Shirley finds her longed-for master in Louis and, like Polly, sits humbly "at his feet" while "tast[ing] a charm" in her lowly position (526). Shirley's uncle, like Mrs. Fairfax and Lucy Snowe, is the disapproving spectator of this prospective union between the wealthy, aristocratic Shirley and her impoverished tutor-cousin. The Victorian term "master" includes these multiple significations of political and educational position and of class difference and is the central term in Bronte's texts. The master-servant intersubjective structure is based on power, upon the dialectics of dominance and submission: this master signifies the law and invariably possesses the attributes of a punishing father.

The master-servant or figurative father-daughter relationship in Bronte's novels has been called by many critics "masochistic." Terry Eagleton and Helene Moglen, for example, both define the sexual relationships in Bronte's novels as "sadomasochistic."[27] Eagleton states provocatively, "Submission is good, but only up to a point, and it is that point which Charlotte Bronte's novels explore"; although Bronte's heroines "habitually welcome male domination as a stimulant to their fiery natures, . . . despotism would be merely oppressive."[28] Whereas Eagleton takes a primarily political perspective on such relationships of power and punishment, Moglen assumes a psychological one. Moglen is remarkably emotionally involved with her subject and seems both sympathetic toward and repelled by the masochism she perceives as the dominant mode of Bronte's experience and of her fiction. Bronte, Moglen believes, "had to examine the scars of confrontation on her own masochistic personality, replacing rationalization with reason. This was to be her personal and artistic goal. It provided the motivating force and the form of her fictions."[29] The cruel combination of sadism and masochism which unsettles these and other critics of Bronte's work takes shape, as Eagleton demonstrates, in the social structures of capitalism and, as Moglen shows, in the individual personality as shaped by relationships in the family. Concepts of the social and individual can be linked, however, only by examining structures of desire in the nineteenth-century family.

I would like to recall the "pricking" and "perverse weapon" which is "almost a skewer" in the girlish hands of Polly Home. The phallic needle penetrates the feminine handkerchief, which is bled upon by the little fingers of the girl who creates this gift for her papa. This act as figure of desire in the father-daughter relationship identifies the daughter not necessarily as "masochistic"—although willingly hurting herself—but primarily as attempting to please her father. Although aside from Mr. Home literal fathers are virtually absent from Bronte's narratives, this scene between Polly and her papa demonstrates that what critics often identify as masochism in Bronte's fiction we may interpret as the structural repetitions and transformations of the father-daughter bond, its figurative pleasings and self-hurts, its gratifications and concomitant punishments. For Bronte, Jane, and Lucy narrate a representative female mythology about desire and punishment in the nineteenth-century patriarchal family and within a phallocentric ideology the privileged intersubjective structure of which is the relationship of father and daughter.

An evocative scene of a daughter's fantasy in *Shirley* confirms this link among paternity, desire, and punishment. The scene begins as Caroline Hilstone breakfasts with her uncle and meditates upon his cynical view of marriage; suddenly, as in a vision, the figure of her dead father appears beside her uncle's—a shape "dim, sinister, scarcely earthly." In Caroline's resulting "dark recollection," her father locks her alone in a room with only a bare, uncurtained bed for furniture; he deprives her of food and comes home at night a madman or an imbecile; Caroline falls ill, and her father threatens to kill her; her screams bring help, and after she is rescued from him, Caroline never sees her father again until she looks upon him in his coffin (114-15). This remarkable trancelike scene associates the father with both seduction and punishment. The garret room represents, like the bowers of the novelettes, a symbolic feminine space; the bed centers the scene spatially and emotionally; events between father and daughter occur at night; and the mad father raves and the daughter falls ill, both metaphors for desire in Bronte's narratives.[30] In this scene, the father verbally abuses and eventually threatens to kill his daughter: Caroline is metaphorically a battered child.

In his essay "A Child Is Being Beaten," Freud articulates desire and punishment with the father-daughter relationship.[31] Freud's predominantly female subjects in this study relate a childhood fantasy with the phrase, "a child is being beaten." In a first phase of the fantasy, the subject comes to recognize the figure who beats the child as her father and then relates the fantasy as "my father is beating the child." In a second phase of the fantasy—a phase never remembered but constructed in analysis by interpretation—the subject accepts the child as herself: "I am being beaten by my father." In the third and final phase, which the subject recalls as occurring in her later childhood, a child among other children watches while someone beats an unknown child: "a child is being beaten." Freud interprets this fantasy as "connected with the incestuous wishes" and as "justified by the persistence of those wishes in the unconscious"; it originates in the struggles of the Oedipus complex and expresses erotic love for the father.

The three phases of this fantasy, Freud also believes, signify different versions of a daughter's love for her father. The subject hates the child who is beaten in the first phase and interprets that child as taking the father's love away from herself; this phase, then, signifies "My father does not love this other child, *he only loves me.*" This early love is jealous and possessive. The father is present in the first phase of the fantasy and the subject is absent. In the second phase both father and daughter are present, and the beating signifies a fantasied substitute for sexual desire of father by daughter as well as punishment for that desire. This phase links all elements of the fantasy, is repressed because its material is dangerous, and so appears only in the language of the unconscious. Being beaten, according to Freud, "signifies a deprivation of love and a humiliation." The daughter desires her father's love and finds herself humiliated by his expression of love or by his rejection of her love. This phase of the fantasy may also signify masochism; the daughter turns her humiliation against herself and sees the father's chastisement as proof or sign of his love and her guilt. In the third phase of the fantasy, the father is absent and the subject-child is an onlooker; the figure who beats the child is a "representative of the father" and comes from the "class of fathers"—a "teacher" or other "person in authority." When the fantasy undergoes transformation and the phase that links desire and punishment is repressed, the child watches the father-substitute punish some other child who is invariably a boy. Although punishment has been displaced onto a child of the opposite gender, the child protects herself from the humiliations and deprivations of love for the father by imagining herself and the father absent from this fantasy, by displacing herself as subject as well as the father as object of her love.

What critics call "masochism" in Bronte's novels, then, we may interpret as stories about the female fantasy in a patriarchal and phallocentric culture, "I am being beaten by my father." The scene in which Caroline remembers her father bears the traces of a fantasy: Caroline experiences this memory in a virtual trance; the figure of the father appears almost as a ghost, as a "shape" across a "wide and deep chasm"; she has seen this vision before—it is a fantasy that recurs (79). This fantasy also appears in various guises throughout Bronte's fiction. The presence of the uncle in Caroline's fantasy about her father links it to Jane Eyre's well-known experience in the red-room. Elements similar to those Caroline remembers appear in Jane's fantasy that her Uncle Reed comes to her in the dark chamber in which he died and in which he and his wife once slept. As Elaine Showalter has demonstrated, the scene in which Jane is punished for rebellion by Mrs. Reed begins with the trappings of sadism and masochism: Bessie and Miss Abbot threaten to tie Jane down with garters—a "preparation for bonds." In that room filled with what Showalter calls symbolic female spaces—secret drawers, wardrobes, jewel-caskets—Jane understands her humiliation: her role is as family pariah. As night falls, she sees a light penetrate the room and thinks the beam a herald of vision; she hears the rushing of wings and is oppressed and suffocated by something near her. She thinks a ghost of her Uncle

Reed has come to console her and to punish those who have punished her (9-16). Jane and the reader learn later in the novel why Jane is punished by her aunt and cast out of her surrogate family: her Aunt Reed resents the affection her husband bestows on the orphan who was born to his sister. Jane's fantasy in the red-room that her uncle consoles while her rival aunt punishes her defines this hallucinated scene as one of displaced desire. Jane desperately needs love from the uncle who once loved her, the uncle who stood in the place of a father, and her desire causes her subsequent haunting and punishment. This trancelike scene in which figurative father and daughter are linked by desire and punishment structures Jane's narrative relationships with Rochester and St. John, causes her desperate search for love and family, and underlies the social relationships in which, as Showalter again points out, women punish other women as the agents of men: Miss Temple for Brocklehurst, Grace Poole for Rochester, Mrs. Reed to avenge her son.[32]

In the three scenes from *Villette*, *Jane Eyre*, and *Shirley* I have discussed, a daughter is punished by or because of or willingly hurts herself for a father or uncle. Polly pricks herself as sign of love for (and by) her father; Caroline imagines her humiliating life with her father while breakfasting with her uncle; Jane wishes her uncle to comfort her, a fatherless daughter who is punished by her rival for her uncle's affection. This intertextual structure links father and daughter in a fantasy of desire and punishment which transgresses the limits even of romance narrative. As such, these iconographic moments resemble the unconscious and repressed material in Freud's exposition of the father-daughter bond. The fantasy of being beaten by the father — verbally or sexually abused and gratified — represents the daughter's humiliation and deprivation at the hands of the father she loves. As Freud points out, this desire becomes conscious only through the language of the unconscious, by linguistic transformation and narrative interpretation. For while Bronte's stories, like the fantasy "I am being beaten by my father," often displace father and daughter, they also tap through language and narrative structure that potentially violent desire in the oedipal family.

I have said this fantasied scene signifies a deprivation of love and a humiliation. Bronte's narratives also appear clearly to link deprivation not only with paternal punishment but also with the father's absence. For the father inevitably abandons his daughter in Bronte's texts. Jane's father dies, and her uncle follows. The scene in which Polly Home sews a gift for her father is immediately followed by his leave-taking. Before his departure, father and daughter speak quietly to one another in a window recess. Although her father promises to return to his Polly, the daughter will endure many more abandonments, as the calmly spectating and disapproving Lucy Snowe correctly conjectures. Polly cries out, "Papa!"

as her father departs, and Lucy rightly interprets her cry as signifying, "Why hast thou forsaken me?" (18-19). In the biblical light of Lucy's phrase, the abandoning father becomes a figure for a withdrawing god.

Narrative structure in Bronte's texts repeatedly enacts this paternal departure, absence, deprivation, and punishment. The narrative structures of the novelettes, for example, consist almost solely of Zamorna's departures from and arrivals at the houses in which his mistresses and wife reside at his pleasure. Because he has so many "easy loves," as Winifred Gérin terms them, he must always leave one scene of desire for another. Indeed, in *Passing Events,* Zamorna rejects his wife, Mary Percy; in *Julia,* he visits Louisa Danci at Evesham; in *Mina Laury,* he leaves his wife and visits Mina Laury; in *Caroline Vernon,* Caroline Vernon journeys to Freetown to be with Zamorna and agrees to become another in the long line of mistresses. Throughout the novelettes, women wait for Zamorna, bemoaning his "Absence — Coldness — total neglect," yet waiting for the presence that defines themselves, their "destinies." Like Lucy Snowe, Mina Laury identifies this presence as godlike: "No tongue could express [my feelings for Zamorna] — they were so fervid, so glowing in their colour that they effaced everything else — I lost the power of properly appreciating the value of the world's opinion, of discerning the difference between right & wrong"; Zamorna, she cries, is "more to me than a human being — he superseded all things. . . . — Unconnected with him my mind would be a blank"; with Zamorna she feels "as weak as a child — she lost her identity — her very way of life was swallowed up in that of another"; she "could no more feel alienation from him than she could from herself" (147, 165, 143). Zamorna represents the transcendental figure of masterful male presence par excellence: he effaces Mina's identity yet renders her life full, connected, a plenitude.

Shirley Keeldar's allegorical narrative of "The First Blue-Stocking" likewise imagines the radiant presence of a heavenly lord to his earthly "handmaiden." The heroine of Shirley's devoir about primitive, tribal life has been deprived of both parents; no one cares for her, feeds or shelters her; she exists "forsaken, lost, and wandering" and lives in hollow trees or chill caverns. Deprived of nurture and love, this lonely girl listens to the profound stillness and hears a deep-voiced oracle call her name:

> "Lord!" she cried, "behold thine handmaid! . . . Lord, come quickly!"
> The Evening flushed full of hope: the Air panted; the Moon — rising before — ascended large, but her light showed no shape.
> "Lean towards me, Eva. Enter my arms; repose thus."
> "Thus, I lean, O Invisible, but felt! And what art thou?" . . .
> "I take from thy vision, darkness: I loosen from thy faculties, fetters! I level in thy path, obstacles: I, with my presence, fill vacancy. . . ."

That Presence, invisible, but mighty, gathered her in like a lamb to the fold; that voice, soft but all pervading, vibrated through her heart like music. Her eye received no image; and yet a sense visited her vision and her brain as of the serenity of stainless air, the power of sovereign seas, the majesty of marching stars, the energy of colliding elements, the rooted endurance of hills wide-based, and, above all, as of the lustre of heroic beauty rushing victorious on the Night, vanquishing its shadows like a diviner Sun. (551-53.)

Shirley's allegorical essay marries Genius and Humanity and climaxes with this rhetoric of desire: the flushing evening, the panting air, the rising moon. The language desires a lordly presence, a voice that speaks comfort, and arms that embrace. Vacancy is filled. Nostalgia for the lost father becomes cosmic. This allegory of lord and handmaiden is a metaphor for the larger intersubjectivities in Bronte's narratives, for the figurative language of sexual relation as desired presence of the sultan, master, feudal lord, captain, king, mentor, and father to the members of a harem, slaves, vassals, lieutenants, worshipers, and children. Just as Eva desires the presence of her "lord," Mina desires her king, Jane her master, Shirley her tutor, Lucy her mentor. Bronte's narratives acknowledge the absence of this figurative paternal figure, yet they nonetheless imaginatively attempt to make him omnipotent and present to the desiring daughter. Rochester, for example, calls Jane to "his presence," and she fears to be exiled from its "sunshine" (248).

This masterful and lordly figure is Freud's paternal "representative." A "representative" is characteristic or typical, stands for others, and depends upon resemblance to that which it represents. In Bronte's narratives, the paternal "representative," a teacher or figure of authority from the class of fathers, not only stands in for the father whom he resembles but differs from him as well. The master is and is not the figurative father. His presence to the woman who desires him replaces the lost presence of the absent father and therefore confirms the father's original presence as a plenitude, as a presence that needs no addition and effaces difference. In this sense, the presence of the "master" in Bronte's fiction attempts to accumulate plenitude, to recover to the adult desiring daughter that childish experience of the father as all-encompassing voice, as all-gathering embrace about which Shirley Keeldar writes in her devoir and which the narrative recalls when Louis Moore recites its text. At the same time, however, the presence of the master at the end of Bronte's novels also confirms while attempting to overcome the father's absence. Jacques Derrida calls this paradoxical overcoming and inscribing of absence by presence the "economy of the supplement." He examines Rousseau's desire for maternal presence: "This presence is at the same time desired and feared. The supplement transgresses and at the same time respects the interdict" against desire.[33] Like the ambiguous figure who disapproves while witnessing desire, Bronte's narrative supplementation of the father allows her heroines to enjoy yet deny the desired presence of the father.

Villette defines Graham Bretton as Papa Home's supplement before his departure. Graham asks Polly one evening why she waits up late. Has she been waiting for him? No, she demurs, for papa. Graham returns, "Very good, Miss Home. I am going to be a favourite: preferred before papa soon, I dare say." Graham then suddenly lifts Polly over his head, while the spectating Lucy comments that "the suddenness, the freedom, the disrespect of the action were too much." Lucy refuses to say what "too much" signifies, but the reader infers from the action that it signifies both an invasion of bodily privacy and an analogue of an action allowed only to papa. For during his stay at Mrs. Bretton's, Mr. Home "frequently lift[s Polly] to his knee" (15-16). Graham's action indeed proves prophetic: Polly almost immediately begins breakfasting with Graham tête à tête and serving him tea as she once served papa. In return, Graham promises Polly a permanent role as his housekeeper. Polly thinks her entire being defined by Graham's presence; Lucy Snowe, the calm spectator, scoffs at the desire for this plenitude which Bronte's narrators once endorsed: "With curious readiness did [Polly] adapt herself to such themes as interested him. One would have thought the child had no mind or life of her own, but must necessarily live, move, and have her being in another: now that her father was taken from her, she nestled to Graham, and seemed to feel by his feelings: to exist in his existence" (21-22). The godlike supplement has so completely overwhelmed Polly's affections that when her father directs her to join him in his travels, Polly wants only to stay with Graham. He whispers, "Polly, you care for me more than for papa, now—"

If the father-supplement kisses and fondles the daughter as did the father, however, he can also hurt and humiliate her as did the father. One day Graham refuses to play with Polly, who therefore becomes stone-faced and silent. Later, "Little Mousie" lies on the carpet "at his feet," and Graham unknowingly kicks her with his foot; she "caress[es] the heedless foot" (23, 27). Lucy thinks Polly fondles Graham in a "strangely rash" and "heedless" fashion and therefore risks repulse worse than a blow. The calm spectator of desire understands the "shocks and repulses, the humiliations and desolations" desire necessarily incurs. As Lucy imagines, the economy of the supplement creates all male-female relationships as displacements of father-daughter desire.

Lucy Snowe's own ambivalent desire defines the economy of the supplement in language. When Dr. John's first letter arrives at the pensionnat, it nourishes Lucy's love: "There was a fulness of delight in this taste of fruition," a taste of sweet "honey-dew," and "elixir" that seems the "juice of a divine vintage." Lucy believes the "cordial core of the delight" in this letter, that Dr. John writes it not only to please her but to "gratify *himself.*" His pleasure in the writing provides Lucy a fulfilled moment in which the letter becomes supplement: "This present moment had no pain, no blot, no want; full, pure, perfect, it deeply blessed me" (195, 216, 209-10). The letter inscribes the fullness of desire yet also prophesies its absence. Lucy's autobiography anticipates abandonment and punishment by men, and the reader understands it does so because Lucy foresees future events by virtue of her perspective as retrospective narrator. Lucy's description of the letter not only recalls her delight and feeling of fullness or nourishment but forecasts her inevitable rejection by and of Dr. John. The presence of the letter inscribes future absence; the writing that attempts to overcome separation will cease with a more permanent separation. In response, Lucy writes two letters: she destroys the letter signifying desire and sends the curt one reason dictates.

The structures I have traced of presence and absence, of supplementation, and of female desire, punishment, and self-punishment as narratively linked to the father appear not only in Bronte's novels but in her biography as well. The central figure in Bronte's imaginative confrontation with her own experience is not Branwell, as Winifred Gérin and Helene Moglen argue, but her father.[34] The death of Charlotte's mother when she was six and the later deaths of her sisters Maria and Elizabeth clearly focused the family structure on Patrick Bronte, who withdrew into reclusion in dismay at the demands he perceived a family of small children would make on him.[35] His grief and loneliness explain at least to some extent his withdrawal: "For the first three months [of Mrs. Bronte's long illness] I was left nearly quite alone, unless you suppose my six little children and the nurse and servants to have been company. . . . Tender sorrow was my daily portion; that oppressive grief sometimes lay heavy on me and [an] agonizing *something* sickened my whole frame. . . . And when my dear wife was dead and buried and gone, and when I missed her at every corner, and when her memory was hourly revived by the innocent yet distressing prattle of my children, . . . I was happy at the recollection that to sorrow, not as those without hope, was no sin" (*Lives,* 1: 58-59). Since Elizabeth Gaskell mythologized him as a tyrant, on the word of a dismissed servant, the figure of Patrick Bronte has been vilified and—the current trend—domesticated.[36] All we know about the father, however, we know from Bronte's imaginings: his paradoxical absence and hovering presence somewhere in the godlike upper stories of the parsonage. When the mother disappeared, the loving father followed. Bronte's fiction plays out the drama of an attempt to recover, to make present through writing, this loved and supportive, this eccentric—perhaps overbearing—father who withdrew, who sent his daughters away to Cowan's Bridge school, who added to rather than healed the void in their experience.

The father's absence also constituted Branwell, Patrick Bronte's namesake and only son, his supplement. If the father's absence signified a deprivation of love to the young and needy daughter, the brother's presence signified a clear humiliation, a punishment not unlike that meted out to the spectating daughter in the third phase of Freud's study of female desire and self-punishment. For Charlotte Bronte's first father-supplement acted out with Lydia Robinson the sexual temptation Charlotte herself so perseverantly resisted with M. Héger. In her letters after Branwell's return to Haworth, Bronte punished him for daring to express the desire she repressed. "To papa he allows rest neither day nor night," she wrote Ellen Nussey; "he is continually screwing money out of him, sometimes threatening that he will kill himself if it is withheld from him. . . . He will do nothing, except drink and make us all wretched" (*Lives*, 2: 96-97). This well-known letter expresses not only anger at Branwell, but surreptitiously at the father for what Bronte perceived as his permissive complicity in Branwell's slow destruction of the family. For while Charlotte vilified Branwell, Patrick Bronte cared patiently for the son, allowing him to sleep in his own room during the final two years of drugs and decline and later idealizing him to Elizabeth Gaskell as "my brilliant and unhappy son" while excoriating Mrs. Robinson as "his diabolical seducer."[37]

M. Héger also resembles the father-supplement, the teacher from the class of fathers in the daughter's fantasy of desire and punishment. And M. Héger, the "father who *persists* in the shape of a teacher" (italics mine), is no more present and available to fulfill the girl's desire than was the literal father. Bronte's desire for the mentor and "master" supplemented her desire for the father and necessarily built into her life another inevitable self-hurt, a chosen rebuff or punishment. As Helene Moglen says, "Hers was not an adulterous wish denied, but rather one which was repressed and never fully confronted"; the relationship "provided an appropriate outlet for Bronte's masochistic tendencies. How else can one explain the extraordinary passivity which allowed her to remain for months in a humiliating situation, not simply unable to fight her dependence upon her 'maitre' but consistently constructing circumstances that would support and intensify that dependence?"[38] Indeed, when the professor and his wife understood Bronte's feelings, M. Héger withdrew from her emotionally. When Bronte left Belgium for the second and final time in 1842, she could neither bear nor fail to recognize the withdrawal that caused M. Héger to stop answering her letters. His letters, like Dr. John's in *Villette*, signified to their hungry receiver the presence of the master's love; their cessation signified its absence, the rebuff the spectating Lucy Snowe comes to expect from all males. Bronte's pleas for a resumed correspondence implicitly recognized the economy of the supplement.

Day and night I find neither rest nor peace. If I sleep I am disturbed by tormenting dreams in which I see you, always severe, always grave, always incensed against me.

Forgive me then, Monsieur, if I adopt the course of writing to you again. How can I endure life if I make no effort to ease its sufferings? . . .

All I know is that I cannot, that I will not resign myself to lose wholly the friendship of my master (*Lives,* 2: 23.)

. . . .

I have been able to conquer neither my regrets nor my impatience. That, indeed, is humiliating—to be unable to control one's own thoughts, to be the slave of a regret, of a memory, the slave of a fixed and dominant idea which lords it over the mind. Why cannot I have just as much friendship for you, as you for me—neither more nor less? Then should I be so tranquil, so free—I could keep silence then for ten years without an effort. . . . Your last letter was stay and prop to me—nourishment to me for half a year. Now I need another. (*Lives,* 2: 70.)

The letter attempts to overcome absence and communicate desire and friendship, but it also confirms absence and inscribes instead humiliation and enslavement, rejection and punishment. The master appears in Bronte's reported dreams as a figure of chastisement: his silence punishes her, as her own must also punish her. The second letter from which I quote is the last extant letter from Bronte to M. Héger; its admission that the pupil desires the teacher more than he cares for her confirms Bronte's future punishment and her own silence.

During this same time, Bronte coped with the failure of her school for girls, the failing eyesight of her father, and the decline of her brother. All three events conspired to keep her at home. Bronte became increasingly close to the father she found impossible to leave—to visit friends, to become a governess, to start her school for girls. In a letter to Elizabeth Gaskell, Mary Taylor recounted a talk she had with Bronte about her refusal to leave home:

She told me she had quite decided to stay at home. She owned she did not like it. Her health was weak. She said she would like any change at first, as she had liked Brussels at first, and she thought that there must be some possibility for some people of having a life of more variety and more communion with human kind, but she saw none for her. I told her very warmly, that she ought not to stay at home; that to spend the next five years at home, in solitude, and weak health, would ruin her; that she would never recover it. Such a dark shadow came over her face when I said, "Think of what you'll be in five years hence!" that I stopped, and said, "Don't cry, Charlotte!" She did not cry, but went on walking up and down the room, and said in a little while, "But I intend to stay, Polly." (*Lives,* 2: 26.)

The decision to stay home centered, of course, on her father, and the relationship grew closer as Mr. Bronte's eyesight grew markedly worse and he became dependent on his daughter.[39] At this time, Charlotte responded to Ellen Nussey's invitation to spend a fortnight with her: "It is quite out of the question. . . . I feel reluctant indeed to leave papa for a single day" (*Lives,* 2: 38). As Anne noted in her diary-paper at about the same time, Charlotte longed to go to Paris but did not; she went instead with her father for his eye operation and nursed him back to health afterward (*Lives,* 2: 52).

The father-daughter relationship culminated in the protracted and well-known battle between Charlotte and Patrick over Arthur Bell Nicholls, whom Charlotte eventually married. Charlotte first reported to Ellen Nussey, "Papa's vehement antipathy to the bare thought of any one thinking of me as a wife" (*Lives,* 4: 30) and later his antipathy to Nicholls in particular, so severe Charlotte could not mention his name to her father. When Patrick found it hard to replace the resigned curate, he finally gave in to the engagement, although he would later refuse the day before the wedding to give his daughter away in church. Moreover, Charlotte stipulated to Nicholls that she "would not leave Papa" (*Lives,* 4: 112), that Nicholls would move into Haworth parsonage with his bride and her father after the wedding, and that Nicholls would take care of Patrick until *his* death should Charlotte die before her husband—a bargain Nicholls faithfully kept.

While Bronte's marriage appears to reestablish the oedipal triangle, the economy of the supplement operated in this family structure as it did earlier in Bronte's life and in her texts. In his professional position of dependence before the marriage and caretaking role after it, Nicholls resembled a son; at Haworth parsonage, he appeared to replace Branwell in the family and so transform the role that son once occupied. Yet Nicholls in fact supplemented Branwell in the oedipal family: he appeared in Branwell's metaphorical place, but was not Branwell. His presence at Haworth recalls Branwell's presence while at the same time it signifies his absence. Nicholls, then, supplements a supplement for the father and so appears a tautological figure who defines the risk of supplementation while enacting its process. Supplementing the father in life and texts must inevitably fail as an effort to recall paternal plenitude and presence, because the doubling or repetition of the supplement confirms absence. Moreover, Patrick Bronte appears to have fulfilled Charlotte Bronte's lifelong desire for the father's presence in this metaphorically oedipal family. Yet the economy of the supplement undercuts this structure of desire. The oedipal family depends upon the father's presence and power as well as his desire for his daughter; while Charlotte's marriage to Nicholls appears to have confirmed paternal presence—she got her father back—it also accused the father of his old absence while attempting to cover it over. Patrick Bronte was still Charlotte's father, but he had lost the authority and power of a father and was now dependent upon his daughter and ultimately upon her husband, his metaphorical son and supplement, for life.

The economy of the supplement disturbs configurations of desire in the oedipal family through the operation of deferral. It guarantees that while seeking gratification of her desire for paternal presence, the supplementing daughter will discover frustration alongside, or instead of, fulfillment. The economy of the supplement in Bronte's life and texts entails repetition of the father-supplement and so becomes tautological. Such redundancy declares the failure of oedipal desire while it attempts to reestablish its pleasures; exposes the daughter's desire and the father's presence as unfruitful while attempting to satisfy both in a secondary way. The tautology of Bronte's father-supplements not only exposes oedipal desire as redundant but blurs the intersubjective structure that desire creates. Desired and powerful father, metaphorical son, and daughter are also dependent and powerless father, husband, and wife. The difference between the two structures, one remembered, the other deferred and nostalgic, constitutes the terrible irony of the daughter's desire for her father, an irony lived out not only by Charlotte Bronte, but by many late-marrying Victorian daughters with widower fathers. Bronte, however, could write about it.

Castration, Sexual Difference, and the Female Imaginary

"Ah! By my word! there is something singular about you," said [Rochester]: "you have the air of a little nonnette; quaint, quiet, grave, and simple, as you sit with your hands before you." — Charlotte Bronte, Jane Eyre

Jane Eyre's autobiographical narrative asserts that she leaves Rochester because she must: the lovers cannot legally marry, and if Jane remains with Rochester as his mistress, she fears he will tire of her. Yet if we trace the interrupted wedding back to its narrative source, we find it in Jane herself. As the wedding approaches and Jane senses disaster, Rochester guiltily cries, "God pardon me . . . and man meddle not with me." Jane responds, "There is no one to meddle, sir. I have no kindred to interfere" (321). Jane's consolatory statement appears innocent enough: it implicitly assumes marriage must be approved by a bride's family if she has one. Yet this statement, almost a *non sequitur* and a bit uncanny on second reading, signifies something in addition to conjugal convention. When Rochester forces Jane to think of herself as Jane Rochester—a person different from her "gray" self, Jane thinks—and attempts to dress her in silks, the figurative language of master and governess identifies Jane as "enslaved," as member of a harem, and "kept" woman. Unlike Mina Laury, Jane resents such metaphors, such sexual politics, and decides to transform the relationship that implicitly takes its tropes from dominance and submission: she will "mutiny." "It would, indeed, be a relief," she thinks, "if I had ever so small an independency; I never can bear being dressed like a doll by Mr. Rochester. . . . I will write to Madeira the moment I get home, and tell my uncle John I am going to be married, and to whom: if I had but a prospect of one day bringing Mr. Rochester an accession of fortune, I could better endure to be kept by him now" (338). Jane assures us parenthetically that she executed this decision the next day.

This curious passage makes assumptions that conflict directly with Jane's assertion that she has no kindred to interfere with her wedding. In fact, the proposal scene occurs immediately following Jane's return to Thornfield from Gateshead, where her dying Aunt Reed has told her about Uncle John in Madeira. Jane's sudden decision to write this uncle who thinks her dead hedges her dependency upon Rochester; despite her willed assertion that she writes her uncles to provide Rochester a fortune with herself as conduit, she writes her uncle to provide herself an "independency"—the rhetorical combination of fortune and self-mastery Jane achieves at the end of her narrative. Although, then, this detail may appear merely to serve the complications of plot, it signals Jane's dissatisfaction with the domineering Rochester and her unconscious desire to forestall her marriage.

Although she reports its probable contents, Jane chooses not to copy her letter to Madeira into her autobiographical text. Jane's missing letter to Uncle John, like Lucy's buried letters from Dr. John, signifies in her narrative not by virtue of its message, but, like Lacan's version of Poe's "purloined letter," by the ways it circulates in the text's intersubjective structure of desire.[40] As the personal letter circulates, however, the sender intends the receiver to become sender and herself then to become receiver: the personal letter demands a response.[41] Indeed, Jane's letter serves as long-delayed response to the letter Uncle John wrote years before, offering his niece adoption while he lives and property and fortune when he dies. Jane's response accepts both and demands a response in turn. That response, however, is unexpected: the receiver dies, and two men appear outside the church on Jane's wedding day. Mason and Briggs answer Jane's letter in person and respond to the surreptitious desire she expresses through the circuit of letters in the intersubjective structure of her text's desire: to flee the scene of her marriage. Briggs tells Jane, "When your uncle received your letter intimating the contemplated union between yourself and Mr. Rochester, Mr. Mason, who was staying at Madeira to recruit his health, on his way back to Jamaica, happened to be with him. Mr. Eyre mentioned the intelligence; for he knew that my client here was acquainted with a gentleman of the name of Rochester. Mr. Mason, astonished and distressed, as you may suppose, revealed the real state of matters. Your uncle, I am sorry to say, is now on a sick bed; from which, considering the nature of his disease—decline—and the stage it has reached, it is unlikely he will ever rise" (372). Jane's resulting flight and eventual independence are caused and originated by her letter, by its nature as the signifier of her desire.

Jane wants not only to defer her wedding, however, but to punish Rochester for his domineering and profligate desire. The narrative figure for Jane's unconscious urge to punish her lover appears in the nighttime deeds of Bertha Mason Rochester: Bertha rends the wedding veil Jane will wear the next day; Bertha tries to burn Rochester in his bed; Bertha burns Thornfield to the ground. Indeed, as Peter Grudin demonstrates, the fire and punishment Bertha perpetrates at the end of the novel is forecast by the remarkable outbreak of "fire and violence" Jane experiences in the red-room at its beginning.[42] Jane's dreams just before her wedding day also prophesy the fiery end of Thornfield. When Mrs. Rochester finally falls from the battlements of the Thornfield she burns, the nearly Mrs. Rochester's dream forecast these events, and so figuratively caused them to happen. As Sandra M. Gilbert and Susan Gubar remind us, Bertha's burning of Thornfield and killing of herself, and the consequent maiming of Rochester, are all unconsciously desired by prim Jane and acted out by her nighttime double.[43]

Richard Chase is the first of many critics to read Rochester's punishment and injury as a "symbolic castration."[44] This conventional Freudian interpretation understandably troubles feminist critics of the novel.[45] Yet Rochester is a figurative "Hercules" or "Samson," Jane an implied Delilah (328). Chase calls upon the metaphor of sight to support his theory of "symbolic castration," recalling Freud's belief that a "substitutive relation between the eye and the male organ" exists in "dreams and myths and phantasies"—the language of the unconscious. Blindness, then, signifies castration in Freud's lexicon, just as the gaze signifies male desire. But Freud implies that symbolic castration punishes incestuous desire: "Anxiety about one's eyes, the fear of going blind, is often enough a substitute for the dread of being castrated. The self-blinding of the mythical criminal, Oedipus, was simply a mitigated form of the punishment of castration—the only punishment that was adequate for him."[46] Rochester, like Oedipus, must pay for his metaphorically incestuous desire for the governess by losing his sight. His symbolic castration represents the daughter's surreptitious punishment of the domineering master-father. In the daughterly autobiographical text—Jane's and Bronte's—castration punishes the punishing figurative father and gains the daughter a qualified mastery over him.

As my first section of this chapter suggests, Freud believed that fear of castration persuades the boy to give up desire for his mother and to accept the father's "no" as law. The girl, however, has no penis and therefore cannot fear losing it. In early psychoanalytic parlance, fear of castration terminates the male Oedipus complex while it ushers in the female. Renouncing her identification with another woman, the girl transfers her love to her father, who possesses a penis; according to Freud's nineteenth-century knowledge of anatomy, she changes the aim of her sexuality from active to passive. As Nancy Chodorow demonstrates, however, Freud's theory of castration assumes a girl's fantasy during this period of her personal history as fact: she does not think or imagine herself castrated or think herself an inferior boy: she is so.[47] Castration, like my other Freudian myths of origin in this book, is metaphorical.[48] A girl understands implicitly that the phallus signifies power and desire, and the boy will not let her forget it; she wants that power yet is told she will never possess it. She understands without being told that she participates in structures of power only by being possessed by someone who possesses the phallus.[49] The female Oedipus complex ushers in, with the metaphor of castration, the daughter's dependence upon the father and his approbation, whereas the male complex encourages identification with the father who goes out in the world and so represents independence from the family and the mother. The daughter's dependence upon fathers is supported by a culture which, like the family, is based upon patriarchal ideology; the teacher-pupil relationship in the realm of education, the father-husband exchange of women in marriage, and the position of the subject in language structures all encourage female dependence upon men from the "class of fathers."[50]

Jeanne Lampl-de Groot and other female psychoanalysts contemporary with Freud initiated a revision of his castration theories. Lampl-de Groot believes the woman subject's phrase, "a child is being beaten," may also signify "a child is being castrated." Thus the female—the daughter—fantasizes herself and her representatives being punished by castration. "She is constantly subjecting herself to castration, for this is the necessary condition of being loved by the father; she is making a fresh effort to get clear of her old love-relations [with her mother] and reconcile herself to her womanhood." In spite of its many "punishments, pains and tortures," Lampl-de Groot believes, the fantasy signifies that "passive, feminine love is victorious."[51] Reading from another perspective, however, we might say the fantasy (and Lampl-de Groot's interpretation) signifies acceptance of a typical wound or scar of the female Oedipus complex; its outcome is a woman's sense of inferiority, a devaluation of her own sexuality, and a belief in the rightness of her cultural subordination to men. Only by freeing herself from desiring dependence upon the father and his representatives can a woman enter the cultural world without this scar.

For in this symbolic realm, castration signifies presence or absence of the phallus—or the father, as I imply in the second section of this chapter. Woman is defined in the dominant ideology as lacking the power associated with the phallus. Freud and Lacan equate this female lack with an equation that appears reductive: the subject may "have" or "be" the phallus.[52] The male "is" the phallus, and the female desires to "have" it; to acquire the phallus she lacks, the girl desires (by a symbolic equation of part-objects) to have a child by her father. Lampl-de Groot interprets this equation from a female perspective: the girl affirms her power, which is apart from the male's, to conceive a child and give birth.[53] The boy will envy this power as the girl envies his powers. This "have" or "be" version of either/or thinking, however, merely justifies the symbolic powerlessness of the female as "castrated." Roland Barthes elaborates Freud's and Lacan's ideology by defining phallic symbolism as fourfold rather than dualistic. In his tour de force, *S/Z*, Barthes proposes this libidinal economy of *Sarrasine:* to be the phallus (the male), to have the phallus (the female), to have and be the phallus (the hermaphrodite), neither to have nor be the phallus (the castrate). He goes on to demonstrate, however, that the opposition active/passive (not castrated/castrated) rather than the opposition male/female structures the Balzacian text: "female" does not necessarily equal "passive" and/or "castrated"[54] —which proves the text more inventive than the sexual dualism enforced by phallocentrism and proves sexuality more diverse—circulatory—than culturally accepted binary opposition.

Bronte's narratives accept a phallocentric and signifying dualism yet also seek to question it. Jane implicitly places herself in the position described by Lampl-de Groot as loving the father and so being "castrated." To free herself from such subservience and self-mutilation, Jane's unconscious desires in her autobiographical text must turn that punishment back on the father. Rather than represent herself as castrated, Jane's narrative castrates the father whose love would symbolically "castrate" her. Jane's master must lose his sight because the eye objectifies and masters.[55] Rochester's mastery creates Jane as a spectacle for male desire, a perspective that defines his own superiority and confirms her lack of power and self-authority. Blinding the eye that gazed at and cutting off the hand that grabbed Jane, her narrative renders the symbolic phallus absent and lops off the option to "be" the phallus. For Rochester at Ferndean has become "powerless" and "dependent," while Jane has grown into an "independent woman," "her own mistress" (556-73). Likewise, the "rigid," "black column," that "shaft," Brocklehurst *is* the phallus, and Jane's narrative relishes his punishment by a school full of women as fully as it demands Rochester's (70). The Jane who vacillates between submission and rebellious "fire and violence" turns her anger against domineering masters from the "class of fathers" who define the female as subservient; the master-servant or father-daughter intersubjectivity in Jane's autobiographical narrative punishes with a cruel fantasy of symbolic castration those characters who interpret mastery as a term in a cultural economy of dominance and submission. This writer of her life must neither "have" the phallus nor be mastered by any male who "is" the phallus: the signifier of phallocentric desire, like the letter, "circulates."

Jane's paradoxical anger and submission resemble Charlotte Bronte's. Blinding as a metaphor for symbolic castration, for dependence, impotence, and lack of self-mastery, appears throughout Bronte's letters as in Jane's fictional autobiography. In her letters to M. Héger, Bronte expressed her own sense of castration, her female subordination to her master, and defined herself as impotent in the face of her dependence upon this man from the "class of fathers": "Now my sight is too weak to write.—Were I to write much I should become blind. This weakness of sight is a terrible hinderance to me. Otherwise, do you know what I should do Monsieur?—I should write a book, and I should dedicate it to my literature-master—to the only master I ever had—to you Monsieur" (*Lives,* 2: 13). In writing *Jane Eyre,* Bronte attempted to define yet master that impotence, that symbolic female castration, by turning castration against fictional fathers; metaphorically dedicated to the master, *Jane Eyre* punishes him for his lack of desire by imagining a master who desires too much and must therefore be castrated as punishment. Yet Bronte also feared that writing narrative would reaffirm her own castration, would make herself as author go "blind." Her well-known correspondence with Robert Southey demonstrates her professed acceptance of female subordination and castration in the patriarchal realm of "letters": writing, she agreed, is not fit work for woman.[56] While Bronte agonized about her master, about writing, and about female castration, Patrick Bronte was in fact going blind from cataracts and so becoming dependent upon his daughter. Bronte feared her father's dependency, yet she, like Jane, also wished it to serve as corrective to her own. Bronte, as Jane, wrote a narrative about castration to punish a father and his masterful representatives for the dependence she felt upon them.

Figurative castration of the phallus appears as narrative resolution not only in *Jane Eyre* but in Bronte's other novels as well. William Crimsworth's unmotivated and mysterious shooting of his son's dog at the end of *The Professor* surreptitiously punishes a son too severely spoiled by his mother. However reasonably the narrator explains his violent actions, the narrative also defines them as excessive via the objection of his son. The repeated references to William's mother's portrait and the emotional charge vested by the narrative in Hunsden's procuring it for William imply that Crimsworth attempts to prohibit in his son his own extreme attachment to a mother and to the feminine, an attachment Crimsworth fights throughout his self-fathering autobiography. A similar yet different metaphorical event occurs at the end of *Shirley:* Robert Moore's shooting. Sandra Gilbert and Susan Gubar believe the workers' burning of the mills surreptitiously acts out female anger against Robert Moore and the capitalist patriarchy; on a Sunday march, the walking columns of women meet head-on the columns of men, their doubles, who, by synecdoche for all workers, burn the mill.[57] The workers also shoot Moore immediately after he confesses his pecuniary motives for proposing marriage to Shirley: another synecdochic female assault on the patriarchal capitalist. Moreover, Robert's injury metaphorically resembles Rochester's. Moore becomes "dependent" upon a woman's care, as though he were an infant (640); his nurse, Zillah, thumps him, "knocks him about," eats his food to starve him, and "fall[s] on him tooth and nail" in the process of making the bed. Martin Yorke, who reports the sounds of beating which emerge from the dark room, links this nurse with Caroline Helstone: "It is queer, . . . Zillah Horsfall is a woman, and Caroline Helstone is a woman: they are two individuals of the same species—not much alike though" (650-52). The narrative pointedly, however, asserts their resemblance: Zillah's pummeling and starving of Moore acts out Caroline's repressed anger at and punishment of the man who rejected her. When Martin reunites Caroline and the wounded capitalist, Moore himself describes his injury as a metaphorical castration: "Unmanned as I am," he says, "I have not the power to cope." Although Moore eventually recuperates, in his weakened state he retains "no iron mastery" (664, 677) and so is now worthy of the quiet but caring Caroline.

Bronte's narrative project not only symbolizes castration as a narrative punishment and resolution but also questions phallocentrism and its ideology of the feminine as different or other. To enter the symbolic realm of culture, as I suggested earlier in this chapter, the child must understand sexual difference, this initial "binary opposition." Sexual difference signifies retroactively to the child the menace of castration, the fear of symbolic loss.[58] To the boy: I might lose it. To the girl: I must have lost it. In *Shirley,* Bronte's novel about industrialism and the "woman question," sexual difference, like metaphorical female castration, signifies a woman's impotence and lack of mastery. "Men and women are so different," Caroline tells Shirley; "they are in such a different position. Women have so few things to think about—men so many: you may have a friendship for a man, while he is almost indifferent to you. . . . I should have learned, in a startling manner, the width of the chasm which gaped between such as he and such as I" (256). Caroline implicitly understands that woman is symbolically castrated in a culture that has no use for woman alone, a culture in which man views woman as enigma.[59] The gaps and chasms between woman and man mean each fails to understand the other. Bronte insists the relationship between the sexes is one of misinterpretation and misreading. Shirley declares:

> "If men could see us as we really are, they would be a little amazed; but the cleverest, the acutest men are often under an illusion about women: they do not read them in a true light; they misapprehend them, both for good and evil: their good woman is a queer thing, half doll, half angel; their bad woman almost always a fiend. Then to hear them fall into extasies with each other's creations, worshipping the heroine of such a poem — novel — drama, thinking it fine — divine! Fine and divine it may be, but often quite artificial — false as the rose in my best bonnet there. If I spoke all I think on this point; if I gave my real opinion of some first-rate female characters in first-rate works, where should I be? Dead under a cairn of avenging stones in half an hour." (395-96.)

Shirley defines man's misinterpretation of woman as a feminocentric but duplicitous fiction: the woman as angel and whore, the male reader as assenting to and so dialectically creating the myth of woman in patriarchal literature. Yet although Shirley also insists that "women read men more truly than men read women," Caroline undercuts Shirley's assertion by declaring her learning deficient to make such judgments. Indeed, given Bronte's cardboard male characters in *Shirley,* the reader tends to think Caroline correct about the discourse of a woman who interprets men.

For *Shirley* stacks the deck against men from its first chapter, in which the narrator satirizes the comradery of clerics as babble and rapaciousness.[60] Mr. Helstone reports he married Mary Cave but failed to notice she soon began dying — presumably from lack of attention. The narrator interprets: "He thought, so long as a woman was silent, nothing ailed her, and she wanted nothing. . . . He made no pretence of comprehending women, or comparing them with men; they were a different, probably a very inferior order of existence" (61). Helstone cannot "abide sense in women: he liked to see them as silly, as light-headed, as vain, as open to ridicule as possible; because they were then in reality what he held them to be, and wished them to be, — inferior: toys to play with, to amuse a vacant hour and to be thrown away" (130). The nonrebellious worker and representative of the deserving poor, Joe Scott, hates "petticoat government" and is the novel's outspoken antifeminist.[61] Caroline insists the apparently devout but non-church-attending Scott misinterprets St. Paul's text about woman's place in the creation myth; about Eve as created from Adam's rib, she says, "If I could read the original Greek, I should find that many of the words have been wrongly translated, perhaps misapprehended altogether. It would be possible, I doubt not, with a little ingenuity, to give the passage quite a contrary turn" (371). Giving the text about men and women a contrary turn, Bronte makes the patriarchal Robert Moore confess to Caroline that "men, in general, are a sort of scum" (97). The end of the narrative proves him correct and refuses to allow his insight to spare him from inclusion in his own category. In another scene of male comradery, Mr. Yorke confesses to Moore that had Mary Cave "loved and not scorned" him, had he been "secure of her affection" and "certain of her constancy," he would probably have abandoned her (615). Immediately thereafter, Moore is shot down and so punished not only for his faithlessness to Caroline but for the untrustworthy and inconstant desire of all men. Bronte's rhetoric of sexual difference in *Shirley* generalizes her anger against men from the "class of fathers" to include virtually all men. Whereas narrative structure surreptitiously symbolizes castration as culminating punishment, this representation of sexual difference speaks the writer's rage openly. Yet Bronte's angry insistence upon a dualistic libidinal economy of men versus women renders meaningless her feminist analysis of the dominant phallocentric ideology that necessitates such anger.

Bronte's rhetoric of sexual difference, her narrative castrations, appear to be an exaggerated attempt to free her heroines from dependence upon fathers. Less excessive metaphors and structures, however, achieve the same desired outcome in several of Bronte's narratives. In *Captain Henry Hastings*, for example, Elizabeth Hastings rejects her father for his rejection of Henry, her brother, and so becomes independent of both her male relations. As governess to Verdopolis's wealthiest families, Elizabeth lives "dependent on nobody—responsible to nobody" (243). Although she longs for home and for the times when she "had been her Brother's & her fathers favourite," she refuses to return to her childhood home and her father. She also refuses to become William Percy's mistress. Elizabeth learns a lesson from the female epigrammatism inscribed on Zamorna's mistress' tombstone, a lesson Jane Eyre will also learn from the long-suffering Helen Burns, a lesson of power normally reserved for the phallus: RESURGAM. Elizabeth rejects father, brother, and lover and chooses the life of a woman alone. Lucy Snowe's autobiographical narrative arranges the same outcome. M. Paul goes to sea, presumably to return to and marry Lucy; she tells the reader with amazement, "Reader, they were the three happiest years of my life. Do you scout the paradox?" (414). We do. The "plenitude" and "nourishment" M. Paul's letters provide fulfill Lucy more adequately than could his real presence. Lucy needs to know herself loved but delights more in the anticipation than the culmination of that love. The equivocal ending of the novel signifies that doubleness or ambivalence of its narrator: Lucy must live alone but feel she has not been forced to do so by circumstance. Elizabeth Gaskell reports that Bronte's father asked her to alter *Villette's* ending, to make the hero and heroine live happily ever after rather than drown M. Paul at sea. Yet "all she could do in compliance with her father's wish," Gaskell confesses, "was so to veil the fate in oracular words, as to leave it to the character and discernment of her readers to interpret her meaning."[62]

Bronte attempted to please her father with her narrative conclusion, yet at the same time refused to do so.

Single-minded rejection of fathers and their representatives from the class of fathers, in fact, appears to be the narrative way out of the reductive choices between castrating the father or being castrated by him, between to "have" or "be" the phallus. Bronte discovered this in several of her narratives, yet failed to find it in her life. I think the case of Elizabeth Hastings shows why: the fictional father rejects the son, forcing the daughter to reject the father in turn. In her own family, Bronte's father supported his son, leaving Charlotte to reject Branwell and so failing to give her an alibi for rejecting the father himself. In terms of family structure and circumstance, Branwell's decline bound Bronte back to her father. She remained emotionally tied to him — dependent upon him, even when he was blindly dependent upon her — for life.

The single woman who rejects fathers, who does not define herself as castrated or lacking the phallus, who does not symbolically castrate fathers, exists primarily on the margins of Bronte's discourse. This woman, repressed and appearing in the narratives only with difficulty, is Bronte's other subject. She is a woman isolated or alone; she is a figure for the heroine; she is a madwoman or a nun. In the grammar of the text, she is "singular": beyond the ordinary, unique or sole; strange or "odd," unable to fit the narrative outcomes reserved for women. Just as Bertha Mason Rochester's madness signifies Jane Eyre's unconscious desire, the figurative "nonnette" of my epigraph to this section signifies her rejection of desire. This nun, whose figure has been widely remarked in *Villette*, appears first in *The Professor*.[63] When William Crimsworth arrives at Zoraide's school for girls, he thinks his students "nun-like." Only Sylvie performs well as a student, yet when Crimsworth discovers her "destined . . . for the cloister," he assumes her "soul warped to a conventual bias." Crimsworth dislikes Sylvie, however, primarily because her "nun-like" devotion secures her against the master's sexual power. "Once I laid my hand on her head," he reports, "in token of approbation; I thought Sylvie was going to smile, her dim eye almost kindled; but, presently, she shrank from me; I was a man and a heretic; she, poor child! a destined nun and devoted Catholic" (78, 87, 104, 125-26). Sylvie interprets the signs of Crimsworth's "approbation" correctly: the professor on the prowl creates his masterful authority by sexualized classroom tyranny. He describes in great detail the physical attractions of Hortense, Eulalie, and Caroline and takes pleasure in humiliating them; Sylvie, whose plainness he terms "ghastly," provides him neither sexual titillation nor the thrill of humiliating her.

The nun has been interpreted as a figure for repression in Bronte's text, largely, of course, because of her necessary link to Bronte's hated Roman Catholicism. If the nun is a figure for repression in *Villette*, however, she also appears a surreptitious figure for desire. For although Bronte attempts to explain the nun in terms of narrative realism, Ginevra's secret courtship with the disguised de Hamal cannot put to rest, as Mary Jacobus suggests, the figurative connection of the nun with Lucy Snowe.[64] Like the letter, the phallus, and the madwoman in and out of the attic, the nun "circulates" and so defines desire by her place in its signifying chain, in the grammar of the narrative. The nun appears to Lucy three times: once as she reads her first letter from Dr. John, once as she buries her letters from him, and once as she talks with M. Paul. The nun heralds Lucy's grief over her loss of Dr. John's love but also defines Lucy's desire to put aside her desire. The nun prophesies Lucy's fraternal kinship with M. Paul and also defines her ambivalence about a sexual relationship with him: "I felt," she writes, "from the first it was me he wanted—me he was seeking—and had I not wanted him too? . . . No sooner did opportunity suddenly and fully arrive, than I evaded it" (325). Although the brother-sister metaphor for relations between the sexes generally prepares the reader of Victorian fiction for the marriage of hero and heroine, in *Villette* it also serves along with the nun to define Lucy's desire to remain single and celibate. For when Mme Beck tells Lucy that M. Paul loves Justine Marie, the dead nun, Lucy finds his "celibacy" congenial to her needs. After discovering that Justine Marie is M. Paul's ward, and not the nun come to life, Lucy flees through Villette and thinks these tortured, often self-deceiving thoughts: "The love born of beauty was not mine; I had nothing in common with it: I could not dare to meddle with it, but another love, venturing diffidently into life after long acquaintance, furnace-tried by pain, stamped by constancy, consolidated by affection's pure and durable alloy, submitted by intellect to intellect's own tests, and finally wrought up, by his own process, to his own unflawed completeness, this Love that laughed at Passion, his fast frenzies and his hot and hurried extinction, in *this* Love I had a vested interest" (395). The metallurgical metaphor in this passage refines and represses desire; in the language at its end, Lucy describes sexuality as cloying and mutable. She simultaneously desires and renounces desire, embracing her cloistered life. It is no surprise, then, that when Lucy enters her dormitory room after this meditation, the nun is in her chaste, single bed. The narrative finally defines the nun as a figure for the singular Lucy herself.

Like the nun, the garden is a figure in Bronte's narratives for the feminine.[65] In the Belgian narratives, the garden becomes associated by William Crimsworth and Lucy Snowe with the female: the hidden space at the center of the city; the space no man may gaze upon; the "forbidden alley" that leads to flowers, bowers, and the tree beneath which Lucy Snowe finds a hollow whose declivity holds her buried letters. In *Shirley,* the garden and the nun come together in Bronte's metaphor for the female, Nunnwood. In this forest dell, the singular female and celibate haunts the surface narrative's concern with marrying and mating, as Caroline explains: "To penetrate into Nunnwood, Miss Keeldar, is to go far back into the dim days of eld. Can you see a break in the forest, about the centre? . . . That break is a dell; a deep, hollow cup, lined with turf as green and short as the sod of this Common; the very oldest of the trees, gnarled, mighty oaks, crowd about the brink of this dell: in the bottom lie the ruins of a nunnery." This wood with the ruins of a nunnery at its center is, like Maggie Tulliver's red deeps, a female sexual landscape complete with metaphorical vagina at its center. And despite Caroline's metaphors of intercourse with masculinity—the gnarled trees, the entry as "penetration"—this female space represents the long-lost love of woman for woman: of woman for herself and woman collectively for other women. Nunnwood serves as a place for strictly female conversation; it celebrates the celibate and/or sexual caring of woman for one another. Shirley invites, "We will go—you and I alone, Caroline—to that wood, early some fine summer morning, and spend a long day there." Alone together, Caroline and Shirley discuss the singular female. "Our power of being happy lies a good deal in ourselves, I believe," Caroline says. Shirley agrees and generalizes: if she were married, she says, "I could never be my own mistress more. A terrible thought!—it suffocates me! . . . When I feel my company superfluous, I can comfortably fold my independence round me like a mantle, and drop my pride like a veil, and withdraw to solitude." "I wonder," Caroline responds, "we don't all make up our minds to remain single" (238-42).

In Bronte's texts, however, the singular and celibate female is feared as well as desired. Although the emotional commitment at the heart of Nunnwood is to the single woman in a bond with her own female likeness, the "masculine" Shirley longs to be mastered by a powerful man, and the passive Caroline fears becoming an "old maid." The two women's attitudes identify Bronte's double narrative representation of the singular female. When Caroline understands Robert Moore has rejected her, she gives up anticipating "the duties and affections of wife and mother" she had assumed would be her "ordinary destiny." Looking in a mirror, Caroline thinks she sees the "signs of an old maid" on her own reflected face; she seeks confirmation or dissent in the looks of two unmarried women, Miss Ainley and Miss Mann—one a hardened "gorgon," the other an emaciated "spectre." Caroline submits without protest to her bitter destiny as a woman alone:

> "Caroline," [Shirley asks], "don't you wish you had a profession—a trade? . . . But hard labour and learned professions, they say, make women masculine, coarse, unwomanly."
> "And what does it signify, whether unmarried and never-to-be-married women are unattractive and inelegant, or not?—provided only they are decent,

decorous, and neat, it is enough. The utmost which ought to be required of old maids, in the way of appearance, is that they should not absolutely offend men's eyes as they pass them in the street." (256-57.)

Moreover, Shirley Keeldar, Esq. and Captain, herself the eponymous hero(ine) of the novel, must be metaphorically castrated at the novel's conclusion: she who desires the trappings and powers of manhood must find herself a woman—a castrate—after all. Immediately after Shirley confesses herself Louis Moore's former student, Shirley is bitten by her hitherto trustworthy dog; she falls ill and fears she will die. Shirley loses her "masculine" power, her rebellious temper, and her position as "master" and owner of the mill once her "master" appears in the narrative. Her resulting illness resembles Caroline's gradual decline and so identifies Shirley as a female like Caroline who depends for her health and happiness upon male approval. Bronte's textual decline into a dualistic libidinal economy of master and servant makes the end of *Shirley* entirely unbelievable.

In that end, Bronte's singular heroines of *Shirley* become plural and marry double patriarchal Moores. This sudden outcome attempts to cover over the an..thesis Bronte has not resolved: the angry denunciation of phallocentrism and its binary oppositions of sexual difference versus the fear those oppositions in fact define the singular female and her metaphorical impotence. Bronte herself suffers this double anger and fear. In her letters about marriage and maidenhood, Bronte, like her heroines, meditated on the enigma of finding herself female, on the "woman question." She refused to discuss it; she feared aloneness; she desired to find that singleness a strength. To Miss Wooler, she wrote,

I have another very egotistical motive for being pleased—it seems that even "a lone woman" can be happy, as well as cherished wives & proud mothers—I am glad of that—I speculate much on the existence of unmarried & never-to-be-married women nowadays, & I have already got to the point of considering that there is no more respectable character on this earth than an unmarried woman who makes her own way through life quietly perseveringly—without support of husband or brother, & who . . . retains in her possession a well-regulated mind—a disposition to enjoy emple pleasure—fortitude to support inevitable pains, sympathy with the sufferings of others, & willingness to relieve want as far as her means extend. (*Lives*, 2: 77.)

To Ellen Nussey, on the contrary, she wrote,

My reserve, however, has its foundation not in design, but in necessity—I am silent because I have literally *nothing to say*. I might indeed repeat over & over again that my life is a pale blank & often a weary burden—& that the Future sometimes appals me but what end could be answered by such repetition except to weary you & enervate myself? The evils that now & then wring a groan from my heart—lie in position—not that I am a *single* woman & likely to remain a *single* woman—but because I am a *lonely* woman & likely to be *lonely*. But it cannot be helped & therefore *imperatively must be borne*—& borne too with as few words about it as may be. (*Lives,* 4: 6.)[66]

Silence and singleness or "respectable" self-support: these are the heart-rending alternatives Bronte offers herself and her doubled heroines in *Shirley*.

Bronte's representation of female desire remains, then, double, as in *Shirley*, or unreadable, as in *Villette*. Jane will never inscribe her desire into her text just as Lucy will bury or refuse to confess hers in her "heretic narrative." Bronte fails or refuses to link her heroine's desire with its circulating signifiers because in a phallocentric system of representation, female desire is spectral. The other side of the "gorgon" whose glance castrates is the "spectre" who fancies or believes herself castrated. *Jane Eyre* defines Bertha Mason Rochester as specter of Jane's desire in the final appearance of madwoman to governess: Bertha looks in the mirror before she rends the wedding veil that will make Jane double of herself on the next morning. As Peter Grudin points out, the presence of the mirror in this scene links it figuratively with the scene in the red-room in which Jane is also haunted by a "ghost" and falls unconscious from terror.[67] In the red-room, Jane passes by a looking-glass and sees there a "strange little figure" who gazes at her with "glittering eyes of fear"; Jane thinks her own reflection "one of the tiny phantoms, half fairy, half imp, Bessie's evening stories represented as coming up out of lone, ferny dells in moors" (16). This strange figure and the mirrored monster from the attic define Jane's desire as demonic and mad but also as other than itself, as spectral.

This moment in which the self becomes specter appears in each of Bronte's novels. The paradigmatic instance occurs in *Villette:*

> At some turn we suddenly encountered another party approaching from the opposite direction. I just now see that group, as it flashed upon me for one moment. A handsome middle-aged lady in dark velvet; a gentleman who might be her son—the best face, the finest figure, I thought, I had ever seen; a third person in a pink dress and black lace mantle.
>
> I noted them all—the third person as well as the other two—and for the fraction of a moment, believed them all strangers, thus receiving an impartial impression of their appearance. But the impression was hardly felt and not fixed, before the consciousness that I faced a great mirror. . . . The party was our own party. (179.)

Like William Crimsworth who sees a thin dark face with sunken eyes as he passes a looking-glass (76), like Caroline Helstone who sees first a charming "spectacle" then an old maid when she looks in the glass (112), Lucy sees herself as others see her: she sees herself as other. In each instance, the subject seeing (him or) herself as other meditates upon desire: will (he or) she be desirable to Zoriade, Robert Moore, or Dr. John? The hero(ine)'s own desire counts for nothing here. The subject looks at herself as other and sees herself as her desired object will see her; she gazes at her reflection with the implied eyes of a male. In fact, Jane Eyre finds her spectral self confirmed by Rochester, who views Jane as the imp, the fairy, the elfin figure she herself saw reflected in the mirror in the red-room. Luce Irigaray defines this specularity of female desire as necessary to a phallocentric and misreading ideology: "The role of 'femininity' is prescribed moreover by this masculine specula(riza)tion and corresponds only slightly to woman's desire, which is recuperated only secretly, in hiding, and in a disturbing and unpardonable manner."[68] Lucy's nun, which Dr. John diagnoses as a "spectral illusion," defines female desire as marginal to the realm of representation open to a woman writer in a phallocentric culture; she must appear surreptitiously and then be explained away by an authoritative male, by the tricks of "realism."

Bronte's heroine therefore appears alienated from her own desire. The signifiers for that desire are the spectral and doubling figures for herself: the ghostly madwoman, the spectral nun, the nun's wood, the letter. Jacques Lacan calls this realm of the double, the specter, and the mirrored image the imaginary. The female enters the symbolic and phallocentric realm of culture through the complex structures of the female Oedipus complex, which signify the doubleness of the aim (active/passive) and object (mother/father) of her desire. The imaginary, then, appears more forcefully in her discourse than in the male's. From the imaginary, she speaks her desire as other, as double. Lacan also locates the imaginary in what he calls the mirror stage. The history of the subject begins with this moment when the child first sees his or her image in the mirror and identifies with the wholeness he or she perceives as essential to that image. The child's sense of insufficiency becomes anticipation; he or she assumes the phantasm in the mirror the self and so precipitates the mediating structure of desire through the other as well as the concept of "identity" which alienates the subject from him or herself.[69] Bronte's adult heroine desires to be that other, and that other defines her desire.

As he or she looks in the mirror, Jane, Caroline, Crimsworth, or Lucy becomes a spectator of his or her own desire. I would like to return to Freud's essay on the fantasy of being beaten to interpret this problematic moment in Bronte's narratives. Freud says about the displacement of the subject in the structural and linguistic transformations of the father-daughter fantasy, "What was originally a masochistic (passive) situation is transformed into a sadistic one by means of repression, and its sexual quality is almost effaced"; the girl "is no longer anything but a spectator of the event which takes the place of a sexual act."[70] Bronte indeed makes her heroine the spectator of her desire to free herself from the erotic demands of the figurative father-daughter relationship. As governesses, Jane Eyre and Lucy Snowe watch events from stairway landings, better to view the activities of others while remaining themselves invisible. Jane retreats to the curtained window recess to symbolize her role as outcast and orphan. Lucy believes herself on the margins of her story, assumes she as first-person narrator is elected to tell everyone's story but her own: the Brettons', Polly Home's, Miss Marchmont's, Ginevra Fanshawe's. The narrative stance of the spectating heroine serves the structural strategy of symbolic castration and sustains the text's circulating signifiers of desire. All three tactics attempt to transform the scars and punishments of a daughter (Freud's "masochism" in the passage I quoted above) into the chastisement of a father (Freud's "sadism"), to liberate the daughter from her dependence on fathers and initiate her into singular femininity.

Language and Mastery

Exhausted by emotion, my language was more subdued than it generally was when it developed that sad theme; and mindful of Helen's warnings against the indulgence of resentment, I infused into the narrative far less of gall and wormwood than ordinary. Thus restrained and simplified, it sounded more credible. — Charlotte Bronte, Jane Eyre

"Let the woman speak out whenever she sees fit to make an objection; — it is permitted to a woman to teach and to exercise authority as much as may be."— Charlotte Bronte, Shirley

In telling the "story of [her] sad childhood," Jane Eyre learns that her audience correlates her restraint and simplicity with narrative credibility. Language must tell the tale of childhood deprivation but must not indulge the intense desires and passions of experience in the telling. In fact, language exists in a different realm from that of emotion; as Jane intuits, storytelling is radically different from experience and shapes while attempting to control experience by its medium, language. Like Jane Eyre, Charlotte Bronte tries to master her past by telling stories about it. As her shifting narrative stances bring Bronte closer to her female experience, she too restrains and makes credible her tale of emotion and resentment, gall and wormwood. She writes first as a man, then as a spectating woman; she bids farewell to Angrian emotionalism, then buries the texts' letters. She regulates past passions. As my second epigraph—Caroline Helstone's "contrary" interpretation of woman's place —implies, a woman's speaking out is the metaphorical vehicle for such self-mastery, and teaching is the concomitant mission. Using language competently gains a woman self-assurance in public as well as private arenas; writing stories about such empowerment is a tool not only for mastering past experience but for acquiring authority in the cultural and symbolic realm. By assuming the uses of language normally reserved for men in her phallocentric culture, Bronte's storytelling heroine—and Bronte herself—tries to master her situation as a powerless female and come to terms with desire and female impotence.

In his discussion of female desire and punishment, Freud demonstrates the ways in which the girl "changes her sex" to free herself from dependence on loving the father and so defining herself as "castrated." The fantasizing girl thus imagines herself a boy in the phase of the fantasy which follows repression of father-daughter desire. In this way, she "escapes from the demands of the erotic side of her life altogether. She turns herself in phantasy into a man, without herself becoming active in a masculine way." Freud generalizes this perception: "When [girls] turn away from their incestuous love for their father, with its genital significance, they easily abandon their feminine role, . . . and from that time forward only want to be boys. For that reason the whipping-boys who represent them are boys too." Freud's rhetorical phallocentrism appears naive today, and his logic appears to enforce masochism on woman despite her apparent "tricks" to escape it; but Freud also taps a central mechanism of displacement in fantasy and the story that relates it which a nineteenth-century woman author could use to master or control her experience: imagining herself male. Freud in fact observes that his female patients who related this fantasy of being beaten by their fathers often elaborated a superstructure of daydreams which grew around (or over) the "masochistic beating-phantasy." The heroes of these daydreams "were always young men; indeed," Freud reports, "women used not to come into these creations at all, and only made their first appearance after many years, and then in minor parts."[71] Freud's patients who "changed their sex" devalued the female and banished it from their narratives.

As I mentioned at the beginning of this chapter, Sandra M. Gilbert and Susan Gubar call this early tendency toward masculine narration in Charlotte Bronte's work "male impersonation."[72] In her Angrian tales and novelettes, Bronte narrates not as "Charlotte Bronte" but as "Charles Townshend." In *Captain Henry Hastings,* Bronte reassumes the male persona she had dropped in *Mina Laury* and writes a masculine narrative of sons rebelling against fathers, of regicide and metaphorical parricide. In *The Professor,* William Crimsworth narrates his fanatical struggle to become a master and father. In *Jane Eyre,* "Currer Bell" "edits" a woman's first-person narrative. Yet in her first published novel, Bronte did not fully "change her sex"; she adopted not a male pseudonym, as did George Eliot, but a genderless name (like "Acton Bell" and "Ellis Bell") that did not specifically signify maleness but was counted upon by the Bronte sisters to be assumed male and so to facilitate publication and reviewing by male critics without gender bias. This equivocal "male impersonation" and its earlier unequivocal versions, however, helped a scribbling girl master her lively passions. Imagining her narrator, herself as author, and her "whipping-boys" male, Bronte removes herself from her erotic father-daughter material. She also accedes to the symbolic realm of culture as would a man and so imagines herself "master" of certain situations in which she as narrator would otherwise be the victim. The best case, of course, is that of William Crimsworth, who, haunted by the feminine, nevertheless uses his position in society as a male to leave his tyrant brother's factory, get a teaching job on the Continent, marry the lace-mender, open a school and get wealthy, move back to England and acquire an "estate," and finally become a patriarch, landowner, and father. Needless to say, a female narrator in the nineteenth century might never have achieved such heights of mastery.

Freud's well-known short discussion of his grandson's *fort-da* game in "Beyond the Pleasure Principle" articulates the ways in which language is a vehicle for mastery. The child throws a wooden reel with a piece of string tied around it into corners, under his bed, and into his bed, while at the same time uttering the phoneme "O" (which Freud interprets as *fort*—"gone"), then reels it back to himself while uttering "A" (which Freud interprets as *da*—"there"). The child does this, Freud hypothesizes, because his mother has gone out; the child repeats and compensates for this unpleasurable absence with the symbolized presence of his wooden toy: he can make it, unlike his mother, return. Active in play rather than passive as in life, he also revenges himself on a symbolic substitute for his absent mother, the reel itself. The child thus constitutes his world into two categories, plenitude and lack of plenitude, and masters his experience (the absence of his mother) through symbol and language.[73]

Freud also believes, however, this symbolic game enacts the child's renunciation of his mother on the level of language. Jacques Lacan develops this aspect of Freud's paradigmatic story of language acquisition by assuming the *fort-da* game also plays out the child's radical alienation from his mother and from himself. The child not only returns the wooden reel, as Freud demonstrates, but occasionally only throws it away. This double game—the repetition of *fort* without *da* as well as of *fort* and *da*—symbolizes the child's vacillation about his relationship with his mother. Indeed, if the child simply mastered his experience by playing the symbolic game and assigning language to its categories, why would he continue to repeat it, to derive pleasure from displeasure over and over again? Lacan answers: the language game represents the child's recurring feelings of alienation and the need to master those feelings which dialectically repeat themselves in the child's daily experience.[74]

Like Freud's grandson, Bronte's spectating narrators attempt both to symbolize and to master their feelings of deprivation and alienation, the repeated absences in their lives. I intend the term "mastery" to imply not only self-control but also public influence, vigor, and power: a heroine finds herself thrust into a setting in which her status as spectator is challenged, and she must demonstrate her ability by asserting her personal authority and confirming her professional competence. Lucy Snowe, for example, that "looker-on at life," finds herself forced by M. Paul Emanuel to act the fop in Mme Beck's *fête* play. "That first speech was the difficulty, she tells her reader; "it revealed to me this fact, that it was not the crowd I feared, so much as my own voice" (120). Lucy's fear of her own woman's voice signifies her lack of authority and her failure to master both herself and her situation. Lucy thinks she deserves no influence or recognition; how could she then speak out with her own voice? Yet Lucy controls her fear of her female voice by speaking in that of the "personage" she represents: the fop. "When [her] tongue got free, and [her] voice took its true pitch, and found its natural tone," she speaks with the voice of a feminized man. She then feels her "own strength," feels the "right power" rise in her body: feels herself in control of the situation. Lucy is also costumed in the equivocal dress of a man; she puts collar, vest, cravat, and palêtot over her prim mauve dress and so signifies her role, her "impersonation," of a man. The female garb she exposes at her hem is the beginning of Lucy's determination to find her own voice as a woman.

The drama Lucy acts out with Ginevra Fanshawe represents desire. Lucy, the fop, attempts to seduce Ginevra, the coquette; but the fop has a rival. Lucy and Ginevra so enjoy the play of desire and the pleasures of triangular rivalry that they retain the drama's "letter" while "recklessly alter[ing] the spirit of the *rôle*" (121). This double drama of letter and spirit taps the desire of the fop Lucy represents—and of herself—to "win and conquer" (121). No wonder Lucy fears her own voice: mastery is an aspect of her desire. This drama of conquest, rivalry, and seduction also appears a metaphor for the buried desires/letters of Lucy's experience outside the drama. Lucy spots the form of Dr. John Bretton among the spectators and acts her part as though the fop she represents rivals Dr. John for Ginevra; in their experience, in fact, she and Ginevra rival one another for Dr. John, and Dr. John rivals de Hamal—Lucy's attic nun! —for Ginevra. As the fop, certainly the opposite of the gray nursery governess, Lucy plays out the delicious desires, rivalries, and conquests she cannot allow herself to play out in her own female voice, in her life. The day after the *fête,* however, Lucy understands the dangers of enacting the letter or language of desire and therefore of pleasing herself. She metaphorically buries her delight in dramatic expression in a locked box, much as she will later bury her letters from Dr. John Bretton.

The vehicle of Lucy's desire and mastery in the *fête* drama is language. This heroine must "find her voice."[75] In *Villette* as in Bronte's other novels, the classroom provides the setting in which the heroine acquires the opportunity to use language as a tool for self-mastery and therefore to gain personal authority. As a teacher, according to Lucy Snowe, a woman finds she may work for herself and so is "spared the pain of being a burden to anybody" (244). The woman teacher acquires an "independence"—an income of her own and a sense of her personal autonomy. Yet Bronte's heroines clearly specify that governessing fails to provide a woman her own voice and authority. The incongruous status of the governess within a family defines the unmarried woman as surrogate nurturer without conferring upon her the privileges and responsibilities of motherhood and denies her authority while demanding she exercise it.[76] The singular female who teaches in a family setting discovers the lack of love in her own life, finds herself under the authority of fathers once more, and so confirms her self-alienation. Lucy therefore refuses to become Polly Home's "companion," Shirley prevents Caroline Helstone from becoming a governessing "slave," and Jane Eyre leaves the nursery first for the drawing room, then for life at Moor House. Indeed, Jane Eyre discovers early in her autobiography the power of her own voice: her "savage, high voice" and rebellious words enable her "first victory" against Mrs. Reed; her confidential and unconventional discourse wins her power in relationships with Rochester and St. John, who cannot imagine "a woman would dare to speak so to a man" (40, 478). When Rochester offers his former governess and nearly wife the opportunity to become his mistress, she refuses; when St. John Rivers asks, however, about a teaching position at Morton, "Will you be this mistress?", Jane willingly accepts. The governess becomes *school*mistress (453).[77]

Bronte's protagonists' first teaching experiences, however, represent the fictions of authority with which teachers attempt to cover up their lack of self-mastery. William Crimsworth and Lucy Snowe both take advantage of their positions at the front and raised above the level of the class; both fear to speak French and so assert their authorities by tearing in pieces the dictées of the handsomest girl in the class. Crimsworth's theory of teaching combines mentorship with tyranny: "When I had shown myself the mildest, the most tolerant of masters—a word of impertinence, a movement of disobedience, changed me at once into a despot. I offered then but one alternative—submission and acknowledgment of error, or ignominious expulsion" (67). Lucy's and Crimsworth's first lessons appear based on Bronte's own at M. Héger's pensionnat; Lucy's story, written at the end rather than the beginning of Bronte's career, demonstrates the advance in understanding of the teaching hero(ine) and the formerly teaching writer. Lucy tells the reader her "want of mastery" in a foreign language drives her to create the fictions of authority: "Could I but have spoken in my own tongue, I felt as if I might have gained a hearing; for . . . nature had given me a voice that could make itself heard, if lifted in excitement or deepened by emotion. . . . I could, in English, have rolled out readily phrases. . . . All I could now do was . . . tear the blotted page in two" (65-69). Lucy understands the links among finding her voice, mastering language, and acquiring the authority of the "master" or "mistress."

Indeed, Lucy Snowe finally represents Bronte's most complex teaching protagonist. To find her voice, become a successful teacher, and constitute herself her own master through language, Lucy, like Freud's grandson, must become active rather than passive, must speak rather than spectate. But Lucy confesses to her reader her own "infatuated resignation," her "diffidence," her "slackness to aspire." To rise from nursery governess to classroom teacher, Lucy needs a mentor who tests and challenges her spectating passivity. She finds one first in Mme Beck —wearing the "aspect" of a man—and second in Modeste's brother and double, M. Paul. Mme Beck challenges Lucy to teach her first class; M. Paul to act the fop, to direct English exams, and to demonstrate her ability as essayist. The mentor also understands Lucy's diffident appearance masks an "aspiring nature," a relish of the "délices de l'autorité," a "petite ambitieuse." In each challenge, Lucy rises to the hiss of her master and herself masters the situation; in each challenge, the medium for mastery is language. Lucy must find her own voice, assert her authority, publicly represent herself "in her own person," and demonstrate her narrative skills (131-34). Only then may she be her own master.

In the meantime, however, she needs the help of her tutor-master. For Lucy's conquests in language and teaching are intimately and causally linked to her relationship with M. Paul Emanuel. He sneers at her weaknesses and so encourages her to strive; he supports and guides her in the difficult task of directing the English exams. Lucy proclaims him a figurative Napoleon, "stern, dogmatic, hasty, imperious," without ties, attachments, dependents, or duties (341). Like Rochester, Crimsworth, and Louis Moore, M. Paul as teacher and mentor chastises and approves of the learning heroine as would a father. He is a figure unmistakably from Freud's "class of fathers" who supplements paternal authority, who is present to the heroine whose own father is absent. If the master masters the heroine in each of Bronte's narratives, then, he or his double also assists her in achieving self-mastery.[78]

In her final test, Lucy Snowe demonstrates she has learned much from her mentor and from her role as teacher. In the presence of her master and two examiners, Lucy undergoes her ultimate and once deferred "show-trial": she must prove herself the writer of an essay on classical learning. As in her first dramatic experience, as in her administering the English exams, Lucy here fears her own voice. She knows little about the classics or French history; when she knows the material upon which she is questioned, she "either *could* not, or *would* not speak." Although she fails to find her speaking voice, however, Lucy does not fail to use language competently. The professors demand she write a dictée on the subject of "Human Justice." Lucy writes an allegorical sketch in which she personifies Human Justice as a selfish, drunken old woman who ignores human suffering, who punishes the strong souls and showers sugarplums on the weak souls who importune her. This woman is a figure for the female spectator and arouses Lucy's contempt. In writing her allegory, Lucy strives to find her angry narrative voice and master the desire to remain a passive and silent, a needy and selfish, looker-on at life. The drunken old woman is a figure for the part of herself Lucy wants to outgrow. M. Paul does not comment upon Lucy's performance, but later in the same chapter he offers her his trust, his companionship, his fraternity. The narrative does not connect these two events causally, but the reader so interprets them: Lucy appears to have earned the respect of her mentor and seems fit for her next task as directress of her own school (335-45).

Language acquisition and female self-mastery, then, appear linked in Bronte's narrative project with the presence of a punishing and approving master who is a figurative father. I would like to look again at Freud's *fort-da* game as a paradigm of the links between language acquisition and parental presence or absence. Although nowhere in his narrative of the symbolic game does Freud mention paternity, Jacques Derrida's deconstruction of the game as paradigm implies that the father indeed structures this symbolic intersubjectivity. Derrida points out what Freud suppresses: his relationship as grandfather to Ernst and as father to Sophie, Ernst's mother. Although Ernst's father is absent—at war on the front—Ernst factors his absent father into the game by representing the father as "gone." The child desires his father's absence. In addition, the playing of this game relies on the presence of the observing, supposedly objective grandfather as the father's triangular substitute and the mother's genealogical father: the father-supplement. Freud's repression of this familial structure defines it as central, as the "censored chapter" in a figurative but untold narrative. Although, then, the mother's absence appears necessary to the child's symbolic game of *fort* and *da,* the (grand)-father's presence and implied approval also sustain the structures of presence and absence the child symbolizes with his wooden reel.[79]

Derrida demonstrates, moreover, that the game depends upon and enhances the (grand)father's authority. For although Freud narrates the game as an event with a determinate interpretation (*"fort"* and *"da"*), it is in fact a speculation, one in which Freud's daughter, Sophie, corroborates her scientific father's authority as interpreter of her child's unintelligible sounds. The writing of "Beyond the Pleasure Principle" carries this self-justification one step further: Freud asserts his status as the founder of psychoanalysis by maintaining that the apparently fundamental compulsion to repeat is nevertheless governed by the pleasure principle. Freud thereby ensures his scientific progeny and genealogy in his meditation with and from his biological family. Derrida also reminds us that Freud's speculation betrays his desire to play, like Ernst, with a symbol of his daughter (Ernst's mother), as well as to master that desire. He would, if playing with the reel, deny himself the supplementary pleasure, the *return* of the reel that symbolizes Sophie, so as not to "risk the wager" that brings the "desired bed into play."[80] Freud's interpretation of his grandson's game tells us not only (Derrida would say unequivocally "not") about the child's use of the signifier to master his experience but about the spectating grandfather's employment of writing to bolster his authority and master his unspeakable desire.

Derrida's categories clarify some implicit contradictions about desire, mastery, and authority not only in the "show-trial" scene but throughout *Villette*. As Lucy Snowe, like Ernst, acquires self-mastery by manipulating symbols and signifiers of desire, M. Paul appears to grow less commanding and Napoleonic. Yet like Freud in Derrida's version of the *fort-da* game, M. Paul enhances his authority while overseeing his pupil and figurative daughter. His power resides in his observation, which, supposedly objective, proves not at all disinterested but, like Freud's, sustained by desire. The gaze of the professor, like that of the psychoanalyst, is not benign but both supportive and domineering. In response to the master's demand she play the fop, for example, Lucy sees "in his vexed, fiery, and searching eye, a sort of appeal behind all its menace" and finds that her lips drop the word "oui" despite her brain's fear of "public display" (115). Moreover, the narrative builds into its structures a mechanism by which to assert the ultimate kindliness of the master's gaze, the appeal behind the menace, and thereby simultaneously avouch Lucy's increasing mastery: the kinship of M. Paul and Mme Beck. Bronte displaces the hostile eye of surveillance and domination from the master, whose sister watches with malignant and castrating gaze the loves and losses of the pupil and schoolteacher she first encouraged to leave the nursery for the classroom. At the climax of the novel, M. Paul masters this mistress, whose "eye graz[es Lucy] with its hard ray like a steel stylet"; he is "roused," and demands Mme Beck leave his presence immediately; Lucy loves his wrath with a newly felt passion (405). M. Paul next proceeds to disentangle the sexual triangle Lucy has inferred: having dismissed his sister and Lucy's implicit rival for his affection, Mme Beck, he declares the mysterious nun, Justine Marie, his ward and proclaims his love for Lucy. The unspoken envies of triangular desire disappear and deflect the reader's suspicion that M. Paul maintains his authority over Lucy. This scene ultimately displaces his mastery: not Paul Emanuel but Lucy will teach in her own school, and the gaze of domineering desire will be banished from her kindly life with the professor.

Villette asserts, then, that Lucy surpasses her mentor's teaching and so earns the right herself to teach and run a school. Yet the master is present, either chastising or approving his student's progress, not only early in the novel but also at its end. In the "show-trial" as in the *fête* play, M. Paul watches Lucy, his brow furrowing and visage darkening when she pronounces herself "dumb," an "idiot." M. Paul rents a school for Lucy, bestows it upon her, and selects her first students. Her grateful response to his generosity reinstates Bronte's early metaphors for the father-supplement: the king and his handmaiden, the lord and his worshiper. "'I will be your faithful steward,'" Lucy promises; "He was my king; royal for me had been that hand's bounty; to offer homage was both a joy and a duty" (410). Bronte's religious analogy confirms the master's figurative fatherhood: like the father in Luke, his letters give Lucy neither a stone nor a scorpion, but "full-handed, full-hearted plenitude" (415). His surname is the name of the Father: inscriber of Epistle and founder of doctrine, signifier of the Messiah. Throughout *Villette*, Bronte prepares Lucy for absence of the master-king-lord-Father, only to achieve for her his metaphorical and emotional presence. In the final equivocal passages of the novel, Bronte's metaphors for presence transfigure M. Paul's presumed death and future absence from Lucy's life. "I thought I loved him when he went away; I love him now in another degree; he is more my own. . . . Here pause: . . . leave sunny imaginations hope. Let it be theirs to conceive the delight of joy born again fresh out of great terror, the rapture of rescue from peril, the wondrous reprieve from dread, the fruition of return" (416-17). Eschewing her responsibility for such metaphors, Bronte nonetheless provides them to cover over and illuminate M. Paul's absence, a lack she understands as necessary to her structural pattern of Lucy's growing mastery. The conclusion of the narrative refuses to untangle the knot of female self-mastery and paternal presence, for Lucy Snowe desires her master even as she desires his absence to enhance her newly found authority.

What Derrida calls in Freud's *fort-da* game the "blurred syntax of the genealogical scene" confirms that desire works within the text's assertion of Lucy's mastery, that mastery is a function of desire. Freud's role in the parable as grandfather and father (in the "place of the son-in-law" as well as genealogical father) and Sophie's role as mother and daughter focus desire on the place Freud as writer occupies in the family scene. These roles also allow the two implicit triangles structured on Freud as fulcrum to resonate with those in his family of origin. Likewise, in the many triangles implicit throughout *Villette* but especially at its end, Lucy finds herself in the place of daughter, "sister," lover, rival, and future wife and so writes her autobiography, her "heretic narrative," from the place at which desire blurs the syntax of the genealogical scene; mastery becomes the necessary assertion the text makes to cover over desire. Moreover, as Derrida reminds us, Freud as narrator in the *fort-da* parable is neither Freud as author nor Freud as observer, yet "Beyond the Pleasure Principle" refuses to admit such difference. This difference calls into play the blurring of the genealogical and familial syntax; the suppression of such difference makes the writer, the father of psychoanalysis, write from the need to master.[81] The scene of Bronte's writing makes a different denial: Lucy as retrospective narrator is different from, older and wiser than, Lucy as observer of the text's events—her role as looker-on at life or spectator—and neither of these Lucys is Bronte. The reader knows, however, the autobiographical basis of Bronte's fiction, knows as well the similarity and difference of writer, narrator, and observer. Charlotte Bronte's implicit narrative denial that she resembles Lucy Snowe, that cold and frosty figure for the writer, calls into play the structure of difference inherent in the scene of autobiographical fictionalizing which blurs the syntax of the familial scene.

Lucy Snowe, however, also becomes an active participant in her autobiographical fiction. Her place in the genealogical scene, then, also resembles Ernst's, yet this "Ernst" is female. This "change of sex" from that of Freud's parable's progeny radically alters the psychoanalytic paradigm of language and culture acquisition. For the symbolic game of presence and absence also represents, as Jacques Lacan describes it, a "self-mutilation." The wooden reel stands for a small part of the subject that "detaches itself from him while still remaining his." This reel becomes the child's first signifier: it is the "first mark of the subject."[82] If I read Lacan's metaphor rightly, this "self-mutilation" is the child's first unknowing encounter with castration. Whereas the threat of castration eclipses the boy's oedipal love for his mother, it initiates the girl's desire for her father: the girl blames her mother for her own symbolic castration and so enters into oedipal love for her father "as though into a haven of refuge";[83] cut off from her mother, she finds in the father the supplemental satisfaction she can no longer obtain from the mother. In throwing the wooden reel, the daughter recalls her mother and unknowingly encounters the metaphorical castration that will later estrange her from her mother and enforce her dependence upon fatherly approval and authority. Moreover, in the symbolic game of *fort* and *da* (presence and absence of the mother, of the wooden reel, of the phallus), castration is the "articulating cut that makes language possible."[84] This "radical cut," which for the boy facilitates relationship with the father, accepts his authority, and initiates the acquisition of language and culture, for the girl marks her inferiority in the linguistic and cultural realm. The first mark of the female subject inscribes her alienation from herself and from her language.

Eugénie Lemoine-Luccioni, following yet revising Lacan's theory of alienation in the *fort-da* parable, depicts self-detachment as intensified by female gender. She believes the girl, who in the mirror stage sees her reflection and identifies that ideal image as herself, also sees the mother who resembles herself (in the mirror, in general) as that ideal image. The girl thus subsitutes for the person of the mother in the *fort-da* game her "own person figured by her body in the specular image."[85] In identifying with the mother in the *fort-da* game, then, the girl acts out her own specularity and radical self-estrangement more fully than does the boy. Later, the same metaphorical castration will confirm her self-detachment and alienation from her desire as she struggles to achieve self-mastery. The girl's symbolic brush with castration in the language game defines the female dialectic of absence and presence, self-alienation and mastery, passivity and activity, as slightly skewed toward the first of these paired oppositions. This is the double bind Lucy Snowe as narrator and participant in her own story writes about.

Lacan also associates alienation in the *fort-da* game with the necessity to repeat as acted out by Ernst, the subject of psychoanalytic investigation. Derrida demonstrates that the father of psychoanalysis, like his subject, struggles with the problems of repetition: just as Freud's paradigmatic tale of the pleasure principle and the compulsion to repeat takes as subject matter repetition, so does his prose get tangled in repetitions.[86] Charlotte Bronte as writer of the story Lucy tells appears in the place Freud occupies in the autobiographical text; as he repeats himself to make the pleasure principle master the repetition compulsion, Bronte repeats herself to make the figure for herself master desire. *Villette* enjoys a unique status in Bronte's career as a repetition of the material in *The Professor*. Lucy's autobiographical novel retells William Crimsworth's, which was published after Bronte's death; that accident of publication, however, fails fully to account for the reasons Bronte wrote *Villette*. Both professorial novels contain some of the same narrative events; the triangular desires of student, master, and mistress structure both texts. At the same time, however, *Villette* differs from *The Professor:* the autobiographer, the writer in the place Freud occupies, is female. This "change of sex" undoes repetition and defines in fact Bronte's attempt not to repeat herself in writing. She exposes the false self-presentation of her earlier narrator as self-serving and embraces the urge to spectate as part of the urge to master.

Villette's difference from *The Professor* also defines its status as a supplemental text. Lucy's story revises Crimsworth's as Crimsworth's revises Bronte's experience in Belgium. Moreover, Bronte's narrative supplement denies the frosty figure for herself the pleasure of the supplement; the author of *Villette* refuses its heretical autobiographer the joy of M. Paul's return and in doing so denies as well Charlotte Bronte's return to England from the Continent. In *The Professor,* on the contrary, Crimsworth enjoys both the rediscovery of his lace-mender and their joint return to Britain. From this perspective, the reader sees the double function *Villette* performs for its writer. It indulges while denying her desire for her master; it undercuts while asserting her mastery of that desire. Writing Lucy's narrative prepares Charlotte Bronte for dependence while declaring her independence; confirms her erotic father-daughter material while asserting her distance from it. *Villette* thus appears a supplementation that would engender repeated supplementation; in an effort to master her experience at M. Héger's pensionnat, Bronte continued to need to write about female mastery.

The economy of the supplement in Bronte's last novel, however, also disrupts oedipal structures and so might have liberated its author from father-daughter desire. Like Bronte's experience with father, brother, and husband after her wedding to Nicholls, the supplementary text about the figurative daughter's urge to master her desire for the father-supplement attempts to define that figure as powerless and tautological and the desire that surrounds him as redundant. Bronte's text cannot earn her heroine this understanding, yet neither, I think, does the writer herself achieve it. Bronte's last novel declares the father-figure absent yet present, the narrator-observer happy yet unhappy with her singularity, and its own structure as complete yet demanding supplementation. The economy of the supplement betrays the fragility of mastery as a narrative and linguistic strategy in Bronte's text about female self-mastery, just as it prophesies the strategy for demystifying daughterly desire.

CONCLUSION

Analysis Terminable and Interminable

THIS BOOK has explored and questioned notions of fatherhood in the work of three mid-nineteenth-century British novelists. Dickens, Eliot, and Charlotte Bronte were all deeply troubled by their relationships with fathers. All three authors wrote about the desire and prohibition characteristic of oedipal material: the daughter's ambivalent desire for the father and the son's ambivalent rivalry with him; the father's prohibitive function as the initiator of law or his failure and so lawlessness; the father's literal or figurative absence. Each writer discovers that fatherhood is necessarily absent, and so his or her origin seems to be in question. Each writer retraces in the stages of narrative sequence the steps of the father, and each recognizes that the father's presence, though desired, cannot be recaptured and must consciously or otherwise be renounced.

In writing about families, and particularly fathers and filiation, Dickens, Eliot, and Charlotte Bronte seek to free themselves from fathers and to confront the problems of authority in the realms of culture, language, religion, and law. Each seeks a mode for achieving his or her own authority, whether in self-engendering, assuming the mantle of male authorship, or mastering desire. Each undertakes authorship unconsciously to perform these self-creating tasks, and each narrates stories about the figures for the self that the process of writing engenders. Dickens, Eliot, and Bronte all achieved a measure of success in their narrative enterprises — as well as, of course, immense worldly success and recognition as the most popular authors of their day. For these writers shared and exposed the filial anxieties of their audience. As they tried to free themselves from the burden of paternal prohibitions, their culture questioned while fearing to overthrow ideologies about fatherhood and the function of paternity in the realm of nineteenth-century thought.

While attempting to write themselves free of fathers and create their own authority, each of my authors tells a story about a different oedipal moment, a different metaphor of self-definition. Together the three tropes imagine the subject's origin in and separation from the mother-father-child triad and the initiation into culture. The primal scene in Dickens's narratives articulates the origin of the child with the symbolic fact of filiation; the scene of seduction in Eliot's retroactively recounts the emergence of daughterly desire; the enigma of castration in Bronte's forces the child to accept him or herself as shaped by a familial and cultural prohibition. Each of these metaphorical turning points reminds its writer of his or her origin in a family while providing a vehicle for escape from that unit. The writer who authors these moments, these origins, understands the inevitable power of the oedipal family; he or she will never cease to struggle with such desire and prohibition, improvidence and criminality, chastisement and approbation. Authoring his or her own mastery while freeing the self from fathers, then, appears to be a paradoxical endeavor, one fraught with the dangers and risks of becoming a subject to oneself and in narrative.

The texts I have examined also play out a struggle for control of the problems of paternity and authority. Each of my authors created strategies for managing desire; each made economic bargains with his or her psyche in the transactional process of producing narrative; each demonstrated the provisional status of self-engendering, acquiring "male" authority, and self-mastering as methods of coping with unmanageable desires. Indeed, Dickens's, Eliot's, and Bronte's strategies for handling oedipal desire confirmed its hold on their lives and their fictions. For each author wrote and rewrote his or her particular version of desire in the family and of the necessity to prohibit it. The inevitable and moving failure of such repression inscribes itself across their texts and in their biographies. The return of the repressed, the failure of language and symbolic confrontation to lay to rest the ghosts of the father, paradoxically empowered the imaginations of my three authors.

Dickens, Eliot, and Charlotte Bronte all struggle as well with symbolic paternity. Their characters, both male and female, enter the realm of culture and signification with the heightened difficulty of fragile selfhood. Their displaced and unacknowledged search for identification with as well as repudiation of paternal authority appears outside themselves, dispersed in their texts as symbolic fatherhood. The necessity to solve the puzzles of their own origins and desires, to find the lost family head, to put the dead or remembered or absent father in his symbolic place are all ways paternity structures my authors' narratives. Moreover, the concept of paternal prohibition prevents linguistic and narrative sequence in the texts of nineteenth-century fatherhood and filiation from regressing into the preoedipal bliss of signification before the oedipal battle — whether enacted by male or female — the language in which self and other appear to be undifferentiated: the "mother tongue" or "baby talk" of gratified desire. This version of desire must be abandoned and the father's negativity accepted or assimilated for Dickens, Eliot, and Bronte paradoxically to free themselves from the force of fatherhood in their lives and fictions. The narrative conventions of nineteenth-century England facilitated and structured this accommodation, and each of my authors struggled to achieve it. Each succeeded to an extent: Eliot questioned her control of such textual issues at the end of her career; Dickens covered over the implications of sequence and origin; Bronte attempted to achieve mastery with her double narrative strategies but inscribed mastery as a version of desire.

The filial entanglements of Dickens, Eliot, and Bronte with literal, figurative, and symbolic fatherhood make sense when interpreted with the tools Freud made available. He articulated, for example, the relationship between fantasies and the texts that inscribe them: dreams, slips of the tongue, jokes, and narratives. He initiated analysis of desire and prohibition in the family by examining his own such unconscious material. He initiated — if only by the force of his female disciples — the study of gender and ideology. The contemporary return to Freud and the articulation of linguistic and structural concerns with his interpretive machinery make possible fresh consideration of literary texts in general and of my Victorian novelists in particular. The role of narrative strategy and sequence in enforcing paternal thematics, the power of metaphor and language in the tasks of the father-haunted nineteenth-century novelist may supplement our thinking with Freud about conscious craft and unconscious motivations in fiction. Considerations of gender and writing, stimulated by the contemporary feminist movement, also extend the ways the critic may use Freud's theories about, for example, sexual difference and desire. The combination of literary criticism with psychoanalysis and contemporary thinking about structure and gender elaborates and enriches — makes more evocative — the ways we may talk about texts.

Finally, I hope this book will send my reader back to those old favorites, the Victorian novels. For reading these long and inhabitable fictions, making the lives of, for example, Esther Summerson or Daniel Deronda or Lucy Snowe, momentarily part of our own still enlivens and refreshes us. It also disturbs us. For the desire and prohibition imagined by my three authors clearly continues to unsettle us, to return as ghosts that haunt our own fragile systems for managing, coping, and repressing. We are all children of families, and like Dickens, Eliot, and Bronte, we all spend our lives outgrowing the hurts of our childhoods.

Notes

Introduction

1. Jean Laplanche and J.-B. Pontalis, "Fantasy and the Origins of Sexuality," *International Journal of Psycho-Analysis* 49 (1968): 11.

2. Ibid.

3. My argument here is largely based on the following sources: "Introduction" and "Mean Household Size in England since the Sixteenth Century," both by Peter Laslett, in *Household and Family in Past Time*, ed. Peter Laslett and Richard Wall (London: Cambridge University Press, 1972), pp. 1-89, 125-58, and Peter Laslett, *The World We Have Lost: England before the Industrial Age* (New York: Charles Scribner's Sons, 1971). Other writings on and histories of the family I have found useful include Philippe Ariès, *Centuries of Childhood: A Social History of Family Life*, trans. Robert Baldick (New York: Alfred A. Knopf, 1962); Claude Lévi-Strauss, *The Elementary Structures of Kinship*, trans. James Harle Bell and Richard von Strumer, ed. Rodney Needham (Boston: Beacon Press, 1969); *The Family in History: Interdisciplinary Essays*, ed. Theodore K. Rabb and Robert I. Rotberg (New York: Harper Torchbooks, 1973); *The Family in History*, ed. Charles E. Rosenberg (Philadelphia: University of Pennsylvania Press, 1975); Edward Shorter, *The Making of the Modern Family* (New York: Basic Books, 1976); and Louise A. Tilly and Joan W. Scott, *Women, Work, and Family* (New York: Holt, Rinehart, & Winston, 1978). For studies of patriarchalism and paternalism, see Peter Laslett, *Patriarcha and Other Works of Sir Robert Filmer* (Oxford: Basil Blackwell, 1949); Gordon J. Schochet, *Patriarchalism in Political Thought: The Authoritarian Family and Political Speculation and Attitudes, Especially in Seventeenth-Century England* (Totawa, N.J.: Rowan & Littlefield, 1974); and David Roberts, *Paternalism in Early Victorian England* (New Brunswick, N.J.: Rutgers University Press, 1979).

4. See especially the chapter on authority in Walter E. Houghton, *The Victorian Frame of Mind* (New Haven: Yale University Press, 1957).

5. Christopher Lasch, *Haven in a Heartless World: The Family Besieged* (New York: Basic Books, 1979), chap. 8, and *The Culture of Narcissism: American Life in an Age of Diminishing Expectations* (New York: W. W. Norton & Co., 1979).

6. Fred Weinstein and Gerald Platt, *The Wish to be Free: Society, Psyche, and Value Change* (Berkeley and Los Angeles: University of California Press, 1969), pp. 143-53.

7. Ibid., pp. 176-96.

8. Ibid. See also Juliet Mitchell, *Psychoanalysis and Feminism: Freud, Reich, Laing, and*

Women (New York: Vintage Books, 1975); Dorothy Dinnerstein, *The Mermaid and the Minotaur: Sexual Arrangements and Human Malaise* (New York: Harper & Row, 1976); and Nancy Chodorow, *The Reproduction of Mothering: Psychoanalysis and the Sociology of Gender* (Berkeley and Los Angeles: University of California Press, 1978).

9. See, for example, Jacques Derrida, "Freud and the Scene of Writing," trans. Jeffrey Mehlman, *Yale French Studies*, no. 48 (1972), pp. 73-117; David Carroll, "Freud and the Myth of the Origin," *New Literary History* 6 (1975): 513-28; Jeffrey Mehlman, "How to Read Freud on Jokes: The Critic as *Schadchen*," *New Literary History* 6 (1975): 439-61; Hélène Cixous, "Fiction and Its Phantoms: A Reading of Freud's *Das Unheimliche* (The 'Uncanny')," *New Literary History* 7 (1976): 525-48; Cynthia Chase, "Oedipal Textuality: Reading Freud's Reading of *Oedipus*," *Diacritics* 9 (1979): 54-68; and Peter Brooks, "Fictions of the Wolfman: Freud and Narrative Understanding," *Diacritics* 9 (1979): 72-81.

10. Augustus Napier and Carl Whitaker, *The Family Crucible* (New York: Harper & Row, 1978).

11. See especially *Ecrits: A Selection*, trans. Alan Sheridan (New York: W. W. Norton & Co., 1977); *The Four Fundamental Concepts of Psycho-Analysis*, trans. Alan Sheridan, ed. Jacques-Alain Miller (New York: W. W. Norton & Co., 1978); *The Language of the Self: The Function of Language in Psychoanalysis*, trans. and commentary Anthony Wilden (Baltimore: Johns Hopkins University Press, 1968; reprinted in paperback as *Speech and Language in Psychoanalysis*, 1981). See also *Returning to Freud: Clinical Psychoanalysis in the School of Lacan*, ed. Stuart Schneiderman (New Haven: Yale University Press, 1980); Jean Laplanche, *Life and Death in Psychoanalysis*, trans., and intro. Jeffrey Mehlman (Baltimore: Johns Hopkins University Press, 1976); Paul Ricoeur, *Freud and Philosophy: An Essay on Interpretation*, trans. Denis Savage (New Haven: Yale University Press, 1970); Sherry Turkle, *Psychoanalytic Politics: Freud's French Revolution* (New York: Basic Books, 1978).

12. See *New French Feminisms*, ed. and intro. Elaine Marks and Isabelle de Courtivron (Amherst: University of Massachusetts Press, 1980); Luce Irigaray, *Speculum: De l'autre femme* (Paris: Editions de Minuit, 1974); Julia Kristeva, *About Chinese Women*, trans. Anita Barrows (New York: Urizen Books, 1977); and Julia Kristeva, *Desire in Language: A Semiotic Approach to Literature and Art*, trans. Thomas Gora, Alice Jardine, and Leon S. Roudiez, ed. Leon S. Roudiez (New York: Columbia University Press, 1980). See also Josette Feral, "Antigone or *The Irony of the Tribe*," *Diacritics* 8 (1978): 2-14; Jane Gallop, "The Seduction of an Analogy," *Diacritics* 9 (1979): 46-51; and Naomi Schor, "Female Paranoia: The Case for Psychoanalytic Feminist Criticism," paper presented at the Modern Language Association Convention, 1979.

CHAPTER 1 Charles Dickens: "Authors of Being"

1. Charles Dickens, *Martin Chuzzlewit* (London: Oxford University Press, 1951), pp. 1-6. Page references to this edition, known as the Oxford Illustrated Dickens, hereafter appear in my text.

2. For a discussion of identity themes in *Oliver Twist*, see J. Hillis Miller, *Charles Dickens: The World of his Novels* (Cambridge, Mass.: Harvard University Press, 1958), pp. 36-84; Steven Marcus, *Dickens: From Pickwick to Dombey* (New York: Simon and Schuster, 1968), pp. 84-91; and Barry Westburg, *The Confessional Fictions of Charles Dickens* (Dekalb, Ill.: Northern Illinois University Press, 1977), pp. 1-31.

3. I am indebted throughout this section about Dickens's obsession with origins and its narrative exposition to Harold Bloom, *The Anxiety of Influence* (New York: Oxford University Press, 1973); Cynthia Chase, "The Decomposition of the Elephants: Double-Reading *Daniel Deronda*," *PMLA* 93 (1978): 215-27; and Patricia Drechsler Tobin, *Time and the Novel: The Genealogical Imperative* (Princeton: Princeton University Press, 1978).

4. Charles Dickens, *A Tale of Two Cities* (London: Oxford University Press, 1949), p. 117. Page references to this edition hereafter appear in my text.

5. For a different yet related account of father-son conflict in this novel, see Albert D. Hutter, "Nation and Generation in *A Tale of Two Cities*," *PMLA* 93 (1978): 448-62. I am indebted throughout this discussion of *A Tale* to Hutter's thinking about embedded story as the retrospective originator of Dickens's narratives.

6. Charles Dickens, *Bleak House*, ed. George H. Ford and Sylvère Monod (New York: W. W. Norton & Co., 1977), pp. 13, 453-54. Page references to this edition hereafter appear in my text.

7. Charles Dickens, *The Old Curiosity Shop* (London: Oxford University Press, 1951), p. 172. Page references to this edition hereafter appear in my text, cited as *OCS* where needed for clarity.

8. For a critical exchange about Sally Brass as the Marchioness's mother, see William C. Bennett, "The Mystery of the Marchioness," *Dickensian* 36 (1940): 205-8; Gerald G. Grubb, "Dickens' Marchioness Identified," *Modern Language Notes* 68 (1953): 162-65; and Angus Easson, "Dickens's Marchioness Again," *Modern Language Review* 65 (1970): 517-18.

9. Imagining himself a woman who writes, Dickens clearly perceived what Virginia Woolf later articulated: that a woman thinks back through her mothers and so seeks a female tradition in literature; see *A Room of One's Own* (New York: Harcourt, Brace, Jovanovich, 1929), pp. 79-96.

10. Taylor Stoehr, *Dickens: The Dreamer's Stance* (Ithaca: Cornell University Press, 1965), pp. 137-70.

11. See Chase, "Decomposition," pp. 217-19.

12. See Peter K. Garrett, "Double Plots and Dialogical Form in Victorian Fiction," *Nineteenth-Century Fiction* 32 (1977): 1-17; see also Garrett's book on the same topic, *The Victorian Multiplot Novel: Studies in Dialogical Form* (New Haven: Yale University Press, 1980).

13. See Dianne F. Sadoff, "Storytelling and the Figure of the Father in *Little Dorrit*," *PMLA* 95 (1980): 235-45.

14. Chase, "Decomposition," pp. 222-23.

15. I modify here Lucien Goldmann's theory of "homologies," in which literary structures resemble the structures of class psychology. For a discussion of Goldmann's ideas, see Fredric R. Jameson, "The Symbolic Inference; or, Kenneth Burke and Ideological Analysis," *Critical Inquiry* 4 (1978): 513.

16. Hutter, "Nation and Generation," pp. 448-50, 454-55; *A Tale of Two Cities*, pp. 303-16.

17. Steven Marcus, "Who is Fagin?" in *Dickens*, pp. 358-78.

18. Laplanche and Pontalis, "Fantasy and the Origins of Sexuality," pp. 9-10.

19. Jacques Lacan, "On a Question Preliminary to Any Possible Treatment of Psychosis," in *Ecrits*, p. 199. See also Julia Kristeva, "The Father, Love, and Banishment," in *Desire in Language*, pp. 148-58.

20. Albert D. Hutter, "Reconstructive Autobiography: The Experience at Warren's Blacking," *Dickens Studies Annual* 6 (1977): 10.

21. Pearl Chesler Solomon, *Dickens and Melville in Their Time* (New York: Columbia University Press, 1975), pp. 125-53. See also Leonard F. Manheim, "The Personal History of David Copperfield," *American Imago* 9 (1952): 21-43, and "The Law as Father," *American Imago* 12 (1955): 17-23; Branwen Bailey Pratt, "Dickens and Father: Notes on the Family Romance," *Hartford Studies in Literature* 8 (1976): 4-22; Lawrence Jay Dessner, "*Great Expectations:* 'the ghost of a man's own father,'" *PMLA* 91 (1976): 436-49; and Albert D. Hutter, "Crime and Fantasy in *Great Expectations*," in *Psychoanalysis and Literary Process*, ed. Frederick C. Crews (Cambridge, Mass.: Winthrop Publishers, 1970), pp. 25-65.

22. Guy Rosalato, "Trois générations d'hommes dans le mythe réligieux et la généalogie," in *Essais sur le symbolique* (Paris: Gallimard, 1969), pp. 59-96. Also, "Du Père," ibid., pp. 36-58.

23. John T. Irwin, *Doubling and Incest/Repetition and Revenge: A Speculative Reading of Faulkner* (Baltimore: Johns Hopkins University Press, 1975), p. 216.

24. See Lacan, "The Signification of the Phallus," in *Ecrits,* pp. 281-91.

25. Edgar Johnson, *Charles Dickens: His Tragedy and Triumph* (New York: Simon and Schuster, 1952), pp. 30-46, 93-100, 254-60, 306-8. See also *The Letters of Charles Dickens,* ed. Madeline House, Graham Storey, Kathleen Tillotson, and Nina Burgis, 4 vols. (Oxford: Clarendon Press, 1965-77), 1: 43-51, 514-28; 2: 207, 214-33; 3: 191, 333-56, 575-602; hereafter cited in the text as *Letters.*

26. See Freud's metapsychological papers, especially "The Unconscious" and "Instincts and Their Vicissitudes," in *The Standard Edition of the Complete Psychological Works of Sigmund Freud,* trans. and ed. James Strachey, 14 (London: Hogarth Press, 1957), 159-215 and 117-40. Hereafter cited as *SE.* See also Jean Laplanche and J.-B. Pontalis, *The Language of Psycho-Analysis,* trans. Donald Nicholson-Smith (New York: W. W. Norton & Co., 1973), pp. 127-30.

27. Charles Dickens, *Pickwick Papers* (London: Oxford University Press, 1947), pp. 74-81, 284-96. Page references to this edition hereafter appear in my text, cited as *PP* where needed for clarity.

28. See J. Hillis Miller's meditation, "The Critic as Host," *Critical Inquiry* 2 (1976): 439-47.

29. Marcus, *Dickens,* pp. 169-212.

30. See Lacan, "On a Question," pp. 215-21.

31. Charles Dickens, *Barnaby Rudge* (London: Oxford University Press, 1954), pp. 602-3. Page references to this edition hereafter appear in my text.

32. Sigmund Freud, "The Uncanny," in *SE,* 17 (1955), 219-52, esp. 232-33.

33. Charles Dickens, *David Copperfield* (London: Oxford University Press, 1948), p. 2. Page references to this edition hereafter appear in my text, cited as *DC* where needed for clarity.

34. This pattern has also been discussed by Westburg, *Confessional Fictions,* pp. 43-48, and Solomon, *Dickens and Melville,* pp. 139-42.

35. Solomon, *Dickens and Melville,* pp. 138-44.

36. Ibid., pp. 149-52. See also Gwendolyn B. Needham, "The Undisciplined Heart of David Copperfield," *Nineteenth-Century Fiction* 9 (1954): 81-107; and William H. Marshall, "The Image of Steerforth and the Structure of *David Copperfield,*" *Tennessee Studies in Literature* 5 (1960): 57-65.

37. See Hutter, "Nation and Generation," p. 453.

38. Charles Dickens, *Great Expectations* (London: Oxford University Press, 1953), pp. 109-10. Page references to this edition hereafter appear in my text.

39. See Stoehr, *Dickens,* pp. 105-9, for further discussion of Pip and George Barnwell.

40. The essential essay on surrogate violence and aggression in Dickens's narratives is, of course, Julian Moynihan, "The Hero's Guilt: The Case of *Great Expectations,*" *Essays in Criticism* 10 (1960): 60-79.

41. Freud, "The Uncanny," p. 226.

42. For a discussion of the relationship between the theater and Dickens's caricaturing aesthetic, see Robert Garis, *The Dickens Theatre: A Reassessment of the Novels* (Oxford: Clarendon Press, 1965).

43. See Westburg, *Confessional Fictions,* pp. 124-25, 198-201.

44. Edward Said, *Beginnings: Intention and Method* (New York: Basic Books, 1975), p. 83. For a critique of Said's masculinist concept of literary engendering to which my own thinking and rhetoric here is indebted, see Sandra M. Gilbert and Susan Gubar, *The Madwoman in the Attic: The Woman Writer and the Nineteenth-Century Literary Imagination* (New Haven: Yale University Press, 1979), pp. 4-5.

45. See Westburg, *Confessional Fictions,* pp. 38-40.

46. For a discussion of the "comic" ending of Pip's narrative in terms of his rebirth as little Pip, see Dessner, *"Great Expectations,"* pp. 447-48.

47. William C. Spengemann, *The Forms of Autobiography: Episodes in the History of a Literary Genre* (New Haven: Yale University Press, 1980), pp. 119-32, thinks only the first fourteen chapters of *Copperfield* "autobiographical," primarily because of David's "rebirth"

at that point in the narrative; the David after rebirth bears little resemblance, Spengemann says, to the David (Dickens) before it. For the complex relationship between Dickensian fiction and autobiography, see Hutter, "Reconstructive Autobiography"; Westburg, *Confessional Fictions,* pp. 179-87; Pratt, "Dickens and Father," pp. 4-8 and 12-17; J. Hillis Miller, "Three Problems of Fictional Form: First-Person Narration in *David Copperfield* and *Huckleberry Finn,*" in *Experience and the Novel: Selected Papers from the English Institute, 1967,* ed. Roy Harvey Pearce (New York: Columbia University Press, 1968), pp. 21-48; Sylvia Manning, "Masking and Self-Revelation: Dickens's Three Autobiographies," *Dickens Studies Newsletter* 7 (1976): 69-74; and Avrom Fleishman, "The Fictions of Autobiographical Fiction," *Genre* 9 (1976): 73-86.

48. For an excellent account of David's economic and oedipal notion of the "self-made man," see Solomon, *Dickens and Melville,* pp. 95-105 and 130-53.

49. See a fine essay by Stanley Tick, "The Memorializing of Mr. Dick," *Nineteenth-Century Fiction* 24 (1969): 124-53; Tick makes some of the same points I do.

50. Bert Hornback, "Frustration and Resolution in *David Copperfield,*" *Studies in English Literature* 8 (1968): 651-67, mentions that a memorial petitions the government for redress of personal grievances.

51. For a discussion of "beheading" as a figure for the imaginative presentation of the self, see Westburg, *Confessional Fictions,* pp. 193-200.

52. Miller, *Charles Dickens,* p. 151, believes Micawber's use of language helps him "escape from reality by transcending it linguistically." "There is," he goes on to say, "a secret identity between the linguistic enterprise of Micawber and that of Dickens himself."

53. See Hutter, "Reconstructive Autobiography," pp. 5-9; Pratt, "Dickens and Father," p. 11.

54. John Forster, *The Life of Charles Dickens,* ed. A. J. Hoppé (London: J. M. Dent & Sons, Ltd., 1966), pp. 19-33.

55. Hutter, "Reconstructive Autobiography," p. 14, also makes this point.

56. Westburg, *Confessional Fictions,* pp. 148-52.

57. Alexander Welsh, *The City of Dickens* (Oxford: Clarendon Press, 1971), pp. 141-228.

58. Coventry Patmore, *The Angel in the House* (Boston: Ticknor and Fields, 1856).

59. Sigmund Freud, "Totem and Taboo," *SE,* 13 (1955), 1-17.

60. Ricoeur, *Freud and Philosophy,* pp. 194-211.

61. Charles Dickens, *Little Dorrit* (London: Oxford University Press, 1953), p. 229. Page references in my text are from this edition.

62. Welsh, *City of Dickens,* pp. 153-54 and 172-73, also discusses the resemblance between father and lover in *Little Dorrit,* and my discussion of this issue is indebted to his.

63. See Alex Zwerdling, "Esther Summerson Rehabilitated," *PMLA* 88 (1973): 429-39; Crawford Kilian, "In Defence of Esther Summerson," *Dalhousie Review* 54 (1974): 318-28; Lawrence Frank, "'Through a Glass Darkly': Esther Summerson and *Bleak House,*" *Dickens Studies Annual* 4 (1975): 91-112; William Axton, "The Trouble with Esther," *Modern Language Quarterly* 26 (1965): 545-57; Martha Rosso, "Dickens and Esther," *Dickensian* 65 (1969): 90-94; and Joan D. Winslow, "Esther Summerson: The Betrayal of the Imagination," *Journal of Narrative Technique* 6 (1976): 1-13.

64. Charles Dickens, *Dombey and Son* (London: Oxford University Press, 1950), p. 845. Page references in my text are from this edition. For an account of the "two spheres" of the novel—male vs. female—see Nina Auerbach, "Dickens and Dombey: A Daughter After All," *Dickens Studies Annual* 5 (1976): 95-114.

65. Julian Moynahan, "Dealings with the Firm of Dombey and Son: Firmness versus Wetness," in *Dickens and the Twentieth Century,* ed. John Gross and Gabriel Pearson (Toronto: University of Toronto Press, 1962), pp. 121-32.

66. René Girard, *Deceit, Desire, and the Novel: Self and Other in Literary Structure,* trans. Yvonne Freccero (Baltimore: Johns Hopkins University Press, 1965), pp. 1-52.

67. Moynahan, "Dealings," pp. 128-30.

68. Welsh, *City of Dickens,* p. 151.

69. Solomon, *Dickens and Melville,* pp. 149-52.

CHAPTER 2 George Eliot: "A Sort of Father"

1. Steven Marcus, "Literature and Social Theory: Starting in with George Eliot," in *Representations: Essays on Literature and Society* (New York: Random House, 1975), pp. 183-213.

2. I am indebted to J. Hillis Miller for details of structure and concept throughout this chapter; Miller's lectures in a National Endowment for the Humanities Summer Seminar at Yale University in 1977 stimulated much of my thinking about gender and paternal thematics in Eliot's narrative project and provided me the enthusiasm to carry through on this speculation.

3. George Eliot, "Amos Barton," in *Scenes of Clerical Life,* in *The Works of George Eliot,* 24 vols. (Edinburgh and London: William Blackwood and Sons, n.d.), 1:99. Page references in my text, cited as *SCL* where needed for clarity, are from this edition, known as the Cabinet Edition.

4. Sigmund Freud, "Family Romances," in *SE,* 9 (1959), 238-39.

5. *The George Eliot Letters,* ed. Gordon S. Haight, 9 vols. (New Haven: Yale University Press, 1954-56, 1978), 2: 406-10. Hereafter cited as *Letters* in my text.

6. See Arthur Efron, "Freud's Self-Analysis and the Nature of Psychoanalytic Criticism," *Review of Psychoanalysis* 4 (1977): 253-80; and Judith Herman and Lisa Hirschman, "Father-Daughter Incest," *Signs* 2 (1977): 737-38. Herman and Hirschman misread to some extent Freud's well-known letter to Fliess and fail to notice that his equation also factors in constitutional causes of hysteria. See also Judith Herman, *Father-Daughter Incest* (Cambridge, Mass.: Harvard University Press, 1981).

7. Elaine Showalter, *A Literature of Their Own: British Women Novelists from Bronte to Lessing* (Princeton: Princeton University Press, 1977), pp. 54-58, 61-65. Showalter's wide-ranging discussion demonstrates that Eliot's relationship with her father is not unique among nineteenth-century daughters who write. For discussion of paternal fantasy as part of the scene of seduction, see also Chodorow, *Reproduction of Mothering,* pp. 117-20, 160-64; Chodorow discusses Marjorie R. Leonard, "Fathers and Daughters: The Significance of 'Fathering' in the Psychosexual Development of the Girl," *International Journal of Psycho-Analysis* 47 (1966): 325-34.

8. Sigmund Freud, "An Autobiographical Study," *SE,* 20 (1959), 33-34.

9. Sigmund Freud, *The Origins of Psychoanalysis: Letters to Wilhelm Fliess, Drafts and Notes: 1887-1902* (New York: Basic Books, 1950), pp. 215-16.

10. Sigmund Freud, "New Introductory Lectures on Psycho-Analysis: Femininity," *SE,* 22 (1964), 120; Laplanche and Pontalis, "Fantasy and the Origins of Sexuality," pp. 1-18.

11. Laplanche and Pontalis, "Fantasy and the Origins of Sexuality," p. 11.

12. Ibid., pp. 13-14.

13. Ruby V. Redinger, *George Eliot: The Emergent Self* (New York: Alfred A. Knopf, 1977), pp. 27-60. See also *Letters,* 1: 135-36, 141-44, 163-68; Gordon S. Haight, *George Eliot: A Biography* (New York: Oxford University Press, 1968), pp. 41-54. Gaskell's terminology appears in *Wives and Daughters,* ed. Frank Glover Smith (Baltimore: Penguin Books, 1969), p. 182.

14. Sandor Ferenczi, "Confusion of Tongues between the Adult and the Child," in *Final Contributions to the Problems and Methods of Psycho-Analysis,* trans. Eric Mosbacher, ed. Michael Balint (London: Hogarth Press, 1955), pp. 157-67.

15. George Eliot, *The Mill on the Floss,* 2 vols. (Edinburgh and London: William Blackwood and Sons, n.d.), 1: 102. Page references in my text are to the Cabinet Edition, cited as *MF* where needed for clarity.

16. George Eliot, *Felix Holt the Radical,* 2 vols. (Edinburgh and London: William Blackwood and Sons, n.d.), 1: 2, 13. Page references in my text are to the Cabinet Edition.

17. George Eliot, *Silas Marner*, 2 vols. (Edinburgh and London: William Blackwood and Sons, n.d.), 1: 255-56. Page references in my text are to the Cabinet Edition. For a different account of the family romance in *Silas Marner*, see Lawrence Jay Dessner, "The Autobiographical Matrix of *Silas Marner*," *Studies in the Novel* 11 (1979): 251-82. In their forthcoming book, Sandra M. Gilbert and Susan Gubar will make some of these same points.

18. Freud, "Family Romances," pp. 237-41.

19. For a discussion of the connections between family romance and the romance mode in American literature, see Eric J. Sundquist, *Home as Found: Genealogy and Authority in Nineteenth-Century American Literature* (Baltimore: Johns Hopkins University Press, 1979). With regard to George Eliot and romance, see U. C. Knoepflmacher, *George Eliot's Early Novels: The Limits of Realism* (Berkeley and Los Angeles: University of California Press, 1968), in which Eliot's realism is tested against Wordsworth's romanticism; Jonathan R. Quick, "*Silas Marner* as Romance: The Case of Hawthorne," *Nineteenth-Century Fiction* 29 (1974): 287-98, for generic discussion of "prose romance"; Joseph Weisenfarth, "Demythologizing *Silas Marner*," *ELH* 37 (1970): 226-44, and "*Adam Bede* and Myth," *Papers on Language & Literature* 8 (1972): 39-52, for an account of the ways in which Eliot's mythologies inform and support her "realism"; and Alexander Welsh, "George Eliot and the Romance," *Nineteenth-Century Fiction* 14 (1959): 241-54, for a discussion of Maggie Tulliver's relation to other romance heroines. See also *Letters*, 3: 339, in which Eliot informs Blackwood she will try to write a "historical romance."

20. See Laura Comer Emery, *George Eliot's Creative Conflict* (Berkeley and Los Angeles: University of California Press, 1976), pp. 69-75. Emery makes some of these same points about fathers and oedipal struggle.

21. George Eliot, *Middlemarch: A Study of Provincial Life*, 3 vols. (Edinburgh and London: William Blackwood and Sons, n.d.), 1: 12. All references in my text are to the Cabinet Edition, cited as *Mid.* where needed for clarity. For discussion of the father-husband and Dorothea's misreading of him see especially Emery, *George Eliot's Creative Conflict*, pp. 157-70; Neil Hertz, "Recognizing Casaubon," *Glyph*, no. 6 (1979), pp. 24-41; J. Hillis Miller, "Narrative and History," *ELH* 41 (1974): 455-73, and "Optic and Semiotic in *Middlemarch*," in *The Worlds of Victorian Fiction*, ed. Jerome H. Buckley (Cambridge, Mass.: Harvard University Press, 1975), pp. 125-45.

22. Alan Mintz, *George Eliot and the Novel of Vocation* (Cambridge, Mass.: Harvard University Press, 1978), pp. 108-13. See also Kathleen Blake, "*Middlemarch* and the Woman Question," *Nineteenth-Century Fiction* 31 (1976): 285-312; and Lee R. Edwards, "Women, Energy, and *Middlemarch*," *Massachusetts Review* 13 (1972): 223-38.

23. See *Letters*, 4: 214-64, 284-302, for Eliot's correspondence with Frederic Harrison and her attempt to master the difficulties of settlement and inheritance law while plotting *Felix Holt*.

24. Lacan, "On a Question," p. 199, et passim. See also Michel Foucault, "The Father's 'No,'" in *Language, Counter-Memory, and Practice: Selected Essays and Interviews*, ed. and trans. Donald F. Bouchard (Ithaca: Cornell University Press, 1977), pp. 80-84.

25. Lacan, "On a Question," pp. 218-19.

26. Redinger, *George Eliot*, pp. 119-28.

27. George Eliot, *Adam Bede*, 2 vols. (Edinburgh and London: William Blackwood and Sons, n.d.), 1: 332. All references in my text are to the Cabinet Edition.

28. See George Eliot, "The Progress of the Intellect," in *The Essays of George Eliot*, ed. Thomas Pinney (New York: Columbia University Press, 1963), pp. 27-45, esp. p. 31. See also a sympathetic rendering of Eliot's concept of the inevitability of temporal progression: Elizabeth Ermarth, "Incarnations: George Eliot's Conception of 'Undeviating Law,'" *Nineteenth-Century Fiction* 29 (1974): 273-86.

29. Marcus, "Literature and Social Theory," pp. 201-4.

30. For different perspectives on Maggie's hunger for love, see Nina Auerbach, "The Power of Hunger: Demonism and Maggie Tulliver," *Nineteenth-Century Fiction* 30 (1975):

150-71; and Bernard Paris, *Experiments in Life: George Eliot's Quest for Values* (Detroit: Wayne State University Press, 1965), pp. 156-68.

31. Emery, *George Eliot's Creative Conflict,* pp. 9-32; David Smith, "Incest Patterns in Two Victorian Novels," *Literature and Psychology* 15 (1965): 144-62.

32. Freud, "Femininity," pp. 129-35; Chodorow, *Reproduction of Mothering,* pp. 165-69.

33. My discussion of the asymmetry of male and female oedipal work is indebted to Herman and Hirschman, "Father-Daughter Incest," pp. 739-40.

34. For a discussion of Eliot's contradictory morality, see I. T. Ker, "George Eliot's Rhetoric of Enthusiasm," *Essays in Criticism* 26 (1976): 39-52; see also the incisive discussion in Calvin Bedient, *Architects of the Self: George Eliot, D. H. Lawrence, and E. M. Forster* (Berkeley and Los Angeles: University of California Press, 1972), pp. 33-98.

35. Redinger, *George Eliot,* pp. 440-59, also defines *Romola*'s publication as unique.

36. Redinger, ibid., p. 433, defines this "strange sequence of fiction" as beginning with "Brother Jacob" and extending through *Romola;* I see this period of struggle as slightly longer.

37. John W. Cross, *George Eliot's Life as Related in Her Letters and Journals,* 3 vols. (Edinburgh and London: William Blackwood and Sons, n.d.), 2: 255.

38. Felicia Bonaparte, *The Triptych and the Cross: The Central Myths of George Eliot's Poetic Imagination* (New York: New York University Press, 1979), p. 10.

39. Quoted by Redinger, *George Eliot,* p. 442.

40. Bonaparte, *The Triptych and the Cross,* pp. 1-33, makes some of these same points about *Romola*'s importance and Eliot's process of composition.

41. Laplanche and Pontalis, *Language of Psycho-Analysis,* pp. 465-69.

42. Sigmund Freud, "Fixation to Traumas: The Unconscious," *SE,* 16 (1963), 273-85, esp. p. 275.

43. Laplanche and Pontalis, "Fantasy and the Origins of Sexuality," pp. 3-11; Laplanche and Pontalis, *Language of Psycho-Analysis,* pp. 404-7; Laplanche, *Life and Death in Psychoanalysis,* pp. 25-47; Sigmund Freud, "Studies in Hysteria," *SE,* 2 (1955), 162.

44. George Eliot, *Romola,* 2 vols. (Edinburgh and London: William Blackwood and Sons, n.d.), 1: 343-52. All references in my text are to the Cabinet Edition.

45. Bonaparte, *The Triptych and the Cross,* p. 116.

46. Carole Robinson, "*Romola:* A Reading of the Novel," *Victorian Studies* 7 (1962): 29-42.

47. Bonaparte, *The Triptych and the Cross,* pp. 188-93, believes Eliot discriminates in *Romola* between the Bacchic law of the aggregate, which protects the individual against the encroachments of others on his freedom, and the Christian law of the community, which binds the individual to concern for the welfare of all. Although Bonaparte discusses Eliot's faith in this Christian law as moral but nondidactic, as descriptive but not normative, I think *Romola* is Eliot's most didactic and normative novel primarily because it taps dangerous memories that must be controlled or repressed to allow its author to go forward in her life and career as a writer.

48. Laplanche and Pontalis, *Language of Psycho-Analysis,* pp. 50-52.

49. As Felicia Bonaparte points out, the public handbills titled "Justice" (which demands execution of the traitors) and "Law" (which urges the appeal be granted) define Savonarola's law as lawless and opposed to the community's interest and morality. See *The Triptych and the Cross,* p. 221.

50. See Robinson, "*Romola,*" p. 41, and Bonaparte, *The Triptych and the Cross,* pp. 229-39.

51. For discussions of uncles in Eliot's novels, see U. C. Knoepflmacher, "*Middlemarch:* An Avuncular View," *Nineteenth-Century Fiction* 30 (1975): 53-81; Joseph Weisenfarth, "Commentary," *Nineteenth-Century Fiction* 30 (1976): 572-73, explicates the allusion in *Middlemarch:* "Der Neffe als Onkel."

52. See Susan R. Cohen, "'The Family Procession': Generational Structures in the Novels of George Eliot" (Ph.D. dissertation, Yale University, 1979).

53. George Eliot, *Daniel Deronda*, 3 vols. (Edinburgh and London: William Blackwood and Sons, n.d.), 3: 104. All references in my text are to the Cabinet Edition.

54. See Joseph Weisenfarth, "The Medea in *Daniel Deronda*," *Die Neuren Sprachen* 22 (1973): 103-8.

55. Henry James, "George Eliot," in *Partial Portraits* (London: Macmillan and Co., 1888), p. 86.

56. Sigmund Freud, "The Ego and the Super-Ego (Ego Ideal)," in *The Ego and the Id*, *SE*, 19 (1955), 28-39.

57. I borrow my terminology from Said's *Beginnings*.

58. For discussions of Judaism in *Daniel Deronda*, see William Baker, *George Eliot and Judaism* (Salzburg: Institut für Englische Sprache und Literatur, Universitat Salzburg, 1975); Avrom Fleishman, "'Daniel Charisi': An Assessment of *Daniel Deronda* in the History of Ideas," in *Fiction and the Ways of Knowing: Essays on British Novels* (Austin: University of Texas Press, 1978), pp. 86-109; Jean Sudrann, "*Daniel Deronda* and the Landscape of Exile," *ELH* 37 (1970): 433-55; and *Daniel Deronda: A Centenary Symposium*, ed. Alice Shalvi (Jerusalem: Jerusalem Academic Press, 1976).

59. Redinger, *George Eliot*, pp. 4-6, et passim. See also Quentin Anderson, "George Eliot in *Middlemarch*," in *From Dickens to Hardy*, ed. Boris Ford (Baltimore: Penguin Books, 1958), pp. 274-93; Edwin J. Kenney, Jr., "George Eliot: Through the Looking Glass," in *Middlemarch*, ed. Bert G. Hornback (New York: W. W. Norton & Co., 1977), pp. 733-50; and Gilbert and Gubar, *Madwoman in the Attic*, p. 452. For an excellent discussion of the reasons nineteenth-century women authors assumed male pseudonyms, see Elaine Showalter, "Women Writers and the Double Standard," in *Woman in Sexist Society: Studies in Power and Powerlessness*, ed. Vivian Gornick and Barbara K. Moran (New York: New American Library, 1972), pp. 452-79.

60. Said, *Beginnings*, pp. 82-84.

61. Sandra M. Gilbert, "Literary Paternity: The Pen as Penis," *Cornell Review*, no. 6 (Summer 1979), pp. 54-65, esp. p. 54. This essay has been reprinted in slightly different form in Gilbert and Gubar, *Madwoman in the Attic*, pp. 3-16. For a perspective on Eliot and the female tradition, see Margaret Anne Doody, "George Eliot and the Eighteenth-Century Novel," *Nineteenth-Century Fiction* 35 (1980): 260-91; and Elaine Showalter, "The Greening of Sister George," *Nineteenth-Century Fiction* 35 (1980): 292-311.

62. See K. M. Newton, "The Role of the Narrator in George Eliot's Novels," *Journal of Narrative Technique* 3 (1973): 97-107; also Michal Peled Ginsburg, "Pseudonym, Epigraphs, and Narrative Voice: *Middlemarch* and the Problem of Authorship," *ELH* 47 (1980): 542-58.

63. George Eliot, *The Impressions of Theophrastus Such* (Edinburgh and London: William Blackwood and Sons, n.d.), pp. 26-27. References in my text are to the Cabinet Edition.

64. Sigmund Freud, "A Case of Paranoia Running Counter to the Psycho-Analytic Theory of the Disease," *SE*, 14 (1957), 263-72; Laplanche and Pontalis, "Fantasy and the Origins of Sexuality," pp. 10-11.

65. Ginsburg, "Pseudonym, Epigraphs, and Narrative Voice," p. 546: "Writing is the process by which a woman — Mary Ann Evans — becomes a man — George Eliot. Writing, the most common metaphor for which is weaving, is the symbolic way by which a woman produces herself a phallus."

66. Miller, "Optic and Semiotic in *Middlemarch*," p. 128.

67. See Dianne F. Sadoff, "'Nature's Language': Metaphor in the Text of *Adam Bede*," *Genre* 11 (1978): 411-26.

68. Chase, "Decomposition," pp. 215-27.

69. See Kenney, "George Eliot," pp. 743-45.

70. See Anthony G. Bradley, "Family as Pastoral: The Garths in *Middlemarch*," *Ariel: A Review of International English Literature* 6 (1975): 41-51, esp. p. 47; and Kenney, "George Eliot," pp. 746-48.

CHAPTER 3 Charlotte Bronte: Masters and Mastery

1. Winifred Gérin, "General Introduction," Charlotte Bronte, *Five Novelettes*, ed. Winifred Gérin (London: Folio Press, 1971), p. 16. Page references in my text are to this edition of the novelettes.

2. Bronte, *Five Novelettes*, p. 17. Also quoted in Winifred Gérin, *Charlotte Bronte: The Evolution of Genius* (London: Oxford University Press, 1969), pp. 104-5.

3. T. J. Wise and J. A. Symington, *The Brontes: Their Lives, Friendships, and Correspondence*, 4 vols. (Oxford: Shakespeare Head Press, 1932), 1: 297. Hereafter cited in my text as *Lives*.

4. Gilbert and Gubar, *Madwoman in the Attic*, pp. 311-17.

5. For a discussion of androgyny as the central concern of Bronte's texts, see F.A.C. Wilson, "'The Primrose Wreath': The Heroes of the Bronte Novels," *Nineteenth-Century Fiction* 29 (1974): 40-57. Helene Moglen, *Charlotte Bronte: The Self Conceived* (New York: W. W. Norton & Co., 1976), pp. 87-104, thinks androgyny as stated in *The Professor* is tested in the later narratives.

6. Stephen Heath, "Difference," *Screen* 19 (1978): 63.

7. See Lacan, *The Language of the Self*, pp. 19-27, and "The Agency of the Letter in the Unconscious," in *Ecrits*, pp. 146-78.

8. Jacques Lacan, "Of the Gaze as *Object Petit à*," in *The Four Fundamental Concepts of Psycho-Analysis*, pp. 67-119.

9. Ibid., pp. 84-85, 83, 88.

10. Sigmund Freud, *SE*, 17 (1955), 231; *SE*, 11 (1957), 211-18.

11. Sigmund Freud, "Jokes and Their Relation to the Unconscious," *SE*, 8 (1960), 98.

12. Sigmund Freud, "Some Psychical Consequences of the Anatomical Distinctions between the Sexes," *SE*, 19 (1961), 252. See also "The Dissolution of the Oedipus Complex," ibid., pp. 175-76; "Female Sexuality," *SE*, 21 (1961), 233; "Femininity," p. 125.

13. Freud, "Anatomical Distinctions," p. 152.

14. Quoted by Heath, "Difference," p. 84. See also Irigaray, *Speculum*, pp. 177-78.

15. Luce Irigaray, "This Sex Which Is Not One," trans. Claudia Reeder, in *New French Feminisms*, ed. Marks and de Courtivron, p. 101. See also Hélène Cixous, "The Laugh of the Medusa," trans. Keith Cohen and Paula Cohen, *Signs* 1 (1976): 881-89.

16. "This Sex," p. 103.

17. See Julia Kristeva, "Oscillation between Power and Denial," trans. Marilyn A. August, in *New French Feminisms*, ed. Marks and de Courtivron, p. 165; and "The Novel as Polylogue," in Kristeva, *Desire in Language*, pp. 159-209.

18. See *Legends of Angria*, ed. Fannie E. Ratchford and William Clyde DeVane (New Haven: Yale University Press, 1933), p. 316.

19. Lacan, "Of the Gaze," pp. 75, 80, 78.

20. Heath, "Difference," pp. 83-92. I am indebted throughout this section of my chapter to Heath's excellent critique of the scopic drive as phallocentric.

21. Charlotte Bronte, *The Professor* (Oxford: Shakespeare Head Press, 1931), pp. 63, 123. Page references in my text are to this edition.

22. Sigmund Freud, "The Medusa's Head," *SE*, 18 (1955), 273-74. On the contrary, Cixous sees Medusa as "beautiful" and "laughing" ("Laugh of the Medusa," p. 885).

23. Charlotte Bronte, *Shirley*, ed. Herbert Rosengarten and Margaret Smith (Oxford: Clarendon Press, 1979), pp. 26, 199-200. Page references in my text are to this edition.

24. Charlotte Bronte, *Villette*, ed. Geoffrey Tillotson and Donald Hawes (Boston: Houghton Mifflin Co., 1971), p. 101. Page references in my text are to this Riverside Edition.

25. Charlotte Bronte, *Jane Eyre*, ed. Jane Jack and Margaret Smith (Oxford: Clarendon Press, 1969), p. 163. Page references in my text are to this edition.

26. The father-daughter or master-servant relationship in Bronte's novels has often been

remarked by critics. See Smith, "Incest Patterns," pp. 135-44; Moglen, *Charlotte Bronte,* esp. pp. 119-28, 174-89, 215-28, 233-40.

27. Moglen, *Charlotte Bronte,* pp. 183-85; Terry Eagleton, *Myths of Power: A Marxist Study of the Brontes* (London: Macmillan Press, 1975), pp. 24-29, 42, 57.

28. Eagleton, *Myths of Power,* pp. 15, 21.

29. Moglen, *Charlotte Bronte,* p. 59.

30. See Wise and Symington, *The Brontes,* 2: 173-74, for a letter to W. S. Williams (4 January 1848), in which Bronte equates sexual desire with mental illness and madness.

31. Sigmund Freud, "A Child Is Being Beaten," *SE,* 17 (1955), 179-204; quotations in this and the following paragraph from this source.

32. Showalter, *A Literature of Their Own,* pp. 112-24.

33. Jacques Derrida, *Of Grammatology,* trans. Gayatri Chakravorty Spivak (Baltimore: Johns Hopkins University Press, 1976), p. 155, also pp. 144-57.

34. See Moglen, *Charlotte Bronte,* pp. 33-59, 75; Gérin, *Charlotte Bronte,* pp. 20-30, 95-100, 136-41, 294-307.

35. Robert Keefe, *Charlotte Bronte's World of Death* (Austin: University of Texas Press, 1979), pp. xi-44, thinks Bronte's mother's death during her fifth year makes the mother the central figure in Bronte's imagination. He notes (as Gérin also points out) that when Bronte became a governess, she invariably disliked the families' wives but found the husbands "pleasant"; this pattern, then, reflects Bronte's oedipal struggle: "For more than fifteen years she had lived without a maternal rival for her father's affections" (p. 17). On the contrary, however, Keefe also believes it "too simplistic" to define Bronte's relationship with Constantin Héger as part of her oedipal material (p. 22).

36. See, for example, Annette Hopkins, *The Father of the Brontes* (Baltimore: Johns Hopkins University Press, 1958), for such a demythologizing. For a justification of Rev. Bronte, see John Lock and Canon W. T. Dixon, *A Man of Sorrow: The Life, Letters and Times of the Rev. Patrick Bronte, 1777-1861* (London: Thomas Nelson and Sons, 1965). Lock and Dixon specifically answer some of Elizabeth Gaskell's charges against Bronte, including his shooting of pistols (pp. 100-115) and the burning of the children's shoes (pp. 253-55).

37. Gérin, *Charlotte Bronte,* p. 300.

38. Moglen, *Charlotte Bronte,* p. 67.

39. See ibid., p. 73; Gérin, *Charlotte Bronte,* pp. 257-58.

40. Jacques Lacan, "The Seminar on 'The Purloined Letter,'" *Yale French Studies,* no. 48 (1972), pp. 39-72.

41. See Joseph Kestner, "The *Letters* of Jane Austen: The Writer as *Emetteur/Récepteur,*" *Papers on Language & Literature* 14 (1978): 249-68.

42. I am indebted for many of my points about the relationship between Jane and Bertha to Peter Grudin's fine essay, "Jane and the Other Mrs. Rochester: Excess and Restraint in *Jane Eyre,*" *Novel* 10 (1977): 145-57. See also Moglen, *Charlotte Bronte,* pp. 124-30.

43. *Madwoman in the Attic,* pp. 354-62.

44. Richard Chase, "The Brontes: A Centennial Observance," *Kenyon Review* 9 (1947): 487-506.

45. Gilbert and Gubar, for example, quote Chase's conclusion that narrative castration demonstrates the "tempo and energy of the universe can be quelled" by a "patient, practical woman," in order to qualify it carefully: "There is an element of truth in this idea," they admit; despite her urge to punish Rochester, however, Jane's goal is "simply to strengthen herself, to make herself an equal of the world Rochester represents" (*Madwoman in the Attic,* p. 368). Carolyn Heilbrun asserts that "Rochester undergoes, not sexual mutilation as the Freudians claim, but the inevitable sufferings necessary when those in power are forced to release some of their power to those who previously had none"; Jane becomes figurative victim for all victims who angrily take revenge on their oppressors (*Toward a Recognition of Androgyny* [New York: Alfred A. Knopf, 1973], p. 59). Adrienne Rich discards this "phallic-

patriarchal notion of [Rochester's] ordeal"; instead she defines Jane's marriage to Rochester as "that of a strong spirit demanding its counterpart in another" ("*Jane Eyre:* The Temptations of a Motherless Woman," *Ms.* 2 [October 1973]: 107). Helene Moglen declares that "Jane's development [can] be maintained only at the cost of Rochester's romantic self-image. Rochester's mutilation is, in the terms of this nascent feminist myth, the necessary counterpart of Jane's independence: the terrible condition of a relationship of equality" (*Charlotte Bronte,* p. 142). It is time, I think, for feminist critics to stop apologizing for Bronte's narrative punishment of Rochester; his punishment indeed represents a "symbolic castration," one that does not signify "equality" but rather a fear of sexual difference and masculine power.

46. Chase, "The Brontes," p. 495; Freud, "The Uncanny," p. 231.

47. Chodorow, *Reproduction of Mothering,* pp. 143-48.

48. See Thomas Ewens, "Female Sexuality and the Role of the Phallus," *Psychoanalytic Review* 63 (1976): 615-37. See also Gilbert and Gubar, *Madwoman in the Attic,* p. 595.

49. For extended discussion, see Herman and Hirschman, "Father-Daughter Incest," pp. 739-42.

50. See Helene Deutsch, "The Significance of Masochism in the Mental Life of Women," in *The Psycho-Analytic Reader,* ed. Robert Fliess (New York: International Universities Press, 1948), pp. 195-207; Freud, "Femininity," pp. 112-35; "Female Sexuality," pp. 225-43. For critiques, see Roy D. Schafer, "Problems in Freud's Psychology of Women," *Journal of the American Psychoanalytic Association* 22 (1974): 459-85; Irigaray, *Speculum,* pp. 51-64; Michael E. Lamb, Margaret Tresch Owen, and Lindsay Chase-Lansdale, "The Father-Daughter Relationship: Past, Present, and Future," in *Becoming Female: Perspectives on Development,* ed. Claire B. Kopp and Martha Kirkpatrick (New York: Plenum Press, 1979), pp. 89-112; Michèle Montrelay, "The Story of Louise," in *Returning to Freud,* ed. Schneiderman, pp. 75-93.

51. Jeanne Lampl-de Groot, "The Evolution of the Oedipus Complex in Women," in *The Psycho-Analytic Reader,* ed. Fliess, pp. 180-94, esp. p. 189.

52. See Freud, "Dissolution of the Oedipus Complex," p. 179; Lacan, "The Signification of the Phallus," in *Ecrits,* pp. 281-91, esp. 289-91.

53. Lampl-de Groot, "Evolution of the Oedipus Complex," p. 186.

54. Roland Barthes, *S/Z,* trans. Richard Miller (New York: Hill and Wang, 1974), pp. 35-39.

55. Heath, "Difference," p. 84, quoting Irigaray.

56. See Gérin's discussion of the correspondence, *Charlotte Bronte,* pp. 109-12.

57. Gilbert and Gubar, *Madwoman in the Attic,* p. 384.

58. For discussion of sexual difference, see Ewens, "Female Sexuality," pp. 625-36.

59. Freud often uses this term and others related to it when admitting his lack of understanding of the female. See, for example, "Femininity," pp. 116, 131. Ewens extends Freud's perception of the "female as other" and shows that for all human subjects, whether male or female, the question of sexuality represents an enigma that must be confronted ("Female Sexuality," pp. 628-30).

60. See Gilbert and Gubar on hunger and eating in *Shirley* (*Madwoman in the Attic,* pp. 372-75).

61. Although my attitude is different from hers, I am indebted in this discussion of feminism in *Shirley* to M. A. Blom, "Charlotte Bronte, Feminist *Manquée,*" *Bucknell Review* 21 (1973): 87-102.

62. Elizabeth Gaskell, *The Life of Charlotte Bronte,* ed. Alan Shelston (Harmondsworth, Eng.: Penguin Books, 1975), chap. 25.

63. For discussion of the nun see Gilbert and Gubar, *Madwoman in the Attic,* pp. 425-38; Charles Burkhart, *Charlotte Bronte: A Psychosexual Study of Her Novels* (London: Victor Gollancz, 1973), pp. 113-17; Robert B. Heilman, "Charlotte Bronte's 'New' Gothic," in *From Jane Austen to Joseph Conrad,* ed. Robert C. Rathburn and Martin Steinmann, Jr. (Minneapolis:

University of Minnesota Press, 1958), pp. 118-32; E.D.H. Johnson, "'Daring the Dread Glance': Charlotte Bronte's Treatment of the Supernatural in *Villette*," *Nineteenth-Century Fiction* 20 (1966): 325-36; and Mary Jacobus, "*Villette*'s Buried Letter," *Essays in Criticism* 28 (1978): 228-44 (a longer version of this essay appears in *Women Writing and Writing about Women*, ed. Mary Jacobus [New York: Barnes & Noble, 1979], pp. 42-60). These critics all view the nun as a figure for self-denial, although Gilbert and Gubar see her as balanced by the figure of the witch, Malevola.

64. For an excellent discussion of the scene in which the narrative posits the nun-in-the-bed as a figure for Lucy, see Jacobus, "*Villette*'s Buried Letter," pp. 235-42.

65. Unlike Charles Burkhart, I do not see the garden (or Eden) as Bronte's "central myth" of "perfect shared sexuality" (*Charlotte Bronte*, pp. 30-31).

66. Five years passed between these two letters; Bronte's optimism about the singular female appears to have been tried and tempered by personal experience.

67. Grudin, "Jane and the Other Mrs. Rochester," pp. 152-55.

68. Irigaray, "This Sex Which Is Not One," p. 104. I include Crimsworth among these heroines because his character, as I implied earlier, links him with the feminine. See also Irigaray, *Speculum*, pp. 183-99; Luce Irigaray, "When Our Lips Speak Together," trans. Carolyn Burke, *Signs* 6 (1980): 69-79; Carolyn Burke, "Introduction to Luce Irigaray's 'When Our Lips Speak Together,'" ibid., pp. 66-68; and Carolyn Burke, "Report from Paris: Women's Writing and the Women's Movement," *Signs* 3 (1978): 843-55.

69. See Jacques Lacan, "The Mirror Stage as Formative of the Function of the I," in *Ecrits*, pp. 1-7. See also Jacobus, "*Villette*'s Buried Letter," pp. 238-44; Heath, "Difference," pp. 75-78.

70. Freud, "A Child Is Being Beaten," pp. 198-99.

71. Ibid., pp. 199, 190-91.

72. Gilbert and Gubar, *Madwoman in the Attic*, pp. 311-35.

73. Sigmund Freud, "Beyond the Pleasure Principle," *SE*, 18 (1955), 14-17. See also Lacan, *The Language of the Self*, pp. 83-87; Jean Laplanche and Serge Leclaire, "The Unconscious: A Psychoanalytic Study," *Yale French Studies*, no. 48 (1972), p. 153.

74. Jacques Lacan, "The Field of the Other and Back to the Transference," in *The Four Fundamental Concepts of Psycho-Analysis*, p. 239.

75. Irigaray, *Speculum*, p. 177. See also Annie Leclerc, *Parole de femme* (Paris: Bernard Grasset, 1974); Cixous, "Laugh of the Medusa," pp. 880-81.

76. See M. Jeanne Peterson, "The Victorian Governess: Status Incongruence in Family and Society," in *Suffer and Be Still: Women in the Victorian Age*, ed. Martha Vicinus (Bloomington: Indiana University Press, 1973), pp. 3-19.

77. Inga-Stina Ewbank, *Their Proper Sphere: A Study of the Bronte Sisters as Early-Victorian Female Novelists* (Cambridge, Mass.: Harvard University Press, 1968), pp. 198-204, and Patricia Beer, *Reader, I Married Him: A Study of the Women Characters of Jane Austen, Charlotte Bronte, Elizabeth Gaskell, and George Eliot* (New York: Barnes and Noble, 1974), pp. 97-105, discuss the convergence of teaching and sexuality but not in the same terms I do. Nina Auerbach, *Communities of Women: An Idea in Fiction* (Cambridge, Mass.: Harvard University Press, 1978), p. 99, defines teaching in *Villette* as a "psychodrama" in which the students represent the teacher's own rebellious urges.

78. This also appears true in *The Professor*, in which William Crimsworth not only tyrannizes over his wife but allows her after their marriage her split life of wife and school directress.

79. Jacques Derrida, "Coming Into One's Own," trans. James Hulbert, in *Psychoanalysis and the Question of the Text*, ed. Geoffrey H. Hartman (Baltimore: Johns Hopkins University Press, 1978), pp. 114-48.

80. Ibid., pp. 115-20, 127-31, quote on p. 130.

81. Ibid., pp. 122-23, 128-29.

82. Lacan, "The Field of the Other," p. 239.

83. Freud, "Femininity," p. 129.

84. Gregory L. Ulmer, "The Discourse of the Imaginary," *Diacritics* 10 (1980): 71. See also Gayatri Chakravorty Spivak, "The Letter as Cutting Edge," in *Literature and Psychoanalysis: The Question of Reading: Otherwise,* ed. Shoshana Felman, *Yale French Studies,* no. 55/56 (1977), pp. 208-66; Robert Con Davis, "The Discourse of the Father," in *The Fictional Father,* ed. Robert Con Davis (Amherst: University of Massachusetts Press, 1981), pp. 4-25.

85. See Heath, "Difference," p. 92, who discusses and quotes from Lemoine-Luccioni's *Partage des femmes.* See also Eugénie Lemoine-Luccioni, "The Fable of the Blood," in *Returning to Freud,* ed. Schneiderman, pp. 61-74. I think it is no accident, in addition, that Bronte's only text that seeks to identify the mother is her most doubling, duplicitous, and specular text, *Shirley.*

86. Derrida, "Coming Into One's Own," pp. 117, 131.

Index

Adam and Eve, 10

Adam Bede: Eliot's doctrine of sympathy, 83; metaphorical structure, 112; narrative structure, 109-10; portrait of Robert Evans, 107; question of interpretation, 111; title, 109

"Amos Barton," 66, 67, 69. See also *Scenes of Clerical Life*

Angrian tales, 159

Author as father, 38 ff., 45, 47, 48

Authority: contradictions in, 165; daughter's lack of, 65; daughter's rebellion against, 80; dependence on father's, 167; and egoism, 113; female, 161; fictions of, 162-63; and figurative father, 131; figures humiliated, 83; *fort-da* game, 164-65; and gender, 80, 104 ff.; of Judaic patriarchs, 103; language and, 39, 80, 159, 170; and law, 80, 170; male, 105; of master, 119; narrative, 104-18; paternal (*see* paternal authority); problems of, 170; and unmarried women, 162; and writing, 165

Authorship: fatherhood through, 110; female, 120

Balzac, Honoré de, 147

Barnaby Rudge: father-son economic in, 27, 29; haunting by father, 29-30; identity of father, 12; oedipal triangle, 55; parricide, 38

Barthes, Roland, 120, 147

Beating fantasy, 133-35, 146, 157

Bell, Currer, 159-60. *See also* Bronte, Charlotte

Bleak House: daughter's role, 52, 59; doubled narrative sequence, 16; father as origin, 17; knowledge of paternity denied, 14

Binding, 91, 95, 98

Blindness as castration symbol, 145, 148

Bonaparte, Felicia, 89, 94

Bracebridge, C. H., 115-16

"Bride from heaven," 51-52

Bronte, Branwell, 120, 139, 140

Bronte, Charlotte, 119-69, 170-72; abandoning father, 135-36; autobiographical basis of fiction, 167; biography, 139; castration metaphor, 3, 9, 143-58, 171; creative process, 120; dialogue in, 125; and father, 141-42, 148, 151, 170; father supplement, 137-38, 143; female desire and power, 129 ff.; gaze metaphor, 121-22, 127-28; and gender, 119; and M. Héger, 140, 141, 148, 162, 169; hero as master, 119; heroine as spectator of desire, 156-58; heroines' attempts at mastery, 159; heroines' desire for fathers, 130 ff.; male impersonation, 127; marriage, 142-43, 155, 169; masochism, 132, 134, 140-41; master, 119, 132, 137, 164; narrative structure, 121, 125, 136; narrator, 159; novelettes, 121, 125, 126, 136, 159; punishment, 133; and rebellion, 120; sexual difference, 149-51; "singular" woman, 152-58, 169; stories, 135; "trance-writing," 120. *See also titles of works*

paternal law, 93; sympathy doctrine, 83, 113-15; writing process, 88 ff. *See also titles of works*

Emery, Laura Comer, 84

Evans, Mary Ann. *See* Eliot, George

Evans, Robert, 68, 69, 80, 83, 86; as model for characters, 107, 115-16

Exhibitionism, 127

Eye, and phallus, 123, 145

Family: desire in, 132-33; oedipal, 55, 135, 171; origins, 10; structural, defined, 5

Family romance: and ambition, 74, 76; in "Amos Barton," 66-67; in Eliot, 72-73; Freud's definition of, 67; and seduction, 67

Family structure: daughter's redemption of, 53; as incestuous, 55, 56; law based on, 78; and therapy, 8; Victorian abstraction, 5; and writing, 46-47

Father: abandoning, 135-36; author as, 39 ff., 45, 47, 48; authority of (*see* paternal authority); betrayal by, 21; Bronte's central figure, 139; daughter's dependence on, 146; daughter's struggle with, 92, 151; dead, 118; economic debt to, 25; fictional, meaning of, 4; figurative, 17, 50, 85, 131, 137; as figure of wish-fulfillment, 71; filial abandonment of, 94; Freud and Lacan's focus on, 8; Freud's "class of," 163; haunting by, 29, 30, 34, 38; as hero, 70, 117; humbling of, 111; as husband, 74; identity of, 12, 14 ff.; initiator of narrative, 13-15; as lawgiver, 79, 84-85, 92, 104; as lover, 55; as master, 131-32; murder of, 24, 28, 86; need to dominate, 127; and origin, 12, 14, 17; and political authority, 6; punishment of, 145; rebellion against, 28; rejection of, 152; return of dead, 29-32; as scapegoat, 97-98; search for, 19; sins of, 14-15; son's renunciation of, 84; suffering inflicted by, 83; superseding, 23. *See also* Parentage; parricide, metaphorical; Paternal; Patriarch

Father-daughter relationship: abuse in, 64; desire and punishment in, 133, 135, 138; in Dickens, 51 ff.; in Eliot, 65; erotic demands of, 157-58; Freud's exposition of, 135; generational reversal in, 56; incest in, 55, 133-34; in *Jane Eyre*, 130; love in, 85, 131; metaphorical marriage in, 57, 74; in *Old Curiosity Shop*, 20; seduction in, 66-67, 70-71, 74 ff.; in *Villette*, 130

Fatherhood: absent, 170; and authority, 78-79; clues to, 17; defined by true feeling, 72; figurative, in writing, 38 ff.; and language, 51; linked to legal rights, 78-79; paradox of, 80; religious analogy for, 166; subdued into brotherhood, 102; through authorship, 110

Father-son economic: conflict in, 24; desire for identification, 28; in Dickens, 26-27, 29; and Freud, 29; *Hamlet* as metaphor for, 33; oedipal guilt and aggression in, 33

Father supplement: in Bronte, 137-38, 140, 143, 166, 169; in Freud's theory, 164; Nicholls as, 142-43

Felix Holt the Radical: cultural decline of paternity, 81; daughterly desire, 78; genealogy in, 78; law as paternal precedence, 78; male memory, 106-7; seduction, 71-73; Victorian morality, 88

Female: authority, 161; authorship, 120; desire and punishment, 133, 140, 156, 159; fantasy, 134; fetishization of, 128; and language, 159, 164, 167; relationships, 138; spectator, 164

Feminine, Freud and Lacan's repression of, 8

Feminists, psychoanalytic, 9

Ferenczi, Sandor, 70

Fetishization of female, 128

Filial service, 69

Fort-da game, 160, 164-68

Freud, Sigmund, 163; beating fantasy, 133-35, 146, 157; castration theory, 146-47; "class of fathers," 163; criticism of, 7; eye and phallus, 123, 145; family romance, 67; father-daughter relationship, 135; father-son economic, 29; female desire and punishment, 133, 140, 159; female psychology, 7; focus on father, 8; *fort-da* game, 160, 164-68; and genealogy, 165; incest taboo, 55; and interpretation of texts, 7; Oedipus complex, 123; paternal representative, 137; primal fantasy, 1-2; psychoanalytic tools, 172; quantifiability of psychic energy, 25; seduction theory, 68; sound in primal fantasy, 107; superego, 85, 101; *Totem and Taboo*, 22, 55, 79; trauma, 90-91; unconscious, 122; as writer, 7-8

Garden as feminine metaphor, 153-54

Gaskell, Elizabeth, 51, 66, 139, 140, 141, 151

Gaze: female, 124, 128, 129; Lacan's theory of, 127; as metaphor in Bronte, 121-22, 127-28;

Gaze (*continued*)
metaphor for sexual aggression, 15; symbolism of, 123, 165-66

Gender: and authority, 80, 104 ff.; in Bronte, 119; and female self-detachment, 168; and visions, 120

Genealogy: agent of suffering, 103; binding and redeeming, 60; and brotherhood, 102; and daughters, 54; and desire, 167; Dickens's concern with, 10-11; and Freud, 165; and identity, 11, 108; and law, 78; and male storytelling, 107; and origin, 11; of patriarchs, 103; and sins of fathers, 15; word as replacement for, 102

Gérin, Winifred, 120, 136, 139

Gilbert, Sandra M., 105, 120, 145, 149, 159

Girard, René, 24, 60

Gorgon image, 129

Great Expectations: author-as-father, 39; as autobiography, 41; dead father, 29, 30, 32; figurative fathers in, 50; representation in, 36

Grudin, Peter, 145, 156

Gubar, Susan, 120, 145, 149, 159

Hamlet: and concept of representation, 35-38; metaphor for father-son economic, 33

Heath, Stephen, 121, 123

Héger, Constantin, 140, 141, 148, 162, 169

Hero as master, 119

"Holy Wars" between George Eliot and father, 80, 93

Horney, Karen, 7

Hutter, Albert D., 21, 23

Identity: and daughters, 53; effaced by masterful male, 136; and father, 12-13; of father, 14 ff.; and genealogy, 11, 108; self-engendered, 38 ff.

Imaginary as feminine, 157

Incest: and castration fear, 124; in *Dombey and Son*, 62; in family structure, 55-56; in father-daughter relationship, 55, 133, 134; as punishment, 63

Irigaray, Luce, 9, 124, 126, 157

Irwin, John T., 24

Jacobus, Mary, 153

James, Henry, 101

Jane Eyre, 143-44, 158; castration, 145, 147-48; father-daughter relationship, 130; female desire, 156; figurative father as master, 131; narrator, 159; power of voice, 162; punishment in, 135, 145; rebellion in, 144, 162; sadomasochism, 134-35

"Janet's Repentance," 113. See also *Scenes of Clerical Life*

Judaism as ideal for Eliot, 102-4

Julia, 121, 122, 136

Kristeva, Julia, 9, 124

Lacan, Jacques, 8, 22, 23, 24, 25, 27, 79, 80, 85, 123, 127, 147, 157, 160, 167, 168

Lampl-de Groot, Jeanne, 7, 146, 147

Language: and authority, 39, 80, 159, 170; and desire, 70, 75, 100, 121, 125; discrepancy with referent, 111; and emotion, 158; and family structure, 47; and fatherhood, 51; and female, 159, 164, 167; as law, 96; as masculine prerogative, 65; mastery of, 126; mystery of, 44; paradox in, 59; and primal scene, 70; as rebellion, 97; separation from referents, 48-49; and signification, 125, 126; and unconscious, 121, 135; as vehicle for making self, 49; as vehicle for mastery, 160, 162-63, 169; as vehicle for worldly success, 43

Laplanche, Jean, 1, 21, 68, 88, 90, 107, 108

Lasch, Christopher, 8

Laslett, Peter, 4, 5

Law: and authority, 80, 170; based on family structure, 78; father as lawgiver, 84-85, 92, 104; and genealogy, 78; language as, 96; language and submission to, 126; as metaphor, 81; moral, 88; narrative as, 98; rebellion against, 97; signified by symbolic father, 79

Lemoine-Luccioni, Eugénie, 168

Lewes, George Henry, 87, 89-90

Lewes, Marian. *See* Eliot, George

Linguistic theories and psychoanalysis, 8

Little Dorrit: double temporality in, 18; embedded narrative in, 19; and incestuous family structure, 55-56; knowledge of paternity denied, 14; search for father, 19

"Looking Backward," 107; See also *Theophrastus Such*

Love: as deadly, 62-63; father-daughter, 85, 131; oedipal, 60; parricide liberating, 35; paternal, 74

Male memory as requisite for storytelling, 106-7

Male persona in Bronte, 159-60; in Eliot, 118

Marcus, Steven, 21, 66, 69, 83

Marriage: as bondage in Eliot, 76; Bronte's attitude toward, 155; Bronte's to Nicholls, 169; Jane Eyre's desire to forestall, 144; symbol of devotion to community, 102; symbolic of father-daughter relationship, 57, 74

Martin Chuzzlewit, 10

Masochism in Bronte, 132, 134, 140-41

Master, in Bronte, 119, 132, 137, 164

Mastery: contradictions in, 165; fragility as narrative, 169; function of desire, 166; implications of term, 161; of language, 126; language as medium of, 160, 162-63, 169; woman's lack of, 149

Memory as male faculty, 106-7, 109

Metaphor: as attempt to control, 113; central, in Dickens, Eliot, Bronte, 3; as delusory, 112; for desire, 121; in Freud, 8; of entry, 122

Middlemarch: composition process, 90; father-daughter seduction, 74 ff.; father's failed authority, 98-99; and fictionalized father, 117-18; filiation and affiliation, 101; and interpretation, 111; and ironic language of desire, 75; and sympathy, 115

Miller, J. Hillis, 112

Mill on the Floss: as autobiography, 90; and cultural decline of paternity, 81; daughter's desire for fatherly love, 77; father-daughter seduction, 71; and language of seduction, 70; and law as paternal precedent, 78; male narrator in, 106; and metaphor as delusory, 112; split father, 85

Mina Laury, 136

Mintz, Alan, 77

Mirror imagery in Bronte, 156-57, 168

Moglen, Helene, 132, 139, 140

Mother, displaced, 69

Moynahan, Julian, 60, 63

"Mr. Gilfil's Love-Story," 82-83. See also *Scenes of Clerical Life*

Napier, Augustus, 8

Narration as structuring primal fantasy, 108

Narrative: authority, 104-18; credibility, 158; dilemma, Eliot's, 87; discontinuity, 126; dual, 16, 46, 71; embedded, 19-20; engendering self through, 46; genealogical correspondence, 109; lack of subject for, 122; as law, 98; power to define subject, 41; as punishment, 67, 115; rebirth through,

40; seduction fantasy as, 70; and spectating female, 158; and unconscious desire, 121

Narrative sequence: created by clues to fatherhood, 17; doubling of, 16; father as source of, 14

Narrative structure: in *Adam Bede,* 109-10; in Bronte's novelettes, 121, 125, 136; and dialogue, 125; and paternity, 171

Narrator: and castration fear, 129; as creator of self, 41; first-person, 39 ff., 59; ironic, 76; male, 106 ff.; male and female, 159, 168; spectating female, 158, 164; as voyeur, 122-23

Nicholas Nickleby: and identity of father, 12; theater as metaphor in, 36

Nicholls, Arthur Bell, 142-43, 169

Nun in Bronte, 152-54

Oedipal: burden, 22; desires, 42, 46, 77, 143; guilt and aggression, 33, 40; identification, 8; love, 60; relationships displaced, 27; situation and primal scene, 60, 64; struggle as economic, 25; triangle, 55, 142-43

Oedipal family: in Bronte's stories, 135; power of, 171; structure as incestuous, 55

Oedipal structures: of desire, 100; displacement of, 27; jealousy and, 64; and supplement, 169

Oedipus complex: asymmetry of male and female, 65, 86; and castration fear, 146; and family romance, 67, 73; female, 68, 85, 86, 157; Freud's late essays on, 123; and seduction fantasy, 68; as theme in Dickens, 64; as theoretical basis for study, 1

Old Curiosity Shop: embedded narrative in, 19-20; father as origin of identity, 14; father-daughter structures in, 20; father-son economic in, 27; figurative fatherhood in, 17; theater as metaphor in, 36

Oliver Twist, primal scene in, 21

Origin: as explaining character, 12; as derived from father, 12; effaced through daughters, 56; father as, 17; and genealogy, 11

Orphanhood: desire to overcome, 74; transcended by daughter, 52

Orphans, in Dickens, 12, 15, 22, 28, 61

Our Mutual Friend, father as ghost in, 30

Parentage: clues to, 17; mystery of, 14-15

Parental authority, child's liberation from, 73

Parricide, metaphorical: in Bronte's novelettes, 159; and daughter, 57, 86; of figurative father, 28; and guilt, 118; liberating love, 35; Romola's wish for, 98; structural, 32; as theme in Dickens, 24

Passing Events, 125, 136

Paternal: affection, signified by seduction, 68; approbation and daughter, 77; betrayal, 49; desire, 133; embrace, 28; law, 92, 96; memories, 107; metaphor, inadequacies of, 28; origin conferring identity, 14; pride, 82; punishment, 135; representative, 137; seduction, significance of, 68

Paternal authority, 6, 11, 24; P. Bronte's loss of, 142-43; comic confusion of, 117; decline in *Romola*, 87; Eliot's acquisition through writing, 110; Eliot's failure to resolve, 97; failure of, 98-99; and language, 39; link with legal rights, 78-79; link of narrative to, 109; loss of, 87; questioned by Eliot, 81-82; redefined by Eliot, 114; seduction justifying, 68; and self-authority, 87; struggle to control, 171; over unmarried daughter, 80; in *Villette*, 163

Paternity: cultural decline of, 81; denial of knowledge of, 14; and desire and punishment, 133; and law, 78; as narrative structure, 171; problem effaced by daughters, 52 ff.; revelation of, 71

Patriarch: Eliot's judgment of, 93; female assault on, 149; and genealogy, 103; idealized figure of, 116

Patriarchal: ideology, 146; structure and Eliot, 110; tradition of storytelling, 107

Patriarchal culture and female fantasy, 134

Patriarchal family: structures of desire in, 133; as Victorian abstraction, 5

Patrimony and legal rights, 78

Pen name: Bronte, 159-60; Eliot, 104-18

Phallocentrism, Bronte's questioning of, 149

Pickwick Papers: betrayal in, 30, 49; economic issues in, 26

Platt, Gerald, 6

Pontalis, J.-B., 1, 21, 68, 90, 107, 108

Primal fantasy: 1, 2; narrator as structuring, 108; seduction as, 68; sound in, 107

Primal scene: and daughter, 58; described, 2; in Dickens, 3, 9, 21, 64, 171; function of, 22; language in, 70; metaphorical, 61; narration as structuring, 108; and oedipal situation, 60, 64; as symbolic, 1, 21

Professor, The: castration in, 148; and the gaze, 128; and male persona, 159; nun figure, 152; repetition in *Villette*, 168-69

Pseudonym. *See* Pen name

Psychoanalysis and literary interpretation, 8, 172

Psychoanalytic terms, defined, 90-91

Punishment: Branwell Bronte signifying, 140; in Bronte's novels, 133; daughter's desire for, 84; of daughter for desire, 87; for desire of father, 134; by father, 83, 94; of father, 145; father's refusal of, 84; of female, 138, 139, 159; incest as, 63; in *Jane Eyre*, 135, 145; for male desire, 151; narrative as, 67, 115; in 19th-century family, 133; paternal, 135; for rebellion, 134; in *Villette*, 135; and women, 63; writing as, 59

Rebellion: Bronte's handling of, 120; in *Jane Eyre*, 144, 162; language as, 97; metaphorical, against father, 28; punishment for, 134

Redemption: as theme in Eliot, 72; through daughter, 53; through genealogy, 60

Redinger, Ruby V., 69, 80, 104

Reform as metaphor for seduction, 72

Representation, concept of, 35-38

Repression: defined, 91; Eliot's ambivalence about, 96; of seduction scene, 104

Ricoeur, Paul, 55

Robinson, Carole, 94, 96

Romola: composition of, 88 ff.; confessional nature of, 90; and male memory, 106; and scene of seduction, 91 ff.; transition in Eliot's career, 89; wish for father's death, 98

Rosolato, Guy, 24

Sadomasochism in Bronte, 132, 134-35

Sarrasine, 147

Saussure, Ferdinand de, 8

Scenes of Clerical Life, 66, 67, 69, 82-83, 113

Seduction: as cause of suffering, 100; in *Daniel Deronda*, 99-100; drama as metaphor for, 161; Eliot's scene of, 3, 9, 171; and family romance, 67; fantasy, 2; fantasy and female Oedipus complex, 68; fantasy as narrative, 70; in father-daughter relationship, 66-67, 70-71, 74 ff., 130; in *Felix Holt*, 71-73; Freud's theory of, 68; meaning of, 66; metaphor for spiritual friendship, 102; paternal, 68; as psychoanalytic term, 67-68; reform as metaphor for, 72; repressed, in *Daniel Deronda*, 104; in *Romola*, 91 ff.; in *Silas Marner*, 71-73; and sound, 107-8; as symbolic, 1

Self-engendering writer as masculine, 65

Sexual: aggression and the gaze, 15; difference, 143-58; meaning obscured in "Amos

The Johns Hopkins University Press

MONSTERS OF AFFECTION

This book was composed in Baskerville text and display type by David Lorton from a design by Lisa S. Mirski. It was printed on S. D. Warren's 50-lb. Sebago Eggshell paper and bound in Kivar 5 by Universal Lithographers.